ASPEN PU

Blond's
LAW GUIDES

CIVIL
PROCEDURE

6TH EDITION

NEIL C. BLOND

JOHN MARAFINO

MARK MONACK

MARK D. PELLIS

LOUIS PETRILLO

Sixth edition revised by

Professor Joel Wm. Friedman

Tulane University Law School
Jack M. Gordon Professor of
Procedural Law & Jurisdiction

 Wolters Kluwer
Law & Business

AUSTIN   BOSTON   CHICAGO   NEW YORK   THE NETHERLANDS

Printed in the United States of America.
1 2 3 4 5 6 7 8 9 0

ISBN 978-0-7355-8606-2

About Wolters Kluwer Law & Business

Wolters Kluwer Law & Business is a leading provider of research information and workflow solutions in key specialty areas. The strengths of the individual brands of Aspen Publishers, CCH, Kluwer Law International and Loislaw are aligned within Wolters Kluwer Law & Business to provide comprehensive, in-depth solutions and expert-authored content for the legal, professional and education markets.

CCH was founded in 1913 and has served more than four generations of business professionals and their clients. The CCH products in the Wolters Kluwer Law & Business group are highly regarded electronic and print resources for legal, securities, antitrust and trade regulation, government contracting, banking, pension, payroll, employment and labor, and healthcare reimbursement and compliance professionals.

Aspen Publishers is a leading information provider for attorneys, business professionals and law students. Written by preeminent authorities, Aspen products offer analytical and practical information in a range of specialty practice areas from securities law and intellectual property to mergers and acquisitions and pension/benefits. Aspen's trusted legal education resources provide professors and students with high-quality, up-to-date and effective resources for successful instruction and study in all areas of the law.

Kluwer Law International supplies the global business community with comprehensive English-language international legal information. Legal practitioners, corporate counsel and business executives around the world rely on the Kluwer Law International journals, loose-leafs, books and electronic products for authoritative information in many areas of international legal practice.

Loislaw is a premier provider of digitized legal content to small law firm practitioners of various specializations. Loislaw provides attorneys with the ability to quickly and efficiently find the necessary legal information they need, when and where they need it, by facilitating access to primary law as well as state-specific law, records, forms and treatises.

Wolters Kluwer Law & Business, a unit of Wolters Kluwer, is headquartered in New York and Riverwoods, Illinois. Wolters Kluwer is a leading multinational publisher and information services company.

Check Out These Other Great Titles:

BLOND'S LAW GUIDES

Comprehensive, Yet Concise . . . JUST RIGHT!

Each Blond's Law Guide book contains: Black Letter Law Outline · EasyFlow™ Charts · Case Clips · Mnemonics · Free Digital Version

Available titles in this series include:

Blond's Civil Procedure

Blond's Constitutional Law

Blond's Contracts

Blond's Criminal Law

Blond's Criminal Procedure

Blond's Evidence

Blond's Property

Blond's Torts

Law school is very different from your previous educational experiences. In the past, course material was presented in a straightforward manner both in lectures and texts. You did well by memorizing and regurgitating. In law school, your fat casebooks are stuffed with material, most of which will be useless when finals arrive. Your professors ask a lot of questions but don't seem to be teaching you either the law or how to think. Sifting through voluminous material seeking out the important concepts is a hard, time-consuming chore. We've done that job for you. This book will help you study effectively. We hope to teach you the law and how to think.

Preparing for Class

Most students start their first year by reading and briefing all their cases. They spend too much time copying unimportant details. After finals they realize they wasted time on facts that were useless on the exam.

Case Clips

Case Clips help you focus on what your professor wants you to get out of your cases. Facts, Issues, and Rules are carefully and succinctly stated. Left out are details irrelevant to what you need to learn from the case. In general, we skip procedural matters in lower courts. We don't care which party is the appellant or petitioner because the trivia is not relevant to the law. Case Clips should be read before you read the actual case. You will have a good idea what to look for in the case, and appreciate the significance of what you are reading. Inevitably you will not have time to read all your cases before class. Case Clips allow you to prepare for class in about five minutes. You will be able to follow the discussion and listen without fear of being called upon.

"Should I read all the cases even if they aren't from my casebook?"

Yes, if you feel you have the time. Most major cases from other texts will be covered at least as a note case in your book. The principles of these cases are universal and the fact patterns should help your understanding. The Case Clips are written in a way that should provide a tremendous amount of understanding in a relatively short period of time.

EasyFlow™ Charts

A very common complaint among law students is that they "can't put it all together." When you are reading 400 pages a week it is difficult to remember how the last case relates to the first and how November's readings relate to September's. It's hard to understand the relationship between different torts topics when you have read cases for three or four other classes in between. Our EasyFlow™ Charts will help you put the whole course together. They are designed to help you memorize fundamentals. They reinforce your learning by showing you the material from another perspective.

Outlines

More than one hundred lawyers and law students were interviewed as part of the development of this series. Most complained that their casebooks did not teach them the law and were far too voluminous to be useful before an exam. They also told us that the commercial outlines they purchased were excellent when used as hornbooks to explain the law, but were too wordy and redundant to be effective during the weeks before finals. Few students can read four 500-page outlines during the last month of classes. It is virtually impossible to memorize that much material and even harder to decide what is important. Almost every student interviewed said he or she studied from homemade outlines. We've written the outline you should use to study.

"But writing my own outline will be a learning experience."

True, but unfortunately many students spend so much time outlining they don't leave time to learn and memorize. Many students told us they spent six weeks outlining, and only one day studying before each final!

Mnemonics

Most law students spend too much time reading, and not enough time memorizing. Mnemonics are included to help you organize your essays and spot issues. They highlight what is important and which areas deserve your time.

TABLE OF CONTENTS

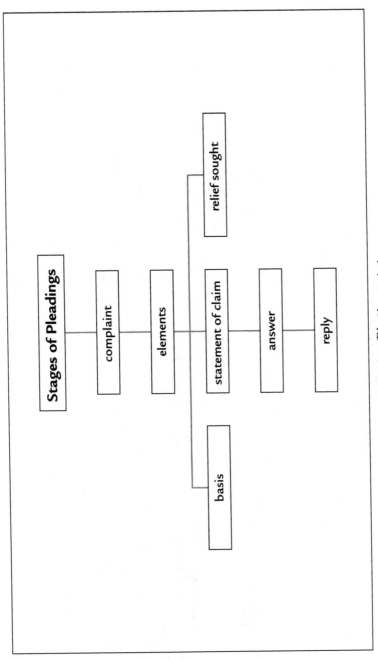

EasyFlow™ Chart 1.1

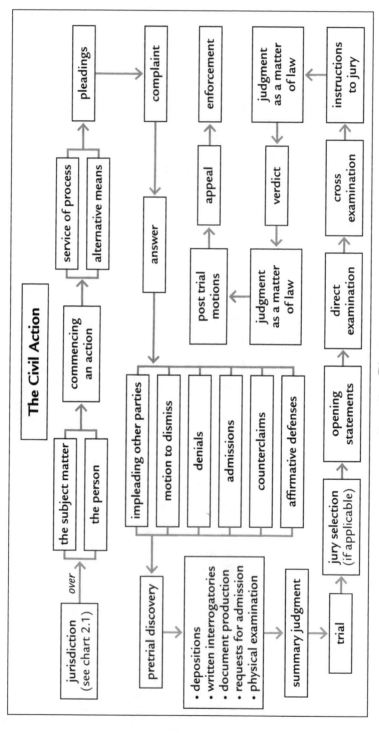

EasyFlow™ Chart 1.2

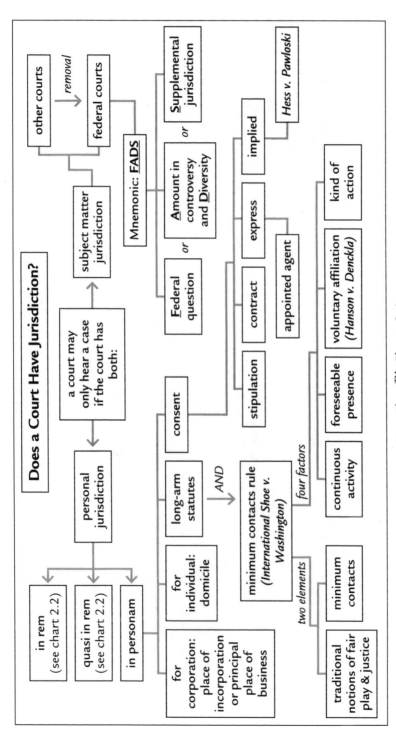

EasyFlow™ Chart 2.1

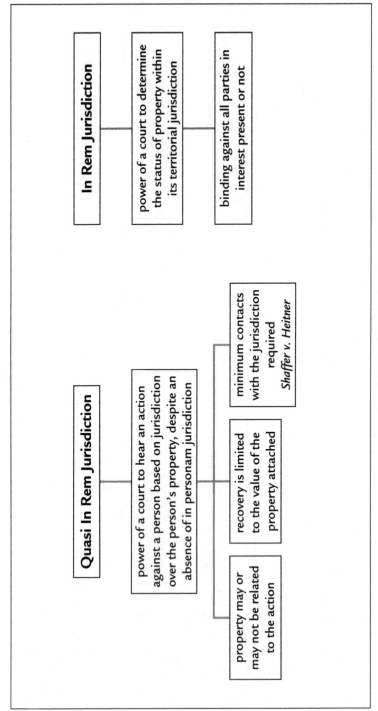

In Rem Jurisdiction

power of a court to determine the status of property within its territorial jurisdiction

binding against all parties in interest present or not

Quasi In Rem Jurisdiction

power of a court to hear an action against a person based on jurisdiction over the person's property, despite an absence of in personam jurisdiction

property may or may not be related to the action

recovery is limited to the value of the property attached

minimum contacts with the jurisdiction required
Shaffer v. Heitner

EasyFlow™ Chart 2.2

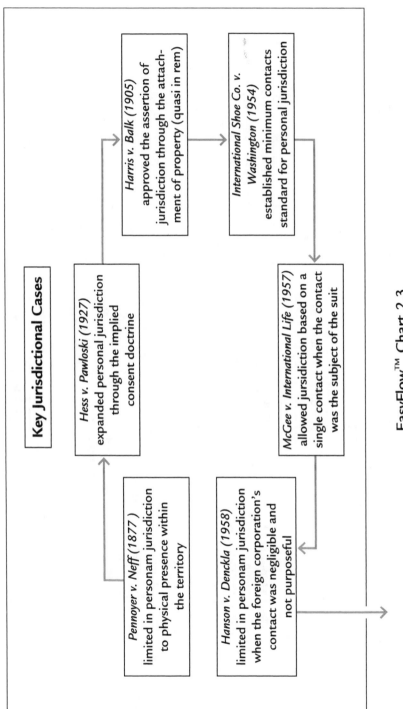

EasyFlow™ Chart 2.3

Key Jurisdictional Cases

Hess v. Pawloski (1927) expanded personal jurisdiction through the implied consent doctrine

Harris v. Balk (1905) approved the assertion of jurisdiction through the attachment of property (quasi in rem)

International Shoe Co. v. Washington (1954) established minimum contacts standard for personal jurisdiction

Pennoyer v. Neff (1877) limited in personam jurisdiction to physical presence within the territory

Hanson v. Denckla (1958) limited in personam jurisdiction when the foreign corporation's contact was negligible and not purposeful

McGee v. International Life (1957) allowed jurisdiction based on a single contact when the contact was the subject of the suit

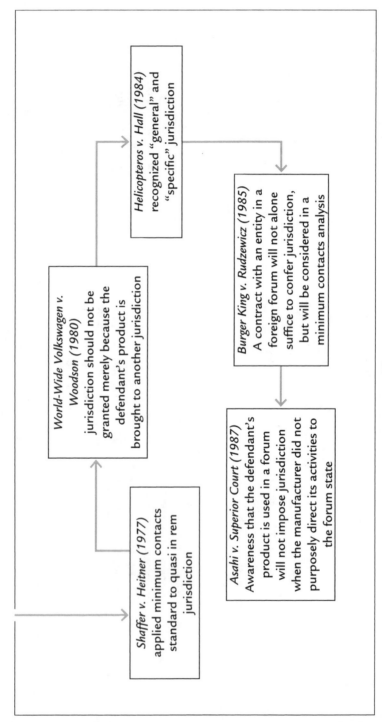

EasyFlow™ Chart 2.4

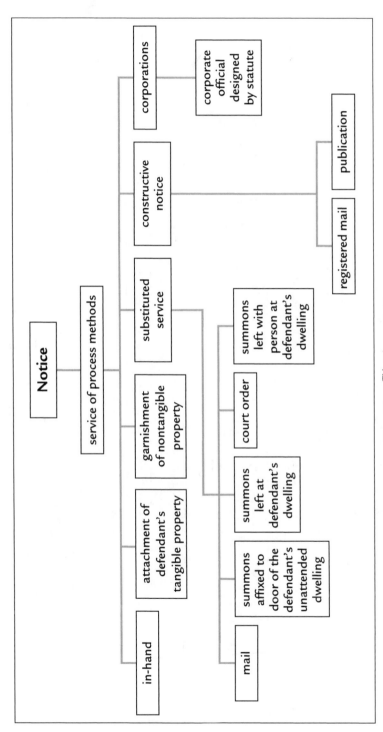

EasyFlow™ Chart 2.5

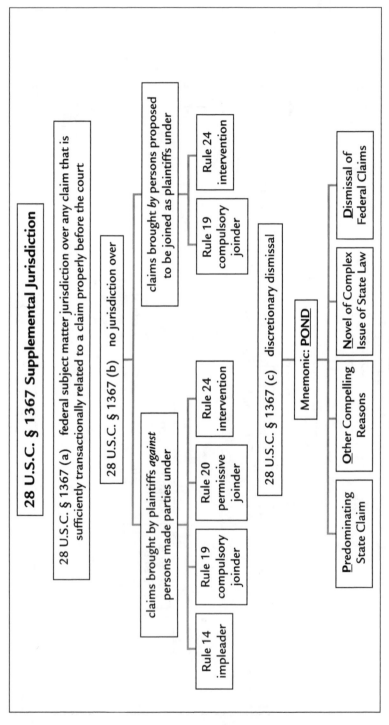

28 U.S.C. § 1367 Supplemental Jurisdiction

28 U.S.C. § 1367 (a)   federal subject matter jurisdiction over any claim that is sufficiently transactionally related to a claim properly before the court

28 U.S.C. § 1367 (b)   no jurisdiction over

claims brought by plaintiffs *against* persons made parties under

- Rule 14 impleader
- Rule 19 compulsory joinder
- Rule 20 permissive joinder
- Rule 24 intervention

claims brought *by* persons proposed to be joined as plaintiffs under

- Rule 19 compulsory joinder
- Rule 24 intervention

28 U.S.C. § 1367 (c)   discretionary dismissal

Mnemonic: **POND**

- **P**redominating State Claim
- **O**ther Compelling Reasons
- **N**ovel of Complex Issue of State Law
- **D**ismissal of Federal Claims

EasyFlow™ Chart 2.6

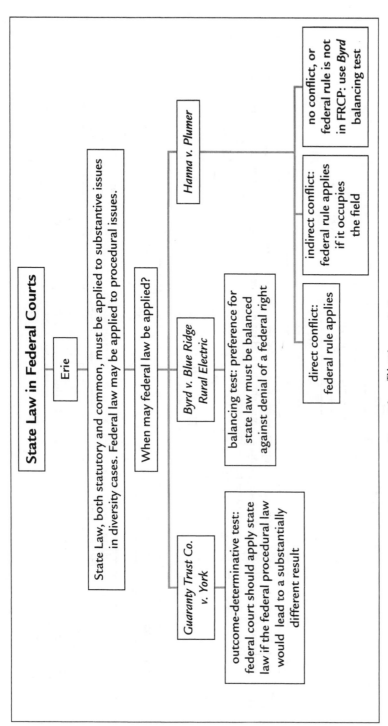

State Law in Federal Courts

Erie

State Law, both statutory and common, must be applied to substantive issues in diversity cases. Federal law may be applied to procedural issues.

When may federal law be applied?

Guaranty Trust Co. v. York

outcome-determinative test: federal court should apply state law if the federal procedural law would lead to a substantially different result

Byrd v. Blue Ridge Rural Electric

balancing test: preference for state law must be balanced against denial of a federal right

direct conflict: federal rule applies

Hanna v. Plumer

indirect conflict: federal rule applies if it occupies the field

no conflict, or federal rule is not in FRCP: use *Byrd* balancing test

EasyFlow™ Chart 3.1

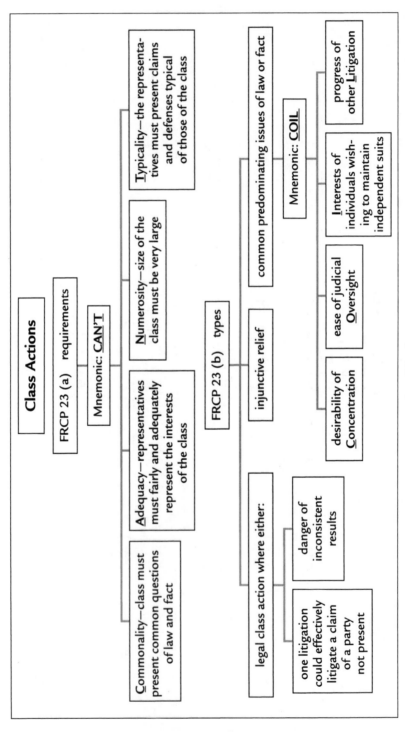

EasyFlow™ Chart 6.1

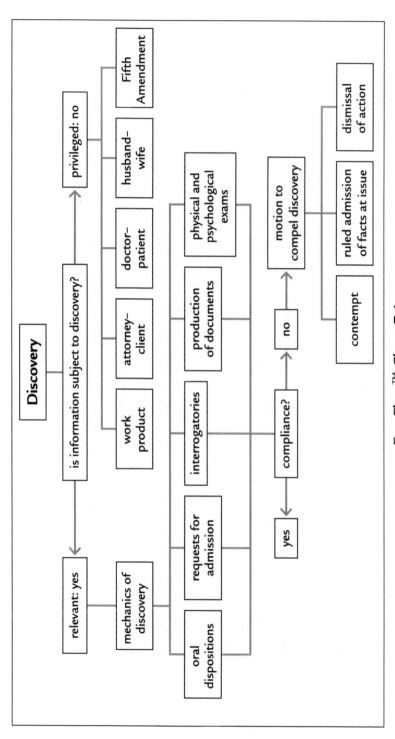

EasyFlow™ Chart 7.1

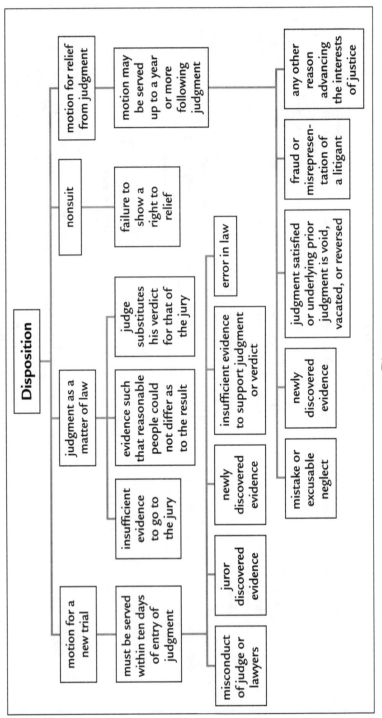

EasyFlow™ Chart 9.1

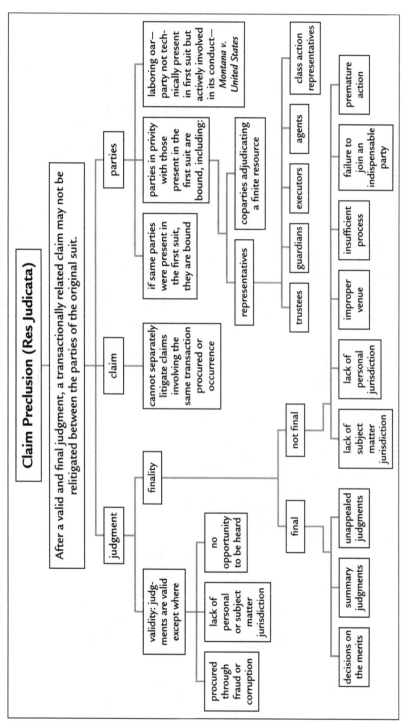

EasyFlow™ Chart 11.1

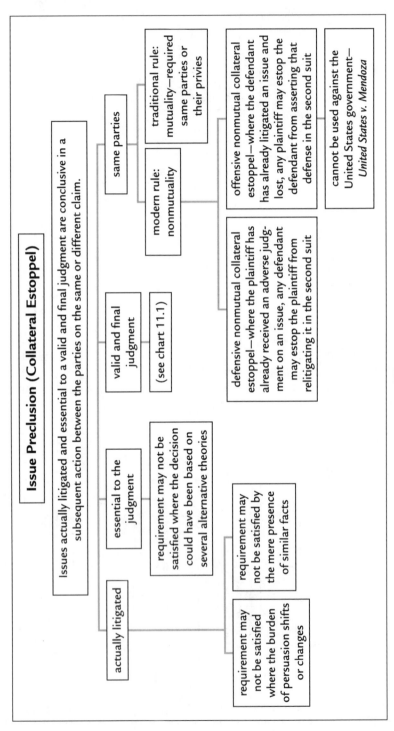

Issue Preclusion (Collateral Estoppel)

Issues actually litigated and essential to a valid and final judgment are conclusive in a subsequent action between the parties on the same or different claim.

actually litigated

essential to the judgment

valid and final judgment

same parties

requirement may not be satisfied where the burden of persuasion shifts or changes

requirement may not be satisfied by the mere presence of similar facts

requirement may not be satisfied where the decision could have been based on several alternative theories

(see chart 11.1)

traditional rule: mutuality—required same parties or their privies

modern rule: nonmutuality

defensive nonmutual collateral estoppel—where the plaintiff has already received an adverse judgment on an issue, any defendant may estop the plaintiff from relitigating it in the second suit

offensive nonmutual collateral estoppel—where the defendant has already litigated an issue and lost, any plaintiff may estop the defendant from asserting that defense in the second suit

cannot be used against the United States government— *United States v. Mendoza*

EasyFlow™ Chart 11.2

CHAPTER 1

Introduction

INTRODUCTION

As an introduction to civil procedure, it is sometimes helpful to look at the process of a civil action, both the procedures and issues involved.

I. COMMENCING THE ACTION

The plaintiff must notify the defendant of the suit being brought, what court is asserting jurisdiction over the case, and something of the nature of the case (although exactly what is needed is unclear and will be discussed in greater detail elsewhere in the book).

There are various methods of commencing the action, but the most common is service of process.

II. PLEADINGS

A. Filing the Complaint

The plaintiff must also notify the court of the impending case. This is done by filing a complaint.

1. Benefits of Being a Plaintiff

As plaintiff, a party has great leeway in framing the structure of the case:

a. The plaintiff gets to choose (at least initially) whether federal or state courts will be used.

b. The plaintiff chooses (also initially) the state or district in which the suit is brought.

c. The plaintiff initially defines the issues involved, including what parties to join as defendants, what relief is sought (injunctive, monetary or both), and how much.

2. Burdens of Being a Plaintiff

a. To the Court

The plaintiff must also carefully frame the nature of the case, for if the plaintiff fails to set forth certain very specific requirements (discussed in detail in Chapter 2), the case may be dismissed.

    b. To the Defendant

    The plaintiff must also set forth in the complaint enough information such that the defendant may identify and respond to the allegations.

B. Responsive Pleadings

What follows from the initial pleadings are a series of responses by both parties.

    1. Purpose

    The pleadings are designed to identify the precise issues disputed by the parties, thereby saving both the court's and parties' time and money that otherwise may have been wasted arguing irrelevant or undisputed issues.

    However, the pleadings may also be used to harass parties or delay the action.

    2. Content

    In the pleadings, a party may:

    a. Amend the Complaint

    b. Assert an Affirmative Defense

    c. Assert a Counterclaim

    d. Implead a Third Party

    e. Make a Motion to Dismiss

    f. Admit and Deny Factual Allegations

III. DISCOVERY

After the pleadings, parties then use various pretrial procedures in order to unearth knowledge in the other party's possession, or in the possession of witnesses. Discovery, however, is not designed to allow a party to discover its opponent's legal strategy, and there are several safeguards and sanctions available to courts and parties to ensure proper discovery.

Some discovery tools available to the litigator are:

A. Depositions

Used to orally interview witnesses.

B. Written Interrogatories

Used to compel written answers to submitted questionnaires.

C. Subpoenas Duces Tecum

Used to compel production of documents in a witness's possession.

D. Medical Examinations

Either physical or psychological, they must be for a specific and necessary purpose, such as determining the extent of injuries, or determining mental capacity.

IV. TRIAL

   A. Jury Trials
      1. Trial by jury is a right in certain actions (criminal trial, most federal court civil suits).
      2. Jurors are usually selected by the judge.
      3. Peremptory challenges (challenges for no reason) to jury selection are allowed.
   B. Trial Procedure
      1. Order of Parties
         The plaintiff always goes first.
      2. Opening Statements
         The parties briefly explain their positions and what they hope to prove.
      3. Questioning of Witnesses
         a. Direct Examination
            Witness's initial questioning. Evidence may be introduced through a witness's reference to it. The evidence must comply with the appropriate rules of evidence (state law or the Federal Rules of Evidence).
         b. Cross-Examination
            Witness's answers to direct examination may be probed, or additional information known to the witness may be brought out.
         c. Redirect
            After cross-examination the party who called the witness may question him about matters brought out in cross-examination.
      4. Motion for Summary Judgment
         If a party has not produced enough evidence to sustain its claim, and the judge feels that no reasonable jury could find otherwise, the judge may summarily dismiss the claim or issue of law involved or, alternatively, direct the jury that the issue involved cannot be decided otherwise.
      5. Closing Arguments
         Parties summarize their version of the case.
      6. Jury Instruction
         Judge tells jury the relevant law, and instructs it as to the relevant burdens of persuasion, as well as any presumptions it may be entitled to make. If there is to be a general verdict with interrogatories or a special verdict, the judge will also instruct the jury on these issues.
      7. Verdict
         a. General Verdict
            Jury decides which party prevails.

      b. General Verdict with Interrogatories
         In complicated cases, a judge may require a jury to answer a
         questionnaire in order to ensure that the jury fully under-
         stood the issues involved.
      c. Special Verdict
         The jury decides only limited factual issues that the judge
         uses to reach a final decision.

V. APPEAL

    A. Reversing the Jury
       A jury's decision may only be overturned where no evidence sub-
       mitted could have resulted in a jury deciding as it did.
    B. Reversing the Judge
      1. Factual Findings
         A judge's findings of fact may be reversed only where "clearly
         erroneous." This standard is supposed to be very high.
      2. Procedural Findings
         A case may be successfully appealed where a judge's procedural
         conclusions constitute an "abuse of discretion."
      3. Legal Findings
         Generally, courts will reverse a trial judge who has misapplied
         the applicable law.

CASE CLIPS

Capron v. Van Noorden (S. Ct. 1804)

Facts: The plaintiff brought an action in federal court without raising a federal question or alleging diversity of citizenship. He lost on the merits. On appeal, he argued that his failure to allege diversity before the federal trial court deprived it of subject matter jurisdiction.

Issue: Can the existence of a federal court's diversity-based subject matter jurisdiction be successfully challenged on appeal even though the plaintiff did not contest jurisdiction and responded on the merits at the trial court level?

Rule: Yes. A federal court cannot act if it does not have subject matter jurisdiction over the case, even if the adverse parties consent to its exercise of authority. Where the requirements for neither federal question nor diversity of citizenship jurisdiction exist, the parties cannot provide the court with subject matter jurisdiction that it does not have. Thus, the trial court's judgment must be reversed on appeal.

Tickle v. Barton (W. Va. Sup. Ct. 1956)

Facts: To obtain jurisdiction over Barton, Tickle's attorney phoned Barton and deceitfully induced him to attend a banquet in the county where Tickle had brought his action.

Issue: Is service of process valid when a party was originally brought within the jurisdiction of the state court by fraud or deceit?

Rule: No. Where a party is brought within the jurisdiction of the court by deceit or fraud, the courts will deem the service of process invalid and refuse to exercise personal jurisdiction.

Case v. State Mutual Automobile Insurance Co. (5th Cir. 1961)

Facts: Three insurance companies had contracted with Case to empower him to act as their agent and the contract included a clause allowing any party to terminate without cause. After the companies cancelled the contract, Case brought suit in federal court alleging wrongful termination. The complaint did not expressly set forth a tort claim alleging interference with Case's performance of the contract, although the facts would have supported such a claim. The trial court dismissed the complaint for failure to state a claim. On appeal, Case argued that the complaint recited facts sufficient to assert a claim for relief.

Issue: When the plaintiff alleges facts upon which a valid claim might be asserted but does not expressly assert that claim in the pleadings, should the court create the claim?

Rule: No. It is the court's duty to adjudicate cases based solely on the pleadings before it. Courts should not create claims that the parties have not raised.

Temple v. Synthes Corp. (S. Ct. 1990)

Facts: After a plate and screw device had been surgically implanted in Temple's back, the screws broke. Temple filed a products liability suit in federal court against Synthes, the device manufacturer, and a separate malpractice and negligence action in state court against the surgeon and the hospital. The trial court granted Synthes's motion to dismiss Temple's federal suit for failure to join necessary parties (surgeon and hospital) per FRCP 19.

Issue: Are joint tortfeasors necessary parties under FRCP 19?

Rule: No. Despite the public interest in avoiding multiple lawsuits, it is not necessary for any or all joint tortfeasors to be named as defendants in a single lawsuit. Joint tortfeasors are only permissive parties and, therefore, failure to join them is not grounds for dismissal under FRCP 19. The dismissal is reversed and the case remanded for further proceedings.

DiMichel v. South Buffalo Railway Co. (N.Y. Ct. App. 1992)

Facts: DiMichel sued South Buffalo in state court for injuries sustained while falling on its premises. During pretrial discovery, DiMichel demanded the production of any surveillance films that South Buffalo had taken of him. When South Buffalo refused on the grounds that such material was undiscoverable work product, DiMichel moved for an order to compel.

Issue: Can a plaintiff obtain a discovery order mandating pretrial production by the defendant of surveillance films taken of the plaintiff that the defendant intends to use at trial?

Rule: Yes. Surveillance films of the plaintiff that the defendant intends to use at trial must be turned over to the plaintiff, but only after the plaintiff has been deposed to avoid permitting the plaintiff to shape trial testimony to the contents of the film.

Alderman v. Baltimore & Ohio R. Co. (S.D. W. Va. 1953)

Facts: While traveling on the defendant's train with a free pass that contained a waiver of liability for injuries to non-paying passengers, Alderman was injured in a derailment caused by a sudden break in a rail. Alderman's federal court complaint initially alleged negligence by the railroad, but in light of the waiver, it was amended to charge the railroad with willful or wanton conduct. The defendant then moved for summary judgment under FRCP 56 claiming that because the complaint failed to allege that the railroad knew of any defect in the rail and in light of the railroad's undenied affidavits that the defect causing the derailment was not visible upon inspection, the plaintiff could not establish the presence of willfulness, an essential element of its cause of action.

Issue: May a court properly grant summary judgment where the undenied facts of the parties' affidavits show that plaintiff cannot substantiate the charge?

Rule: Yes. A court must grant summary judgment for defendant where the facts are undisputed and, as a consequence, the plaintiff will be unable to prove at trial a requirement element of the claim asserted in its complaint.

Alexander v. Kramer Bros. Freight Lines, Inc. (2d Cir. 1959)

Facts: In a negligence case brought in federal court, the defendant raised the issue of contributory negligence in its answer, but never requested a jury charge on that subject nor objected to the judge's instruction that the defendant bore the burden of establishing contributory negligence. The defendant appealed an adverse jury verdict on the ground that the judge had erred in its jury charge.

Issue: Can a party challenge a faulty jury charge on appeal when it failed to make a timely challenge to that charge on the record to the trial judge?

Rule: No. Per FRCP 51, a party who fails to timely object to a jury charge at trial in federal court waives that issue on appeal.

Diniero v. United States Lines Co. (2d Cir. 1961)

Facts: At the close of the evidence in a tort case filed in federal court, the judge provided the jury with eight interrogatories to be returned as a special verdict. After the jury informed the court that it found one of the judge's interrogatories ambiguous, the judge rephrased the interrogatory. But when the jury ultimately informed the judge that it was unable to reach agreement on an answer to that question, the judge withdrew all the interrogatories and, over the defendant's objection, reinstructed the jury to return a general verdict. The jury returned a general verdict for the plaintiff and the defendant appealed, claiming error in the judge's decision, over its objection, to withdraw the interrogatories and to demand a general verdict.

Issue: Is it an abuse of discretion for a federal trial judge to withdraw all written interrogatories from jury consideration for the purpose of eliminating confusion as to one such interrogatory?

Rule: No. Withdrawing written interrogatories is not an abuse of a trial judge's discretion where the defendant is not thereby prejudiced.

Note: Distinguish this case from one in which the jury simply delays in returning answers to interrogatories, and the trial judge withdraws the interrogatories. That is prejudicial to the defendant, and constitutes reversible error.

Texas Employers' Insurance Association v. Price (Tex. Ct. Civ. App. 1960)

Facts: During jury deliberations in a personal injury action filed in state court, one of the jurors related his personal experiences in an effort to persuade the jury to the plaintiff's cause. The jury returned a large verdict in favor of the plaintiff and the defendant appealed on the ground of juror misconduct.

Issue: Is a juror's effort to persuade a jury by relating his personal experiences reversible error?

Rule: Yes. It is misconduct and reversible error for a juror to relate to other jurors his own personal experiences as original evidence of material facts to be considered in their deliberations.

Lavender v. Kurn (S. Ct. 1946)

Facts: In a state court action under the Federal Employers Liability Act, the administrator of the decedent's estate alleged that the decedent had been killed by a mail hook protruding from the side of defendant's railway car while the defendants claimed that the deceased had been murdered. On appeal, the jury's verdict in favor of the estate was overturned by the state supreme court on the ground that the jury's conclusion that the deceased had been struck by the hook was based purely on speculation.

Issue: May an appellate court reverse a jury's decision on the grounds that the jury must have used speculation and conjecture in reaching its decision?

Rule: The standard of appellate review of a jury verdict is the "clearly erroneous" rule, i.e., that verdict must be upheld when there is an evidentiary basis for it. Under this standard, a verdict can be reversed only when there is a total absence of probative facts to support it. Where sufficient evidence exists that reasonable jurors can reach different inferences, the jury is entitled to engage in some speculation in choosing the most reasonable inference.

Hicks v. United States (4th Cir. 1966)

Facts: In an action brought in federal court under the Federal Tort Claims Act, the administrator of the decedent's estate charged a navy doctor with negligence based on his failure to exercise "ordinary care" in the deceased's treatment. In a court trial, the judge relied upon the testimony of the government's expert witness in determining that the doctor had exercised "average judgment," and entered judgment for the defendant.

Issue: In light of FRCP 52(a), when may a court of appeals reverse a trial judge's finding of negligence, as opposed to a finding of fact, which may only be set aside where "clearly erroneous"?

Rule: An appellate court may freely review a trial judge's ruling on the issue of negligence as it is a question of law, not of fact. Thus, the "clearly erroneous" standard of FRCP 52(a) is inapplicable.

Des Moines Navigation & R. Co. v. Iowa Homestead Co. (S. Ct. 1887)

Facts: An Iowa plaintiff sued an Iowa defendant and several New York defendants in state court. The New Yorkers removed the case based on diversity of citizenship. The plaintiff never objected to the removal (including before the U.S. Supreme Court) and contested the merits and a verdict was rendered for the defendants. The plaintiff subsequently refiled the same claim in state court and sought to avoid claim preclusion on the grounds that the federal court judgment was void for lack of subject matter jurisdiction.

Issue: Is a federal court judgment entitled to preclusive effect when that court lacked subject matter jurisdiction but where the judgment loser never challenged the existence of subject matter jurisdiction at trial or on appeal?

Rule: Yes. A party who fails to challenge a court's subject matter jurisdiction at trial or on appeal is bound by the preclusive effect of that judgment even if the rendering court did not possess subject matter jurisdiction.

Bell v. Novick Transfer Co. (D. Md. 1955)

Facts: In a negligence action arising out of an auto accident that was originally filed in state court and then removed, the defendant subsequently moved to dismiss on the grounds that the complaint did not allege specific acts of negligence, but only that the defendant's agent negligently drove its truck into the car in which the plaintiff was riding, thereby injuring the plaintiff.

Issue: What information must a complaint contain?

Rule: Under FRCP 8, which applies to removed cases (Maryland rules of procedure would have applied if the case had not been removed), a complaint need only contain a short and plain statement of the claim showing that the pleader is entitled to relief. This complaint met that standard. Motion to dismiss denied.

Houchins v. American Home Assurance Co. (4th Cir. 1991)

Facts: Mr. Houchins was missing for over seven years and, by law, presumed dead. He had two life insurance policies, both of which required that the insured's death be accidental to be entitled to coverage. When the insurer refused to pay, Mrs. Houchins filed a breach of contract suit in federal court. American Home moved for summary judgment on the ground that Mrs. Houchins offered no evidence either of her husband's death or that it was accidental.

Issue: May a party defeat a motion for summary judgment by offering only an inference as evidence of an essential element of the claim as to which that party has the burden of persuasion?

Rule: No. FRCP 56(c) provides that summary judgment must be granted against a party that fails to make a showing sufficient to establish the existence of an element essential to that party's case as to which it bears the burden of persuasion. Although the plaintiff was entitled to a presumption that the husband had died, merely showing his disappearance (the fact generating the presumption) was insufficient to enable a reasonable factfinder to conclude that the death was accidental. Thus, since the plaintiff did not establish the existence of a genuine issue of fact on this essential element of her claim, the defendant was entitled to summary judgment.

Norton v. Snapper Power Equipment (11th Cir. 1987)

Facts: Norton, a gardener, was injured by a power lawnmower manufactured by Snapper when a blade sliced off his fingers. He sued Snapper in federal court on a strict liability theory. After the jury returned a verdict in favor of Norton, the trial judge issued judgment notwithstanding the verdict on the grounds that there was insufficient evidence from which a jury could have found that a blade-stopping device would have reduced or prevented Norton's injuries.

Issue: What is the standard for granting a judgment notwithstanding the verdict?

Rule: A verdict cannot be based on speculation and conjecture. However, a jury can reach a verdict by reconstructing events by drawing inference upon inference. A court should grant judgment notwithstanding the verdict only where the evidence, when viewed in the light most favorable to the nonmoving party, so strongly points in favor of the moving party that reasonable people could not find otherwise.

CHAPTER 2

Jurisdiction

I. OVERVIEW

A court may only hear a case if the court has both:

A. Subject Matter Jurisdiction

Power to adjudicate the kind of case presented.

1. Power to Act
2. The defendant must be provided with adequate notice and opportunity to be heard.

B. Personal Jurisdiction

Power over the parties or property involved.

1. In Personam Jurisdiction

The court has jurisdiction due to its power over the defendant itself.

2. In Rem Jurisdiction

The court has jurisdiction due to its power over the property (*res*) in question.

3. Quasi in Rem Jurisdiction

The court has jurisdiction by seizing property that belongs to the defendant but that is not the subject of the litigation.

II. SUBJECT MATTER JURISDICTION

A. Defined power of a court to decide the kind of action before it. Mnemonic: **FADES**

B. Federal Question Cases (28 U.S.C. §1331)

1. Federal courts have jurisdiction over "all civil actions arising under the Constitution, laws, or treaties of the United States."
2. A case meets this constitutional standard if either federal law creates the cause of action or the plaintiff's right to relief under a state law-created claim necessarily depends upon resolution of a substantial question of federal law and that exercise of federal jurisdiction does not alter the allocation of labor between federal and state courts that was envisioned by Congress.

3. A claim can be created by federal law either expressly or by implication.

C. Diversity (28 U.S.C. §1332)

   1. **Amount in Controversy**

      a. This rule does not apply to federal question cases.

      b. The party seeking federal jurisdiction must show that his claim was made in good faith and that it is possible the amount in controversy exceeds $75,000. The party is not required to prove the actual value of the amount in controversy.

      c. The party challenging the jurisdiction will only prevail if he shows with "legal certainty" that the claim will be adjudicated for less than $75,000.

      d. The jurisdiction may not be challenged if the actual recovery turns out to be less than $75,000.

      e. Under the majority rule, the amount at stake must exceed $75,000 to either the plaintiff or the defendant.

      f. Multiple plaintiffs or defendants:

         i. One plaintiff may aggregate several claims against a single defendant to reach the statutory minimum.

         ii. One plaintiff may not aggregate several claims against several defendants nor may he join claims against other defendants when he has aggregated several claims against one defendant to reach the statutory minimum.

         iii. Multiple plaintiffs will qualify for federal jurisdiction when at least one plaintiff's claim is valued at $75,000.

         iv. Jurisdiction will not be allowed when the aggregate of several plaintiffs' claims meets the statutory minimum but no single claim meets the statutory minimum. **Exception:** Two or more plaintiffs enforcing the same right or interest that they share or own.

         v. The same rules apply for class action suits.

   2. **Diversity of Citizenship**

      a. Complete Diversity

      Each plaintiff must be a citizen of a different state than each defendant. However, co-plaintiffs and co-defendants may be citizens of the same state. This is a requirement of §1332, not of Article III of the U.S. Constitution.

      b. Minimal Diversity

      In federal interpleader cases, there is diversity where one or more plaintiffs are from a different state than one or more of the defendants.

      c. Citizenship is measured at the time the suit is brought, not at the time of the event in controversy.

D. Enumerated Areas
1. Constitution

The Constitution enumerates various areas where the federal courts have original jurisdiction, such as admiralty and cases involving ambassadors and public ministers. None of these cases require the amount in controversy.

2. Statutes

Congress has also passed statutes granting federal courts exclusive and original jurisdiction over certain areas of the law, including patent and copyright law, antitrust law, and cases where the United States is a party. With the exception of cases where the United States is a defendant, no amount in controversy requirement need be met.

E. Supplemental Jurisdiction (28 U.S.C. §1367)
1. Pre-existing Doctrines of Pendent and Ancillary Jurisdiction

Prior to the passage of the Federal Judiciary Act of 1991 (28 U.S.C. §1367), nondiverse state law claims that otherwise would have to be adjudicated in a state court due to lack of federal subject matter jurisdiction might be joined with a valid federal question or diversity claim by virtue of doctrines known as pendent and ancillary jurisdiction.

a. Pendent Jurisdiction

Encompassed claims that do not fall within the federal court's original jurisdiction that are contained in the plaintiff's complaint.

b. Ancillary Jurisdiction

Encompassed claims that do not fall within the federal court's original jurisdiction that are asserted by parties other than the plaintiff as a cross-claim, counterclaim or third-party claim. The distinction between the two is largely academic because the rules governing both types of jurisdiction are identical, and in any event, they have both been rendered moot by the supplemental jurisdiction statute.

c. Impact of Enactment of 28 U.S.C. §1367

The concepts of pendent and ancillary jurisdiction were rendered moot as they were supplanted by the doctrine of supplemental jurisdiction codified at 28 U.S.C. §1367.

2. Statutory Provisions
a. What Is Covered? (28 U.S.C. §1367(a))

Federal courts may now hear a claim that is part of the same "case" as a claim within the court's original jurisdiction, i.e., that this supplemental claim arises out of the same transaction, occurrence or series of transactions or occurrences as the claim properly before the court.

b. What Is Not Covered? (28 U.S.C. §1367(b))
Claims that are either
  i. Brought by necessary parties (FRCP 19) and intervenors (FRCP 24); or
  ii. Brought by any plaintiff against any party joined under FRCP 14, 19, 20, or 24
may not be attached to an existing diversity claim unless there is independent satisfaction of the diversity of citizenship requirement.

c. Discretionary Dismissal (28 U.S.C. §1367(c))
Even if a claim is not prohibited under §1367(b), a court may still dismiss a supplemental claim at its discretion if:
Mnemonic: **POND**
  i. **P**redominating State Claim
    When the state claim predominates over the federal case it would be fairer to have a state court decide the case.
  ii. **O**ther Compelling Reasons
    The statute requires "exceptional circumstances."
  iii. **N**ovel or Complex State Law
    State courts are more qualified than federal courts to resolve novel or complex issues of state law.
  iv. **D**ismissal of Federal Claims
    All claims within the court's original jurisdiction have been dismissed, leaving only the supplemental claims for disposition.

III. PERSONAL JURISDICTION

A. In Personam
  1. Physical Presence
    a. *Pennoyer v. Neff* (S. Ct. 1877)
    A state court cannot assert in personam jurisdiction over a nonresident defendant unless the defendant was personally served with process in the state or voluntarily appeared before the court. But a state court may exercise jurisdiction over a nonresident defendant's property, even if the property is not related to the action at hand, if the property is located within the territorial limits of the forum state.
    b. Kinds of Jurisdiction
      i. In Personam
      Where the proceeding involves an adjudication of the defendant's rights and obligations and where jurisdiction is based on the defendant's own presence within the territorial limits of the forum state.

       ii. In Rem
         Attachment of defendant's in-state property when the
         defendant is out of state and the property is located within
         the territorial limits of the forum state.
    c. Transient Presence
       Jurisdiction may be asserted over any person entering the
       state for even a brief moment such as persons passing
       through by car or flying over in a plane.
2. Domicile
    a. Relevance
       A court may exercise in personam jurisdiction over an
       individual though the person is not physically within the
       jurisdiction if that person was domiciled within the forum
       state.
    b. Determination
       Domicile is determined by:
         i. Party's intent to permanently locate there, and
        ii. An affirmative act expressing such intent.
    c. Limitation
       A person may only have one domicile, even though he has
       more than one residence.
3. Jurisdiction Based on Consent
    a. A court may render a binding enforceable judgment against a
       party who consents to the jurisdiction of the court even if the
       court would not have had jurisdiction over the individual
       absent his consent.
    b. Kinds of Consent
        i. Express Consent
           (1) Defendant stipulates court's jurisdiction in advance of
              litigation.
           (2) Parties to a contract may specify or limit the jurisdic-
              tion(s) in which suit can be filed through a forum
              selection clause.
           (3) Parties to a contract appoint an in-state agent to
              accept process.
           (4) An appearance on the merits (general appearance).
        ii. Implied Consent
          State statutes may specify that persons engaging in certain
          activities will impliedly consent to that state's jurisdiction.
        iii. Motorist Statutes
          Hess v. Pawloski (S. Ct. 1927)
          A state statute can confer implied consent to jurisdiction
          upon any motorist operating a vehicle within the state
          with respect to any dispute arising out of the use of an

automobile on the state's highways where the defendant received actual notice of the suit.

4. Jurisdiction over Corporations
   a. A corporation is subject to the jurisdiction of the state in which it is incorporated.
   b. For purposes of personal jurisdiction, a corporation is resident in the state in which it is incorporated. For federal subject matter jurisdiction based on diversity of citizenship purposes, a corporation is considered a citizen of both its state of incorporation and the state where it maintains its principal place of business.
   c. Unlike an individual, a corporation will not fall under a state's jurisdiction by the mere presence within the state of a corporate employee or officer.

5. Minimum Contacts Rule
   a. *International Shoe Co. v. Washington* (S. Ct. 1945)
      In order to subject a defendant to in personam jurisdiction in a state where the defendant is neither resident nor present, there must be certain minimum contacts between the defendant and the forum such that maintenance of the suit does not offend traditional notions of fair play and substantial justice embodied in the Due Process Clause of the Fourteenth Amendment to the U.S. Constitution.
   b. Two-Step Analysis
      i. Does the defendant have minimum contacts with the forum? If so,
      ii. Will asserting jurisdiction comply with traditional notions of fair play and justice?
   c. *Hanson v. Denckla* (S. Ct. 1958)
      Jurisdiction may not be invoked when a defendant's contact with the forum state is negligible and not purposeful.
   d. Specific Jurisdiction — *McGee v. International Life Insurance Co.* (S. Ct. 1957)
      A defendant's activities in the forum may subject the defendant to personal jurisdiction, even if sporadic or a single act, as long as the action arises from that single act (specific jurisdiction).
   e. General Jurisdiction — *Helicopteros Nacionales de Colombia, SA. v. Hall* (S. Ct. 1984)
      Where the defendant's in-forum activities do not give rise to the plaintiff's cause of action, the constitutional due process standard will be met only if the defendant's in-forum activities are substantial.

    f. *Kulko v. Superior Court* (S. Ct. 1978)
      A parent does not have minimum contacts with a state because he allowed a child to live with the other parent in the forum state.

    g. *World-Wide Volkswagen v. Woodson* (S. Ct. 1980)
      Conduct in a forum, not expectation of revenue, is how jurisdiction is determined. The fact that the defendant derived revenue from use of its product in the forum state was not sufficient to confer jurisdiction where the product was brought into the state by the plaintiff. In addition to the *International Shoe* contacts-based analysis, a state court also must evaluate the fairness of exercising jurisdiction over the nonresident defendant based on an assessment of the interests of the plaintiff, forum state, defendant, and judicial system.

    h. *Asahi Metal Industry v. Superior Court* (S. Ct. 1987)
      Where the defendant has no direct linkage to the forum state, in determining whether it created a constitutionally sufficient relationship with the forum state, one must examine the stream of commerce. Two separate four-member groups of Justices offered different formulations of the stream of commerce theory. One opinion (Justice O'Connor) requires that the defendant put the product in the stream of commerce and take some affirmative act to direct it toward the forum state. The other opinion (Justice Brennan) requires only that the defendant place the product in the stream of commerce and that it is aware that the product is being marketed in the forum state.

    i. *Burger King v. Rudzewicz* (S. Ct. 1985)
      Jurisdiction is not conferred solely because one party to a contract resides in the forum.

B. In Rem Jurisdiction
  1. Definitions
    a. In Rem Jurisdiction
      Jurisdiction based on a court's power over a thing (*res*), not a person. The action is technically against the property, not a person. The subject of the litigation is related to the property.

    b. Quasi in Rem Jurisdiction
      Jurisdiction based on an action against a person. Since the court is unable to obtain in personam jurisdiction over the defendant, jurisdiction is obtained by seizing the defendant's property. The property is NOT related to the action. The action is against the person, not the property. Quasi in

rem actions may force the sale of real property, garnishment of wages, or assignment of a debt.

2. *Rush v. Savchuk* (S. Ct. 1980)
   Quasi in rem jurisdiction over an insurer may not be based on its obligation to defend a policy holder.

3. *Shaffer v. Heitner* (S. Ct. 1977)
   All assertions of personal jurisdiction, including in rem and quasi in rem jurisdiction, may only be asserted when the defendant has the "minimum contacts" with the forum state that satisfy the requirements for in personam jurisdiction as defined by *International Shoe.* Although this ruling has negligible effect on the continued availability of in rem jurisdiction, it substantially limits the availability of quasi in rem jurisdiction.

IV. NOTICE AND OPPORTUNITY TO BE HEARD

A. Generally
   A court that has proper jurisdiction over a case may only proceed when the defendant has proper notice of the proceedings against him. Proper notice usually entails service of "process" consisting of a summons to appear and a copy of the complaint. The defendant need not necessarily receive actual notice of the suit but the procedures followed must be "reasonably likely" to provide notice. The defendant must have adequate time to prepare his defense.

B. Waiver of Personal Service
   FRCP 4 imposes an affirmative duty upon competent children, adults, corporations, partnerships, and unincorporated associations within the United States to waive personal service in favor of service by mail or its equivalent. If such a defendant refuses to execute a waiver, the federal district court shall assess plaintiff's costs in effecting service unless the defendant convinces the court that it had good cause for failure to waive service.

C. Methods of Service Where Waiver Unavailable or Not Executed
   1. Personal Service
      Defendant is physically handed a summons.
   2. Attachment
      Defendant receives notice by the attachment of his tangible property. Statutes typically require additional notice such as mailing the summons or publication.

3. Garnishment
Garnishment of a debt or other nontangible property will satisfy
the notice requirement in quasi in rem cases. Statutes require
that further notice be provided.
4. Substituted Service
Modern statutes often allow substituted service so that justice
will reach a defendant avoiding personal service. Some types of
substituted service generally allowed are:
a. Mail
b. Summons affixed to door of the defendant's unattended
dwelling
c. Summons left at defendant's dwelling
d. Court order
e. Summons left with a person of "suitable age and discretion"
residing in the same dwelling as the defendant
5. Constructive Notice
a. Registered or certified mail
b. Publication
c. Electronic transmission
6. Corporations
a. Designated Corporate Official
The statute will designate the official to receive process.
b. *Mullane* Rule
Expense and availability of the names and addresses of the beneficiaries to numerous small trust funds should be taken into
account in determining the sufficiency of notice by publication.
Subsequent cases have required notice by mail to all parties.

V. REMOVAL

A. Generally
A defendant may remove an action to a federal court when the
action fell within the court's original subject matter jurisdiction
but was asserted in a state court.
B. Exception
A diversity action may only be removed when no defendant is a
citizen of the state in which the action was filed.
C. Defendant's Right
The right of removal can only be asserted by defendants, even when
the plaintiff is a counter-defendant to a counterclaim that falls
within the federal court's original subject matter jurisdiction.
D. Valid State Court Jurisdiction Unnecessary
A case can be removed from a state court that did not possess
subject matter jurisdiction over the action (28 U.S.C. §1441(f)).

VI. CHALLENGES TO JURISDICTION

A. Special Appearance
   1. Traditional View
      Since presence is one way of asserting personal jurisdiction over a defendant, without a special appearance, any appearance in court, even to challenge jurisdiction, would invite a court to assert jurisdiction over the party. With a special appearance (as opposed to a general appearance that is an appearance to challenge the merits of the case and that constitutes a waiver of objection to personal jurisdiction), a party appears for the limited purpose of challenging personal jurisdiction. If the challenge is successful, the case is dismissed, and the suit must be refiled with a new assertion of jurisdiction. If the challenge fails, the party has not waived its right to challenge the merits of the case.
   2. Modern Terminology
      In the federal and most state court systems, the term "special appearance" has been replaced by the use of a motion to dismiss for lack of personal jurisdiction. In these courts, a defendant challenges jurisdiction by filing a motion to dismiss for lack of jurisdiction without being deemed to have consented to the exercise of jurisdiction over it. Many courts also allow a limited appearance for in quasi in rem actions where the defendant can challenge the merits but limit its liability to the value of the property seized as the basis for exercising personal jurisdiction over it.
B. Collateral Attack
   A defendant defaulting on an action may collaterally attack a default judgment asserted in another jurisdiction on the grounds that the first action was asserted in a forum without proper jurisdiction. This often occurs where a default judgment granted in one jurisdiction is sought to be enforced in a second jurisdiction.

VII. VENUE

A. Defined
   The place within a jurisdiction where an action is brought.
B. State and Local Courts
   Local rules establish venue. The location where the cause of action arose, the residence or place of business of the parties, and the site of property involved in the action are among the most commonly used factors.

C. Federal Venue

Under the federal venue statute, 18 U.S.C. §1391, venue lies in a district where the defendants reside or where the claim arose. Where no district in the United States would meet either of these requirements, venue lies in a district where a defendant is subject to personal jurisdiction (in pure diversity cases) or where the defendant may be found (in cases involving a federal question claim). A corporation resides for venue purposes in any jurisdiction where it is subject to personal jurisdiction. An alien may be sued in any district.

D. Transfer of Venue

A federal trial court can transfer a case to another federal district where it could have been brought if either venue did not lie in the chosen forum (28 U.S.C. §1446) or if venue did lie in the chosen forum but an alternative forum in which the action might have been brought is substantially more convenient to the parties and witnesses, and is in the interest of justice (28 U.S.C. §1404).

E. Forum Non Conveniens

A court may decline jurisdiction and dismiss a case over which it had subject matter jurisdiction and involving defendants over which it could exercise personal jurisdiction and where venue lies if there is an alternative forum in which all requirements for jurisdiction and venue also are met and where the plaintiff's chosen forum is highly inconvenient to either the defendant(s) or the chosen forum.

CASE CLIPS

Pennoyer v. Neff (S. Ct. 1877)

Facts: Mitchell brought an action against Neff in an Oregon state court to recover legal fees. He served Neff, a nonresident, by publication and obtained a default judgment. Thereafter, Neff learned of the sale of his real property in Oregon to satisfy the judgment. He sued Pennoyer, who had obtained title from the purchaser, in federal court in Oregon to recover his property. Neff argued that the state court judgment that resulted in the sale of his property was void because that court did not have personal jurisdiction over him.

Issue: Is service by publication sufficient to give a state court in personam jurisdiction over a nonresident?

Rule: No. A personal judgment against a nonresident served only by publication is invalid. For a court to exercise in personam jurisdiction over a nonresident defendant, that defendant must come within the court's jurisdiction either by receipt of personal service within the state or by appearing in the action. In rem jurisdiction may be exercised by timely attaching the in-state property of an out-of-state defendant who otherwise could not be brought into the jurisdiction by in personam jurisdiction. To promote the sovereignty of states within the United States, each state has exclusive power over persons and property located within its territorial boundaries.

Hess v. Pawloski (S. Ct. 1927)

Facts: In a Massachusetts court, the plaintiff of Massachusetts sued the defendant of Pennsylvania for injuries arising from an auto accident in Massachusetts. Process was served in compliance with a state statute that appointed the state registrar of motor vehicles as a nonresident's agent for receipt of service of process in suits arising out of the use of an automobile on the state's highways.

Issue: May a state enact a statute that deems a state official to be appointed in advance as a nonresident's agent on whom process may be served for claims arising out of automobile accidents occurring within the state?

Rule: Yes. Since a state has the right to regulate and promote safety on its highways, it may deem a nonresident motorist to have appointed one of its officials as his agent on whom process may be served in proceedings arising out of such highway use as long as the defendant receives actual notice of the suit.

International Shoe Co. v. Washington (S. Ct. 1945)

Facts: The state of Washington brought suit to collect unemployment taxes from a company that did not have an office in Washington and that was incorporated in another state, but that did have a sales force of 11 to 13 people in Washington who regularly solicited business.

Issue: What contacts are required for the courts of a state to exercise in personam jurisdiction over a nonresident defendant?

Rule: The Due Process Clause of the Fourteenth Amendment requires that state courts can exercise in personam jurisdiction over a nonresident defendant only when that defendant has "the minimum contacts with the forum state such that maintenance of the suit does not offend traditional notions of fair play and substantial justice." The extent of the relationship between the nonresident defendant and the forum state will have to be significantly more substantial if the plaintiff's cause of action does not arise out of the defendant's in-forum activities than when it does arise out of those activities.

Concurrence: (Black, J.) The Due Process Clause imposes only a procedural requirement that parties have fair notice of suits brought against them. It does not impose any limitation on a state's power to exercise jurisdiction over parties to litigation.

Gray v. American Radiator & Standard Sanitary Corp. (Ill. Sup. Ct. 1961)

Facts: Gray was injured in Illinois when a water heater exploded. She sued Titan, the manufacturer of a safety valve, an Ohio corporation that did no business in Illinois. Gray relied on Illinois's long-arm statute, which provided for the exercise of personal jurisdiction over a defendant who committed a tortious act in Illinois.

Issue: Does a state long-arm statute providing for the exercise of personal jurisdiction over a defendant who commits a tortious act within the forum state extend to a situation where the allegedly negligently manufactured product was manufactured outside of the forum state but caused injury inside the forum state and, if so, does application of this statute meet the constitutional due process requirement for the exercise of personal jurisdiction?

Rule: The alleged negligence cannot be separated from the resulting injury and, therefore, the presence of the injury in the forum state satisfies the statutory requirement. Since the cause of action arose out of the defendant's in-forum contact (the occurrence of the injury), the level of contacts required by *International Shoe* have been met by the commission of a single tort particularly where, as here, the defendant did not claim that the present use of its product in the forum state was an isolated instance.

World-Wide Volkswagen Corp. v. Woodson (S. Ct. 1980)

Facts: The Woodsons of New York bought an Audi in New York. After being injured in a crash while driving through Oklahoma, they brought an action in Oklahoma state court against the New York dealer and the New York area distributor of the car for defective design. Neither defendant had any business connection to Oklahoma. The trial court and state supreme court upheld the exercise of jurisdiction over the defendants.

Issue: May a state exercise personal jurisdiction over a nonresident corporation that has no direct connection with the forum state but that places its product into a "stream of commerce" and a consumer brings that product into the forum state?

Rule: (White, J.) No. To meet the contacts standard of *International Shoe*, a defendant must purposefully avail itself of the privilege of conducting activities within the forum state and this standard is not met when the product arrives in the forum as the result of the unilateral action of a third party (here, the plaintiffs). Under these circumstances, the defendant's forum contacts are so attenuated that it would not reasonably anticipate becoming subject to the forum state's jurisdiction Additionally, beyond the contacts analysis of *International Shoe*, which focuses on the reasonableness of imposing the burden of defending upon the defendant, the court also should consider the interest of the forum state, the plaintiff, and the interstate judicial system in assessing the overall fairness of exercising personal jurisdiction.

Dissent 1: (Brennan, J.) As long as the defendant purposefully injected its product into the stream of commerce and its use in the forum is predictable, the court also should examine the non–defendant-related fairness factors set forth by the majority.

Dissent 2: (Marshall, J.) By being part of a nationwide auto marketing network, the defendants could reasonably expect to be required to defend in the forum state.

Asahi Metal Industry Co. v. Superior Court (S. Ct. 1987)

Facts: In a personal injury suit filed in California state court, Zurcher, a Californian, sued Cheng Shin, a Taiwanese tube manufacturer. Cheng Shin, in turn, sought indemnification from Asahi Metal, the Japanese manufacturer of a component part. Zurcher and Cheng Shin subsequently settled, leaving only the claim by Cheng Shin against Asahi. The state courts all upheld the exercise of personal jurisdiction over Asahi. Asahi did not ship any of its products directly to the United States. Asahi knew that some of Cheng Shin's tubes containing its valves were sold throughout the United States, including California, but insisted that it never imagined that this would subject it to jurisdiction in California.

Issue: Under what circumstances is the constitutional requirement for personal jurisdiction satisfied when a foreign corporation manufactures products outside the United States that end up in the forum state via the stream of commerce?

Rule: (O'Connor, J.) The defendant must not only have placed its product in the stream but also taken some affirmative act to purposefully direct it toward the forum state.

Concurrence 1: (Brennan, J.) To satisfy the *International Shoe* reasonableness (via contacts) portion of the due process test in a stream of commerce case, it is sufficient for the defendant to have placed its product in the stream of commerce and to be aware that the final product (of which its product is a component part) is being marketed in the forum state. Under such circumstances, the defendant benefits from the retail sale of the final product in the forum and indirectly benefits from the state's laws that regulate commercial activity.

Concurrence 2: (Stevens, J.) It is not always necessary to engage in the *International Shoe* inquiry about the existence of contacts by the defendant with the forum state when, as here, inquiry under the fairness factors set forth in *Volkswagen* independently establishes the unfairness of exercising personal jurisdiction.

Burger King Corp. v. Rudzewicz (S. Ct. 1985)

Facts: Rudzewicz, a Michigan resident, contracted with Burger King, a Florida corporation, to operate a franchise in Michigan. The contract stated that Florida law controlled and required monthly rental payments to be sent to Burger King headquarters in Florida. When Rudzewicz fell behind on his rental obligations, Burger King brought suit in Florida.

Issue: May the forum state exercise in personam jurisdiction over a nonresident defendant who has entered into a contract with a corporation from the forum state?

Rule: Yes. The sending of rental payments to the forum constitutes direct and continuous contacts with the forum state sufficient to satisfy the *International Shoe* standard of due process. These actions by the defendant were sufficient to put him on notice that he might be subject to suit in the forum state.

Dissent: (Stevens, J.) Enforcing a boilerplate franchise contract in which the franchisor unilaterally chose the forum for litigation violates the fundamental fairness principle embodied in the Due Process Clause.

McGee v. International Life Insurance Co. (S. Ct. 1957)

Facts: McGee, a California citizen and beneficiary on a life insurance policy issued by Texas-based International Life, brought suit in California state court when the insurer failed to pay when the insured, another California resident, died. International Life had no office and solicited and transacted no business in California except for the policy as to which McGee had been paying policy premiums from California to

International Life in Texas. McGee obtained a default judgment and brought an enforcement action in Texas state court. The Texas court refused to enforce it on the ground that the California court lacked personal jurisdiction over the Texas-based insurer.

Issue: Does the Due Process Clause permit the exercise of personal jurisdiction over a nonresident corporation based on a single set of transactions in the forum state when the plaintiff's claim arises out of those transactions?

Rule: Yes. Where the court is exercising specific jurisdiction (i.e., the claim arises out of the defendant's forum activities), a lower threshold of contacts is required to meet the *International Shoe* test. Since the plaintiff's claim arose out of a contract that was paid for by premiums sent from the forum and the forum state had a significant interest in providing a forum for its residents denied payment for foreign insurers, asserting jurisdiction is not a denial of due process.

Perkins v. Benguet Consolidated Mining Co. (S. Ct. 1952)

Facts: Perkins, a nonresident of Ohio, sued Benguet, a Philippine mining corporation, in Ohio state court for failure to pay her stockholder dividends and to issue her stock certificates. Although Benguet maintained a continuous and systematic part of its mining business in Ohio, this cause of action did not arise out of any of its activities in Ohio. The trial court dismissed the action for lack of personal jurisdiction.

Issue: May a state court assert in personam jurisdiction over a foreign corporation regarding a cause of action not arising in the state, nor related to the systematic and continuous activities of the corporation in that state?

Rule: Yes. When a foreign corporation has sufficient and substantial business in a state, the Due Process Clause does not preclude (nor require) the state court's exercise of general jurisdiction, i.e., jurisdiction in a case involving a cause of action that does not arise out of the defendant's in-forum activities.

Helicopteros Nacionales de Colombia, S.A. v. Hall (S. Ct. 1984)

Facts: Hall brought a wrongful death action in Texas state court against Helicopteros, a Colombian corporation engaged in transportation services outside the United States. Although Helicopteros had no agents in the United States, it sent executives to Texas to negotiate a contract, purchased spare parts from a Texas company, trained personnel in Texas, and received checks from Texas banks. None of these activities related to the helicopter crash that generated the plaintiff's suit.

Issue: When a party purchases parts, trains personnel, and negotiates a contract in a state, has it established the necessary contacts to subject itself to the state's in personam jurisdiction not arising out of those forum activities?

Rule: No. In a case of general jurisdiction, the extent of a defendant's forum activities must be more substantial than in a suit that arises out of those forum-related contacts to pass muster under *International Shoe*. Purchases and isolated trips are not sufficiently continuous and systematic to meet that standard.

Dissent: (Brennan, J.) This cause of action did arise out of the defendant's forum-related contacts and so the state could constitutionally exercise personal jurisdiction, despite a lack of systematic and continuous contacts.

Shaffer v. Heitner (S. Ct. 1977)

Facts: Heitner brought a shareholder's derivative suit against Greyhound, a Delaware corporation, and 28 of its officers and directors in Delaware state court. Jurisdiction was based on sequestration of the individual defendants' Greyhound stock, which was deemed, pursuant to Delaware state law, to be located in Delaware.

Issue: Absent other contacts of a defendant with a state, will sequestration of the defendant's property that is deemed to be located in that state provide a state court with a basis for quasi in rem jurisdiction over the property owner?

Rule: All assertions of personal jurisdiction, whether in personam, in rem, or quasi in rem, now must be subjected to the *International Shoe* test of constitutional fairness. And though the presence of the property inside the forum constitutes a contact for due process purposes, where, as in quasi-in-rem cases, the cause of action is unrelated to that contact, the mere presence of the property in the forum state often will not provide a sufficiently substantial degree of purposeful activity to meet the constitutional standard.

Concurrence 1: (Powell, J.) Cases asserting quasi-in-rem jurisdiction based on the presence of real property arguably should meet the constitutional standard, without more.

Concurrence 2: (Stevens, J.) Agreed with the result in this case and with Justice Powell's comments about cases involving real property, but suggested that the Court's application of *International Shoe* to all quasi-in-rem cases may be too broad because "other long-accepted methods of acquiring" quasi-in-rem jurisdiction should not be subject to a test that requires more than the presence of that property in the forum.

Concurrence and Dissent: (Brennan, J.) This is an advisory opinion — since the majority struck down the state jurisdictional statute there was no reason to discuss to what extent constitutional analysis also should be applied in cases involving quasi-in-rem jurisdiction. Moreover, the plaintiff never had the opportunity to present evidence of the defendants' forum contacts since he had no reason to believe that evidence of anything other than the presence of their property in the forum was necessary to establish jurisdiction.

Burnham v. Superior Court of California (S. Ct. 1990)

Facts: Mr. and Mrs. Burnham were living in New Jersey when they separated. Mrs. Burnham moved to California with their children. While Mr. Burnham was in California to conduct business and to visit the children, he was served with a copy of his wife's divorce petition that had been filed in California state court. He moved to quash the service of process on the grounds that the court lacked personal jurisdiction over him because his only contacts with California were a few short visits.

Issue: May a court exert jurisdiction over a nonresident who was personally served while temporarily in a state in a suit unrelated to his activities in that state?

Rule: Physical presence alone is sufficient for a state to exercise jurisdiction over a person; due process requirements are satisfied. Since personal service within the forum state (i.e., physical presence) always has been viewed as a fair basis for exercising jurisdiction, regardless of whether the claim did or did not arise out of the defendant's presence in the forum, exercising jurisdiction based solely on such physical presence comports with "traditional notions" of fair play and substantial justice, as required by *International Shoe*.

Concurrence: (Brennan, J.) Although historical pedigree is relevant, it is not dispositive of the question of whether a particular basis for jurisdiction satisfies due process requirements. All jurisdictional rules must satisfy contemporary notions of due process. Nevertheless, a consideration of all relevant factors demonstrates that, as a rule, exercising personal jurisdiction based solely on the defendant's voluntary presence in the forum does satisfy the requirements of due process.

Pavlovich v. Superior Court (Cal. Sup. Ct. 2002)

Facts: Pavlovich, a Texas-based computer systems operator who had other direct contact with California, operated a passive web site that neither solicited or transacted any business nor permitted interactive exchange of information between user and operator. It provided site visitors with the source code that allowed them to copy movies from DVDs. Pavlovich was sued for misappropriation of trade secrets in California state court by a nonprofit trade association with its principal place of business in

California. Pavlovich sought to have the case dismissed for lack of personal jurisdiction.

Issue: Does the creation of a passive web site subject the site operator to in personam jurisdiction in a state where visitors have access to the site?

Rule: No. In order to meet the constitutionally mandated standard of contacts set forth in *International Shoe*, a web site must be more than a passive site that merely provides information to the viewer. For the web site operator to be said to have purposefully availed itself of forum benefits, the site must be assessed as to the level of its interactivity and, in particular, commercial activity. Since the instant web site was totally passive and there was no evidence of any California-directed content, nor any evidence that any Californian ever "hit" the site, the fact that the defendant may have known that his conduct could disadvantage California-based companies was an insufficient basis for the exercise of in personam jurisdiction.

Carnival Cruise Lines, Inc. v. Shute (S. Ct. 1991)

Facts: The Shutes (Washington State citizens) purchased tickets for a cruise with Carnival (a Florida corporation) through a Washington travel agent. Each ticket included a clause in fine print that named Florida as the forum state for any and all disputes arising from the cruise. During the cruise, Eulala Shute slipped and fell on a deck mat. The Shutes sued Carnival in the federal court in Washington. Carnival moved for dismissal based on the enforceability of the forum selection clause of the cruise tickets.

Issue: Is a forum consent clause in a form contract for passage on a cruise enforceable?

Rule: Yes. A forum consent clause is presumptively enforceable, particularly where the clause is a vital part of the agreement entering into the parties' practical and economic calculations. A party claiming that such a clause is unfair bears a heavy proof burden to rebut the presumption of enforceability. The forum selection clause in this case was reasonable because the cruise line had a high efficiency interest in conducting all litigation in a single forum. The passengers, too, derived an important benefit from the clause in the form of a reduced fare and conceded that they had notice of the selection provision in the contract.

Dissent: (Stevens, J.) Forum selection clauses in passenger tickets are unenforceable because the parties do not have equal bargaining power.

Insurance Corp. of Ireland, Ltd. v. Compagnie des Bauxites de Guinee (S. Ct. 1982)

Facts: The Compagnie des Bauxites de Guinee of Delaware sued various foreign insurance companies for breach of contract in federal court. Most of the foreign defendants contested personal jurisdiction and so Compagnie attempted to obtain the facts to establish jurisdiction via discovery. But when the companies failed to comply with the court's orders for production of the requested information, the trial court, per FRCP 37(b)(2)(A), issued an order presuming valid in personam jurisdiction.

Issue: May a court presume a valid assertion of jurisdiction pursuant to FRCP 37(b)(2)(A) due to a party's failure to produce requested documents during discovery?

Rule: Yes. Since the defendants challenged the exercise of personal jurisdiction over them, they could not block the plaintiff's reasonable efforts to establish the facts sufficient to justify the exercise of jurisdiction. Sanctioning their refusal to comply with the court's order by presuming the existence of personal jurisdiction does not violate due process.

Mullane v. Central Hanover Bank & Trust Co. (S. Ct. 1950)

Facts: Known and unknown nonresident beneficiaries of a trust fund were given notice of the application for judicial settlement of the account by publication in a local newspaper.

Issue: Is notice by publication of the pendency of an action adequate when attempting to inform known parties who could be apprised more effectively by mail or other means?

Rule: The fundamental requisite of due process is the opportunity to be heard. Due process requires that notice be reasonably calculated to apprise interested parties. Although notice by publication to nonresidents whose identity or location is unknown is adequate, it is not sufficient by itself where known interested parties can practicably and easily be informed by other means.

Jones v. Flowers (S. Ct. 2006)

Facts: After paying off his mortgage, Jones moved out of his house but stopped paying his property tax and never informed the state of his new address. Subsequently, he was informed of his delinquency by certified letter to him at that house. But no one signed for the letter nor appeared at the post office to retrieve it and so it was returned to the state agency as "unclaimed." Thereafter, notice of a public sale of the property was published in a local newspaper and a second certified letter was sent to the house informing Jones that the house would be sold if the taxes went unpaid. That letter also was returned as unclaimed and the house was sold to Flowers. Jones brought suit in state court alleging that the state's failure to provide additional forms of the tax sale violated the Due Process Clause.

Issue: Is service by certified letter sufficient to meet constitutional due process requirements when that letter is returned to the sender as unclaimed?

Rule: The government sender's knowledge that the letter was returned as unclaimed is a factor to consider in applying the *Mullane* standard of notice reasonably calculated to apprise interested parties. A reasonable person interested in informing a property owner of a tax sale would take additional steps to notify that person when a certified letter is returned as unclaimed, such as resending the letter by regular mail or posting it on the front door. And the fact that the defendant failed to provide the state with an updated address did not forfeit his right to constitutionally sufficient notice.

National Equipment Rental, Ltd. v. Szukhent (S. Ct. 1964)

Facts: Szukhent, a Michigan citizen, leased farm equipment from National Equipment Rental, Ltd. of New York. The contract provided that attorney Florence Weinberg would accept service in New York for claims arising from the contract. When Szukhent defaulted on payment, National Rental sued in federal court in New York. It served the agent, Weinberg, who then mailed the complaint to Szukhent.

Issue: If the person designated as agent for receipt of process in a contract is unknown to that party, is chosen by the adverse party, and is not required by the contract to forward a copy of the complaint to the named party, does this meet the requirement of service upon an "agent authorized by appointment" under FRCP 4(e)(2)?

Rule: Yes. A party to a private contract may agree that any litigation under the contract shall be conducted in a particular state and may appoint an agent to receive service of process, even if the agent is not personally known to the party and the agent has not expressly undertaken to transmit notice to the party. The single requirement of a valid agency is transmittal of the service to the party.

Dissent: (Black, J.) Although there is no due process issue in this case because the defendant did receive actual notice of the summons and complaint, the possibility for abuse of such clauses exists where large companies may force customers to come to a forum state the seller prefers and so such service should not be sanctioned.

State ex rel. Sivnksty v. Duffield
(W. Va. Sup. Ct. App. 1952)

Facts: Petitioner Sivnksty, a nonresident, was arrested and jailed on criminal charges of reckless driving following an accident involving Duffield. While in jail awaiting trial, Sivnksty was served with process in the civil case. He moved to dismiss on grounds of lack of personal jurisdiction since his presence in the forum was the product of his forced incarceration.

Issue: Can a nonresident who is confined in jail on criminal charges be validly served in prison with notice of a civil suit?

Rule: Yes. A nonresident party who is incarcerated on criminal charges or imprisoned as the result of a conviction can be served with process in a civil case if he was voluntarily in the jurisdiction at the time of the arrest and the confinement. However, a nonresident would be immune from civil process if he was served while in the jurisdiction under criminal process to take part in a criminal trial.

Wyman v. Newhouse (2d Cir. 1937)

Facts: Newhouse of New York was induced by Wyman's fraud to enter Florida whereupon he was served with process.

Issue: Can a state court properly exercise personal jurisdiction over a defendant who was lured into the forum state by fraud and then served with process?

Rule: When a defendant is fraudulently induced to enter the jurisdiction for service of process, the court lacks personal jurisdiction over him, and any judgment against him is null and void.

Fuentes v. Shevin (S. Ct. 1972)

Facts: Fuentes purchased a stove and other household goods from Firestone under an installment conditional sales contract. When a dispute arose over the servicing of the stove, the seller sued for repossession of all of the goods. Before the complaint had been served on Fuentes, Firestone obtained a writ of replevin authorizing the sheriff to seize the disputed goods at once. Fuentes challenged the state statute authorizing prejudgment replevin, for which Fuentes was offered neither notice nor a hearing in advance of seizure.

Issue: Do prejudgment replevin procedures that allow property to be seized without notice or an opportunity for a hearing to challenge the proposed taking violate due process where a hearing is granted after the property is taken?

Rule: Yes. It is fundamental to due process that there be notice and an opportunity to be heard at a meaningful time and in a meaningful manner before there is a significant taking of property by a state. To be meaningful, the notice and hearing must be granted when the deprivation or property can be prevented. Thus, an individual must be granted notice and a hearing before he is deprived of a significant property interest, except for extraordinary circumstances that justify postponing the hearing until after the taking has occurred. Even a temporary, non-final deprivation of property violates the Due Process Clause in the absence of timely notice and opportunity for hearing.

Dissent: (White, J.) In these situations the importance to the creditor of being able to repossess the items while they are still able to be located may outweigh the danger of an erroneous repossession. The availability of a bond posted by the plaintiff sufficiently guards against the assertion of frivolous claims and wrongful temporary deprivations.

Connecticut v. Doehr (S. Ct. 1991)

Facts: In connection with a tort suit, DiGiovanni submitted an ex parte request in Connecticut state court for prejudgment attachment of Doehr's home. The relevant state statute provided for ex parte prejudgment attachments of real property upon verification that there was probable cause to sustain the plaintiff's claim, but did not require a demonstration of extraordinary circumstances justifying prejudgment attachment. Based on the ex parte application, i.e., without notice to the property holder, the attachment order was issued by the state court. Thereafter, Doehr filed suit in federal court claiming that the ex parte attachment statute violated the Due Process Clause of the Fourteenth Amendment.

Issue: Does a state statute that allows prejudgment attachments of real estate without prior notice or hearing in the absence of a showing of exigent circumstances violate the Due Process Clause of the Fourteenth Amendment?

Rule: Yes. There can be no prejudgment attachment of realty without notice and hearing absent a showing of exigent circumstances. A prejudgment remedy statute that concerns deprivation of real property must satisfy a three-part inquiry: (1) consideration of the private interest affected by the measure, (2) examination of the risk of erroneous deprivations of that private interest; and (3) assessment of the interest of the party seeking the remedy. Property owners have obvious interests in continuous possession of their property and attachment severely limits the owner's opportunity to alienate or encumber it. Ex parte proceedings present serious risks of erroneous deprivations of property and absent exigent circumstances, the plaintiff has no compelling interest in controlling the property pending receipt of a judgment.

Lacks v. Lacks (N.Y. Ct. App. 1976)

Facts: A husband was granted a judgment of divorce by a New York State court even though he had not been a resident of New York for one full year preceding the commencement of the proceeding, as required by state law. Two years later, the former wife moved to vacate the judgment on the grounds that the court lacked subject matter jurisdiction to entertain the divorce action because of the husband's nonresident status.

Issue: Is a final judgment unenforceable on the grounds of lack of subject matter jurisdiction when the trial judge erroneously determined that all the elements of the cause of action were present?

Rule: No. The rule that lack of subject matter jurisdiction makes a final judgment void only applies when the court lacked jurisdiction over the subject matter of the suit as set forth by statute. It does not apply when one of the elements of the cause of action is missing. The absence of an element of the claim goes to something other than subject matter jurisdiction. This case fell within the court's statutorily created subject matter jurisdiction.

Mas v. Perry (5th Cir. 1974)

Facts: Jean Paul Mas, a citizen of France, and Judy Mas, a Mississippi citizen, moved to Louisiana after their marriage to continue their education, without intending to remain there permanently. Once in Louisiana, they rented an apartment from Perry, a Louisiana citizen, and subsequently sued him in federal court in Louisiana on a state law invasion of privacy claim, basing federal jurisdiction on diversity of citizenship.

Issue: What is the definition of citizenship for diversity purposes within the meaning of 28 U.S.C. §1332?

Rule: For purpose of diversity, citizenship is determined by "domicile," which, in turn, means one's fixed and permanent home, which can be changed only by residing in another state with the intention to remain there. Mere residence in another state, without demonstration of intention to remain, does not equate to domicile/citizenship. Thus, as neither plaintiff had demonstrated an intention to change their domicile from France and Mississippi to Louisiana, they were both diverse from the Louisiana defendant. Diversity jurisdiction over the claim by the French Mr. Mas existed under §1332(a)(2) (alienage) and over the claim by Mississippi plaintiff Mrs. Mas under §1332(a)(1).

A.F.A. Tours, Inc. v. Whitchurch (2d Cir. 1991)

Facts: Whitchurch's former employer, AFA, brought a state law claim of misappropriation of trade secrets against him in federal court asserting diversity jurisdiction. In its complaint, AFA sought an injunction and damages "in an amount which is not presently ascertainable, but which is believed to exceed the sum of $50,000" (the then existing amount in controversy requirement) and punitive damages of "no less than $250,000." The court *sua sponte* raised the issue of whether the value of the claims exceeded the amount in controversy requirement. It then concluded that it did not and dismissed the case for lack of subject matter jurisdiction.

Issue: What is the proper test for determining whether a plaintiff meets the minimum amount requirement for diversity jurisdiction set forth under 28 U.S.C. §1332?

Rule: In a diversity suit, the proper test governing the amount in controversy is whether the sum claimed by the plaintiff is made in good faith. It must appear to a legal certainty that the claim is for less than the minimum amount to justify a dismissal. The district court erred here in resolving the issue without allowing the plaintiff an opportunity to brief the issue; in most cases the legal certainty inquiry cannot be resolved on a record without briefing.

Note: The amount in controversy requirement for diversity jurisdiction subsequently was raised from in excess of $50,000 to in excess of $75,000 in 1996.

Kramer v. Caribbean Mills, Inc. (S. Ct. 1969)

Facts: In a dispute between Panama and two defendants — a Panamanian corporation and Caribbean Mills, a Haitian corporation — the Panamanian corporation assigned 95 percent of its interest to Kramer, a citizen of Texas, who had no other connection with the matter, and who agreed to return the recovery, if any, to the assignor. The sole purpose of the assignment was to create complete diversity for federal subject matter jurisdiction purposes.

Issue: When has a party been "improperly or collusively" joined to invoke the jurisdiction of the federal court within the meaning of 28 U.S.C. §1359?

Rule: Where an assignee lacks previous connection with a suit and simultaneously reassigns most of the interest back to the original owner it is evident that such party was improperly and collusively joined to manufacture federal jurisdiction.

Louisville & Nashville R.R. v. Mottley (S. Ct. 1908)

Facts: Mottley brought an action in federal court alleging that the opposing party had breached a contract by revoking a pass for free transportation. Mottley asserted federal question jurisdiction based on the railroad company's anticipated defense that an act of Congress proscribed free passes.

Issue: Does the anticipated assertion by the defendant of federal law as a defense to a state law-created cause of action suffice to provide federal question jurisdiction; i.e., is this a case "arising under" federal law as required by 28 U.S.C. §1331?

Rule: The federal law issue must be part of a "well-pleaded complaint"; i.e., it must be a part of the plaintiff's prima facie claim and not enter the case through a defendant's answer or as a plaintiff's reply to an anticipated defense.

Merrell Dow Pharmaceuticals, Inc. v. Thompson (S. Ct. 1986)

Facts: Families from Canada and Scotland brought a state tort action against Merrell Dow to recover damages for their children's birth defects allegedly caused by the mother's ingestion of Bendectin during her pregnancy. The negligence element of the plaintiffs' prima facie case alleged Dow's violation of a federal statute. Dow removed the case to federal court on the grounds that the action turned on an interpretation of federal law, and subsequently moved for dismissal of the case on the grounds of forum non conveniens, which the trial court granted. The appellate court reversed the forum non conveniens ruling. Instead, it held that the presence of a federal statutory issue in a state law-created claim when the relevant federal statute did not create a private right of action, did not meet the "arising under" standard for federal question jurisdiction and ordered the case remanded to state court.

Issue: Does pleading a violation of a federal statute as an element of a state cause of action create federal question jurisdiction under 28 U.S.C. §1331?

Rule: A claim that alleges a violation of a federal statute as an element of a state cause of action does not create federal question jurisdiction if Congress withheld a private right of action when enacting the statute. Because the federal statute that was implicated in the negligence element of the plaintiff's state law tort claim did not provide for a private right of action, federal question jurisdiction did not exist over the plaintiffs' claim and removal to federal court was improper.

Dissent: (Brennan, J.) The fact that Congress withholds a private federal damages remedy when crafting a statute does not mean that Congress intends to withhold federal jurisdiction from a suit alleging a violation of that statute as an element of a state claim. Federal jurisdiction over such claims would further the important federal interest of uniformity in interpretation and application of the federal statute at issue. Where, as here, an element of the plaintiff's claim depends upon an interpretation of federal law, federal question jurisdiction exists.

T.B. Harms Co. v. Eliscu (2d Cir. 1964)

Facts: There was a disagreement between the parties regarding ownership of a copyright. Harms brought an action in federal court seeking equitable and declaratory relief.

Issue: Does an action to determine ownership of a copyright "arise under" the laws of the United States, thereby conferring jurisdiction on the federal courts?

Rule: An action arises under federal copyright law only if it deals with (a) infringement; (b) royalties for reproduction; (c) a claim requiring construction of the Act; or (d) a distinctive policy of the Act requiring that federal principles should control. Issues of ownership do not arise under federal copyright law; they are issues of state contract law and are, therefore, insufficient to invoke federal question jurisdiction.

Grable & Sons Metal Products, Inc. v. Darue Engineering & Manufacturing (S. Ct. 2005)

Facts: Grable's real property had been seized by the IRS to satisfy a tax delinquency. Although federal law required the government to provide the taxpayer with notice of the seizure by personal service, it did so by certified mail. Years after the land was sold, Grable brought a state law quiet title action in state court challenging the purchaser's title on the ground that Grable had not received service as required by federal law. The buyer removed the case based on federal question jurisdiction. The trial court denied the plaintiff's motion to remand, holding that the state law-created claim presented a "substantial" question of federal law and, therefore, met §1331's "arising under" requirement for federal question jurisdiction.

Issue: Is a state law claim that incorporates a federal statutory question properly removable on the basis of federal question subject matter jurisdiction; i.e., does it "arise under" federal law?

Rule: Yes, sometimes. A state law-created claim can meet the "arising under" requirement for federal question jurisdiction, but only if (1) it depends upon the resolution of a contested and substantial federal issue and (2) exercising federal jurisdiction will not disrupt the congressionally defined allocation of authority between federal and state courts under §1331. Here, an essential element of the plaintiff's prima facie case was whether the federally required notice had been given, so the first test was satisfied. And since very few state law title cases will raise a contested matter of federal law, allowing those few that do to be heard in federal court will not have any meaningfully disruptive impact on the federal-state division of judicial labor. Thus, federal jurisdiction was proper. With reference to *Merrell Dow*, the absence of a federally created cause of action is not dispositive of the question of the existence of federal question jurisdiction.

United Mine Workers of America v. Gibbs (S. Ct. 1966)

Facts: Gibbs brought an action in federal court, asserting both a federal claim, under the Management Relations Act, and a nondiverse state law claim, conspiracy to interfere with a contract.

Issue: Do federal courts have jurisdiction to hear nondiverse state law claims if they are brought together with federal claims?

Rule: Where a plaintiff with a federal question claim against one defendant also brings a nondiverse state law claim against that defendant, federal courts have discretion to exercise "pendent jurisdiction" over the state law claim if it and the federal question claim are deemed to form part of the same "case," i.e., are derived from a common nucleus of operative facts. The court can decline to exercise pendent jurisdiction over pendent claims where they predominate over the federal claims or where they involve complex and/or novel questions of state law.

Exxon Mobil Corp. v. Allapattah Services, Inc. (S. Ct. 2005)

Facts: This is a consolidation of two separate cases. In one, several plaintiffs brought a state law claim in federal court on the basis of diversity of citizenship. Although all adverse parties were of diverse citizenship, only one of the plaintiffs asserted a claim that alleged damages sufficient to meet the amount in controversy requirement. The other suit was a state law-based class action brought by Exxon dealers alleging that Exxon Corporation overcharged for fuel that the dealers had purchased from it. In this suit, all adverse parties were of diverse citizenship but not all class members' claims met §1332's amount in controversy requirement. In the class action suit, the Eleventh Circuit upheld the exercise of supplemental jurisdiction over the claims of those class members whose claims did not fall within the court's original jurisdiction for failure to meet the jurisdictional amount requirement. In the non–class action, the trial court dismissed all claims on the ground that none met the amount in controversy requirement. The First Circuit ruled that although one plaintiff's claim did meet the jurisdictional minimum, since at least one other plaintiff's claim did not meet that requirement, this destroyed diversity jurisdiction entirely in the case and, consequently, in the absence of any original jurisdiction, there was no basis upon which to exercise supplemental jurisdiction.

Issue: Can a federal district court exercise supplemental jurisdiction over a state law claim between diverse parties when that claim does not meet the amount in controversy requirement when there is a state law claim in the case between adverse parties that does meet the amount in controversy requirement?

Rule: Yes. In order to exercise supplemental jurisdiction, there must be a related claim in the case that falls within the federal district court's original jurisdiction. As long as there is complete diversity between all adverse parties, and as long as there is one state law claim that meets the amount in controversy requirement, the court can exercise supplemental jurisdiction over those state law claims between diverse parties that do not independently meet the amount in controversy requirement as long as these claims meet the same "case" requirement of the supplemental jurisdiction statute, 28 U.S.C. §1367(a). The contamination theory only applies where one of the parties destroys complete diversity. In a suit that does not contain a federal question claim, the presence of but one nondiverse party contaminates the entire case, thereby destroying diversity-based original jurisdiction over the rest of the case.

Borough of West Mifflin v. Lancaster (3d Cir. 1995)

Facts: Two plaintiffs who had been arrested after refusing to leave a shopping mall sued several nondiverse defendants in state court alleging a variety of state law claims and one federal civil rights claim. The defendants removed and the federal court remanded the entire case on the grounds that the state law claims predominated.

Issue: When a case involves a federal question claim and nondiverse state law claims, when can the entire case be removed pursuant to 28 U.S.C. §1441(c)?

Rule: Removal of the entire case is permitted under §1441(c) where the claims not within the court's original jurisdiction are separate and independent from a federal question claim in the case. Here, the state and federal claims arose out of the same core set of facts and thus were not separate and independent within the meaning of §1441(c). Thus, while not removable under §1441(c), for the precise reason that the state claims form part of the same "case" as the federal question claim, they do qualify for the exercise of supplemental jurisdiction under §1367. But since the trial court did not remand on the basis of the discretionary factors set forth in §1367(c), but only on its interpretation of §1441(c), a writ of mandamus is issued ordering the trial court to reverse its remand order. The trial court can consider whether to remand the entire case or only those claims in which state law predominates under §1367(c).

American Fire & Casualty Co. v. Finn (S. Ct. 1951)

Facts: Fire damaged Finn's Texas home. She sought recovery under state law in a Texas state court against some diverse defendants and some nondiverse defendants. Two diverse defendants removed the entire case. One of the losing defendants moved to vacate the judgment on the grounds that removal was improper because of a lack of complete diversity, i.e., original jurisdiction.

Issue: What is the meaning of the "separate and independent" language of 28 U.S.C. §1441(c)?

Rule: Where a plaintiff's claims against various defendants arise out of a "single wrong" that devolves from an interlocked series of transactions, the claims are not separate and independent within the meaning of §1441(c) and so removal is improper.

Bates v. C & S Adjusters, Inc. (2d Cir. 1992)

Facts: Bates, a New York resident, brought an action in the Western District of New York against C&S, a Pennsylvania company, claiming that a C&S collection letter he had received for a debt incurred in Pennsylvania violated the federal Fair Debt Collection Practices Act. C&S sent the letter to Bates's former residence in Pennsylvania, but it was forwarded by the post office to Bates's New York address. The trial court granted the C&S motion to dismiss for improper venue.

Issue: Is a district in which a debtor resides and to where a bill collector's payment notice has been forwarded a proper venue in a federal question case under 28 U.S.C. §1391(b)(2)?

Rule: 28 U.S.C. §1391(b)(2) allows an action to be brought in "a judicial district in which a substantial part of the events or omissions giving rise to the claim occurred." Since the receipt of a collection notice is a substantial part of the events giving rise to a claim of this type, that standard was met even though the defendant did not voluntarily direct the notice into the forum.

Hoffman v. Blaski (S. Ct. 1960)

Facts: Blaski and other citizens of Illinois brought a patent infringement action against Hoffman and a Texas corporation controlled by Hoffman, in federal district court in Texas. Hoffman moved, under 28 U.S.C. §1404(a), for a transfer of venue to the Northern District of Illinois. The court granted the motion despite the fact that the district court in Illinois would not have had personal jurisdiction over the defendants had the case originally been brought there.

Issue: May a federal district court in which a civil action is properly brought transfer the action under 28 U.S.C. §1404(a) to a district court in which the plaintiff did not have a right to bring the action in the first place if the defendant agrees to waive objections to the transferee court's lack of venue over the case and to submit to personal jurisdiction?

Rule: No. The power to transfer an action to another district depends not upon the wish or waiver of the defendant but upon whether the transferee district was one in which the action "might have been brought" by plaintiff, which means that the transferee court must have subject matter and personal jurisdiction, and satisfy the relevant venue requirements.

Ferens v. John Deere Co. (S. Ct. 1990)

Facts: Ferens, a Pennsylvania citizen, wanted to bring a state law tort claim for damages against Deere, a Delaware citizen, in federal court in Pennsylvania. Ferens could not bring the action in Pennsylvania, because the statute of limitations had run out on the claim. So he brought the tort claim in federal court in Mississippi, where, under governing choice-of-law rules, the claims were not time-barred. Ferens then successfully moved to have the suit transferred to Pennsylvania under 28 U.S.C. §1404(a), but the Pennsylvania federal court ruled that the Pennsylvania statute of limitations governed and dismissed the complaint.

Issue: Can a plaintiff initiate a transfer under 28 U.S.C. §1404(a), and, if so, what choice of law rules must the transferee court apply?

Rule: Yes, and the transferee court must apply the law of the transferor district. There is no language in §1404 limiting the opportunity to transfer to a defendant. But since transfer under §1404(a) presumes that the transferor court was a district in which venue was proper, transfer for the sake of convenience and justice will result in a change of court but not a change of the governing law. Section 1404(a) should not be interpreted in such a way as to create forum shopping or substantive changes in applicable law. In a §1404-based transfer, the transferee court must apply the law that would have been applied by the transferor court.

Piper Aircraft Co. v. Reyno (S. Ct. 1982)

Facts: Reyno sued in federal district court in California as administratrix on behalf of the estates of five Scottish passengers killed in a plane crash that occurred in and all of whose victims resided in Scotland. Both Piper Aircraft Co., manufacturer of the plane, and Hartzell Propeller, Inc., manufacturer of the propellers, were American corporations. The district court dismissed on the grounds of forum non conveniens. The court of appeals reversed, principally because Scottish law was less favorable to plaintiffs.

Issue: In exercising its discretion on whether to dismiss a case for forum non conveniens, should the trial court deny the motion solely on the ground that the law of the alternative forum would be less advantageous to the plaintiff?

Rule: No. Unless the other jurisdiction is so clearly inadequate or unsatisfactory as to fail to provide for any recovery at all, the possibility of application of less favorable substantive law cannot support a refusal to dismiss on forum non conveniens grounds. The court should consider the private interests involved, convenience to the parties and witnesses, location of the evidence, and where the event in controversy occurred.

Sinochem Int'l Co. Ltd. v. Malaysia Int'l Shipping Corp. (S. Ct. 2007)

Facts: A Malaysian shipping company brought an admiralty claim against a Chinese importer in federal court. The trial court determined that it possessed subject matter jurisdiction over the admiralty claim. It also concluded that though personal jurisdiction over the Chinese defendant was unavailable under the forum state's long-arm statute, permitting limited discovery might unearth information sufficient to permit personal jurisdiction under FRCP 4(k)(2). Nonetheless, it did not permit such discovery. Instead, it granted the defendant's motion to dismiss on forum non conveniens grounds.

Issue: Can a federal district court dismiss on forum non conveniens grounds prior to resolving whether or not it has both subject matter and personal jurisdiction?

Rule: A federal district court has the discretion to dismiss on forum non conveniens grounds regardless of whether or not it has either subject matter or personal jurisdiction. Although it cannot rule on the merits before determining that it possesses both forms of jurisdiction, there is no mandatory sequencing of non-merits grounds for dismissal, including forum non conveniens. Although a court cannot dismiss on forum non conveniens grounds after determining that it lacks personal or subject matter jurisdiction, where it has not ruled on a jurisdictional (non-merits) question, it has the discretion to consider the forum non conveniens motion. In exercising the discretion to resolve a forum non conveniens motion ahead of a jurisdictional issue, where resolution of the jurisdictional issue would not be arduous, considerations of judicial economy and solicitude for the plaintiff's choice of forum ordinarily should impel the court to resolve the jurisdictional issues before the forum non conveniens motion. But where jurisdictional issues are arduous, expensive, or time consuming, and where the forum non conveniens factors weigh heavily in favor of dismissal, the court can deal first with the forum non conveniens motion.

CHAPTER 3

Erie Doctrine

I. INTRODUCTION

A. Explanation

A common conflict arising from the federal system is determining what procedures to use when a state claim is asserted in federal courts, and when federal claims are asserted in state courts. Further complicating matters is the frequently amorphous line between procedure and substance that plays an important role in choice of law analysis. The *Erie* doctrine, developed in *Erie Railroad* and its many progeny, sets forth a framework, however convoluted, for determining which law to apply.

B. Policy Considerations

1. Forum Shopping

Insofar as federal procedural law might be more favorable to litigants than state procedural law, courts attempt to prevent litigants from using the federal courts as a method of finding the most favorable jurisdiction.

2. Uniformity

Having two sets of laws may create confusion among citizens, especially where one law may direct a citizen to do that which another law discourages.

3. Federalism

Despite the Supremacy Clause, federal courts are wary of treading too harshly on state autonomy in drafting their own substantive remedies.

4. States as Laboratories

State legislatures often take the initiative on various legislation that Congress may later incorporate into its own laws. Forcing uniformity may impede such inventiveness.

II. STATE LAW IN FEDERAL COURTS

A. History
  1. Rules of Decision Act
     Located in §34 of the Judiciary Act of 1789, the Rules of Decisions Act directed federal courts to apply "the laws of the several states, except where the Constitution, treaties, or statutes of the United States shall otherwise require or provide. . . ."
  2. *Swift v. Tyson* (1842)
     Justice Story's decision held that:
     a. State law should be applied in federal court only when ruling on matters of purely local concern (e.g., real estate).
     b. Federal courts were free to evolve their own "general" common law regarding state laws.
  3. The Advent of Forum Shopping
     The creation of federal common law encouraged forum shopping. Since litigants could choose between two distinct bodies of common law, the party would choose the forum (i.e., federal or state court) with the most favorable law. This unsatisfactory state of affairs lasted for nearly a century.
B. *Erie Railroad Co. v. Tompkins* (1938)
  1. The Holding
     Justice Brandeis's decision ended the *Swift v. Tyson* era in its tracks. There the Court:
     a. Held that state law, including both statutory and common law, must be applied to substantive issues in cases based on diversity jurisdiction.
     b. Expressly overruled *Swift v. Tyson* as "an unconstitutional assumption of powers by the Courts of the United States."
     c. Eradicated federal general common law.
  2. Underlying Policies
     a. Elimination of uncontrolled forum shopping, and
     b. Avoidance of inequitable administration of laws.
  3. What *Erie* Did Not Change
     Federal law still applies in some diversity cases when a federal statute or federal question is involved and other requirements have been satisfied.
C. Federal Procedural Laws
  1. Conformity Act (1872)
     Federal courts must follow the procedure of the courts of the state in which they are located. This law has been replaced by the Enabling Act of 1934.
  2. Enabling Act (1934)
     The Supreme Court may now formulate general rules of procedure for the federal courts. The Act stated that the procedural

rules were not to "abridge, enlarge, nor modify the substantive rights of any litigant." However, substance and procedure are not easy to distinguish.

3. Federal Rules of Civil Procedure (1938 – same year as *Erie*) provided general rules of procedure in accordance with the Enabling Act.

D. Scope of the *Erie* Decision

Following *Erie*, the Supreme Court formulated a series of tests to help the federal courts decide whether a given state law is substantive or procedural.

1. *York* Outcome-Determinative Test

    In *Guaranty Trust Co. v. York* (1945), a federal court in a diversity case should apply state law if application of federal law would lead to a substantially different result. The court in *Guaranty* applied the state statute of limitations because the application of a statute of limitations so affects the result of litigation as to require the application of state law.

2. *Byrd* Balancing Test

    In *Byrd v. Blue Ridge Rural Electric Cooperative, Inc.* (1958), Justice Brennan's decision held that the preference for state law must be balanced against denial of the federal right. If a state law in a diversity action would deny a party a strongly protected federal right, the federal rule or policy should be followed even if it would lead to a substantially different outcome.

3. *Hanna* "Smart Person" Test

    In *Hanna v. Plumer* (1965), Chief Justice Warren set out what is currently the definitive test for ascertaining the applicable law.

    a. Presumption of Procedure

        Outcome determinativeness is no longer dispositive of the choice of law inquiry. But federal rules must be followed to the exclusion of a state law if the federal rule is sanctioned by the Rules Enabling Act.

        i. It does not "abridge, enlarge, nor modify the substantive rights of any litigant."

        ii. Note that no federal rule has yet been held to infringe on a litigant's rights. This is due in part to Chief Justice Warren's assertion that the FRCP were enacted by "smart people" who would know better.

    b. Conflict with the State Law

        i. Direct Conflict

            If the federal rule is in direct conflict with the law of the state, the federal rule must still be followed.

        ii. Indirect Conflict

            Even if there is no direct conflict with state procedural law, the federal rule will preclude the use of a state statute if it

occupies the field of operation of the state statute (see
Burlington Northern Railroad Co. v. Woods).

   iii. No Conflict

If there is no conflict at all, or if the rule in question is not
in the FRCP, *Hanna* does not apply.

(1) Some courts employ the analysis of *Erie* and the balancing test of *Byrd*.

(2) Justice Scalia, dissenting in *Stewart Organization Inc. v.
Ricoh*, would prefer to apply the *York* outcome determinative test, but his approach does not yet command
a majority of the Court. Several lower courts have
applied *York*, however.

(3) Some courts have held that *Hanna* has overruled *Byrd*,
and that unless a rule is in the FRCP, state law must
apply, and if it is in the FRCP, the federal and state
rules will be applied simultaneously.

(4) The Harlan Concurrence

Justice Harlan's concurrence in *Hanna v. Plumer*
provided a stricter test. In deciding whether to apply
a state or federal rule, a court must determine if the
choice of rule would substantially affect those primary
decisions respecting human conduct that our constitutional system leaves to state regulation. So far, this
test has had no impact on the law, although it has been
supported by several scholars.

E. The Problem of Ascertaining State Law

Federal courts adjudicating a state claim must predict how the
highest court of the state would decide the claim.

  1. State Authority

Statutes and constitutions of the state must be applied as interpreted by the state's highest court. If there is no holding in the
highest court, lower court decisions should be consulted as per-
suasive authority.

  2. Certification

The question may be certified to the state's highest court.

  3. Analogy

If the issue has not been undertaken by the state before, other
authorities may be consulted to help discern how the highest
court would rule. Federal courts can also consider analogous
rulings and policies if the most recent case law on point is outdated or unclear.

  4. Conflicts of Law

Federal courts must also apply the conflicts of laws rules of the
state in which it is sitting (see *Klaxon v. Stentor Elec. Mfg. Co.*).

F. Residual Federal Common Law

Even though *Erie* declares "there is no federal general common law," there are situations where federal common law is employed to avoid subjecting strong federal interests to the inconsistencies of the laws of the several states.

1. Federal common law is followed in most federal question cases:
2. Mnemonic: **FLUID**
   a. **F**oreign relations matters.
   b. Federal statute of **L**imitations applied where analogous state statutes of limitations either do not exist, or do not adequately protect the interests Congress wished to protect.
   c. **U**nited States is a party.
   d. **I**nterpreting federal statutes, treaties, or the Constitution.
   e. **D**isputes between the states.
3. Federal common law is also followed in some diversity cases:
   a. Federal defense is raised, or
   b. Federal interests outweigh state interests. Incidental federal concerns are not sufficient to compel the use of federal common law in a purely private litigation (see *Bank of America Nat'l Trust & Sav. Ass'n v. Parnell*).

III. FEDERAL LAW IN STATE COURTS (REVERSE *ERIE*)

A. Supremacy Clause

When a federal claim is brought in a state court, the Supremacy Clause of the Constitution (Art. VI) compels the application of federal law.

B. Federal Defense

A federal right may be relevant to a state action if it is interposed as a defense to a state action.

C. Superseding State Law

State rules of procedure must not be followed if they impose unnecessary burdens on federal rights of recovery (see *Brown v. Western Ry. of Alabama*).

CASE CLIPS

Erie Railroad Co. v. Tompkins (S. Ct. 1938)

Facts: As Tompkins walked on Erie Railroad Company's land, a freight train injured him. While Pennsylvania common law would have denied Tompkins relief as a trespasser, federal common law did not regard Tompkins as a trespasser. No Pennsylvania statute applied to the issue of trespassing. In *Swift v. Tyson* (S. Ct. 1842), Justice Story held that the Federal Judiciary Act required federal courts to apply state statutes, but not state common law, in diversity cases. Accordingly, the district court applied federal common law in this diversity case and awarded damages to Tompkins.

Issue: Which law, federal or state, must be applied to substantive issues arising in a diversity case?

Rule: Under the Constitution, only state law, both common law and statutory law, may be applied to substantive issues arising in a diversity case. The federal courts have no constitutional or statutory authority to create substantive rules of common law. There can be no federal general common law.

Concurrence: (Reed, J.) This case need only be decided by expanding the word "law" in §34 of the Federal Judiciary Act to include common law as well as statutes. Absent the Federal Judiciary Act, it is unclear whether federal courts may, under the Constitution, develop their own common law.

Dissent: (Butler, J.) The Court erred here because no constitutional issue was raised by the parties nor did the Attorney General of the United States receive the statutorily required notice that the constitutionality of a federal statute was being raised.

Guaranty Trust Co. v. York (S. Ct. 1945)

Facts: York, who could not sue in state court because the statute of limitations had run, brought suit in federal district court on the basis of diversity against the Guaranty Trust Company, alleging a breach of fiduciary duty. York claimed that the statute of limitations was a procedural matter to be governed by federal law. The court of appeals ruled that the fact that the action was brought in equity meant that the federal court could disregard the state rule.

Issue: When is a federal court hearing a state claim in a diversity case bound by state law?

Rule: A federal court in a diversity case should follow the state rule if not following state law would lead to a substantially different result than if the suit had been brought in state court. Using this "outcome-determinative" test, the Court applied the state statute of limitations, finding it substantive for *Erie* purposes.

Dissent: (Rutledge, J.) Whether or not the action may be barred depends not upon the law of the state that creates the substantive right, but upon the law of the state where suit may be brought.

Byrd v. Blue Ridge Rural Electric Cooperative, Inc. (S. Ct. 1958)

Facts: After being injured on the job, Byrd brought a federal diversity action against his employer, Blue Ridge Electric, alleging negligence. A state workmen's compensation statute gave certain employers immunity from suit. Under state law a judge, not the jury, decides whether an employer fits within the statute's immunity. In this federal action, the jury decided all the factual issues, including whether Blue Ridge fit within the statute's immunity.

Issue: When should a federal court sitting in diversity follow a federal rule or policy even though the suit would lead to a substantially different outcome had it been prosecuted in state court?

Rule: A federal rule or policy should be applied to the exclusion of state law that would mandate a different result where the federal interest at stake outweighs any countervailing state interest, coupled with the desire for uniform application of the laws. Applying this "balancing test," the Court found that the federal interest in jury decisions outweighed the state's interest in uniform application of the law, particularly where, as here, the state law concerned the "form and mode" of remedy (i.e., trial by jury or judge) and not the substantive right giving rise to a remedy. But the Court remanded the case to allow Blue Ridge to introduce evidence showing it fit within the statutory immunity.

Hanna v. Plumer (S. Ct. 1965)

Facts: Osgood and Hanna of Ohio were involved in an auto accident in South Carolina. Hanna of Ohio sued Plumer, executor of Osgood's estate, in a federal diversity action in Plumer's home district of Massachusetts. In compliance with FRCP 4(d)(1), copies of the summons and complaint were left with Plumer's wife at his residence. Plumer moved for summary judgment on the ground that service was not sufficient because the complaint was not personally served upon him, as required by Massachusetts state law.

Issue: Does the *Erie* substantive issue standard for applying state law extend to questions involving both substantive and procedural considerations when resolution of that question can be outcome determinative per *Guarantee Trust*?

Rule: No. Where federal procedure and state law conflict, the federal procedure will be applied in federal court, as long as it has been validly enacted under the Federal Enabling Act and does not violate constitutional principles. Where they do not conflict, the *York* "outcome-determinative" test should be applied to determine whether the federal rule should be applied at all.

Concurrence: (Harlan, J.) State rules should be applied in lieu of a contrary federal rule where the state law directs a "private primary activity." This state law does not address any primary interest.

Walker v. Armco Steel Corp. (S. Ct. 1980)

Facts: Armco claimed that Walker's federal personal injury suit, brought in diversity, was time barred because the state statute of limitations provided that suit is not commenced until the defendant is served and the limitations period had expired by the time Armco had been served. Walker argued that the suit should be allowed to proceed because FRCP 3 governs the tolling of the statute of limitations and it provides that an action is deemed commenced when suit is filed, rather than when the defendant is served. The trial court dismissed the action, applying the state limitations period, and the circuit court affirmed.

Issue: Should a federal court sitting in diversity follow state law or FRCP 3 in determining when an action commences for the purpose of tolling the state statute of limitations?

Rule: In diversity actions FRCP 3 governs the date from which various timing requirements of the *federal* rules begin to run, but does not affect the *state* statute of limitations. No language of FRCP 3 indicates that it was intended to toll a state limitations period nor displace state tolling rules for limitations period purposes. So the dismissal is affirmed.

Stewart Organization, Inc. v. Ricoh Corp. (S. Ct. 1988)

Facts: Stewart, Inc., an Alabama corporation, brought a breach of dealership contract suit in federal court in Alabama against Ricoh Corp., a New Jersey corporation. Ricoh moved for a transfer of venue under 28 U.S.C. §1404 to the southern district of New York, as specified in the contract's forum selection clause. Stewart opposed the transfer on the grounds that Alabama state law disfavored forum selection clauses. The district court agreed with Stewart, applied state law, and denied the transfer.

Issue: Should a federal court sitting in diversity apply state or federal law in deciding whether to transfer venue?

Rule: When a federal rule under consideration (§1404) is a statute, the court will apply it as long as it was enacted within Congress's constitutional authority. Since the federal venue transfer statute mandating some consideration of the forum selection clause applied to the case, it was a procedural rule under *Hanna*, and since it fell within Congress's Article III authority as augmented by the Necessary and Proper Clause, it properly governed the venue dispute.

Gasperini v. Center for Humanities, Inc. (S. Ct. 1996)

Facts: Gasperini, a California journalist, brought a diversity action against the Center in a New York federal court, alleging that it had lost transparencies it had agreed to return to him. The Center admitted liability and the jury issued a damage award, which the Center appealed as excessive under New York state law, which permitted state appellate courts to review jury verdicts and order new trials when the award was excessive. The federal circuit court applied state law and vacated the damage award. Gasperini appealed to the Supreme Court on the grounds that the Seventh Amendment of the U.S. Constitution precluded such judicial review of a federal jury's decision.

Issue: Does the Seventh Amendment to the U.S. Constitution preclude a federal circuit court from reviewing a federal trial judge's decision not to set aside a jury's damage award pursuant to state law that provides state appellate courts with authority to overturn a jury award?

Rule: No. A damage award in federal court can't be significantly greater than what would be tolerated in state court. Application of the much more restrictive federal rule for overturning jury verdicts would result in substantial variations between state and federal judgments. So the standard in a diversity case for reviewing jury awards should be the one set forth in state law. But that decision should be made in the first instance by the federal district court, with the court of appeals limited to an abuse of discretion standard of review. So the Court vacated the circuit court's judgment and remanded to the district court for application of the state standard of review of jury damage awards.

Dissent: (Stevens, J.) The circuit court already applied the state statutory standard so no reason to remand to the trial court. Affirm the circuit court's judgment.

Dissent: (Scalia, J.) This ruling contradicts longstanding and well-established precedent by this Court that prohibited federal circuit courts from reviewing a district judge's refusal to set aside a civil jury damage award as contrary to the weight of the evidence.

Mason v. American Emery Wheel Works (1st Cir. 1957)

Facts: Mason, a citizen of Mississippi, filed suit against American Emery, a Rhode Island corporation, in Rhode Island federal court based on diversity. Mason claimed American's negligently manufactured product injured him in Mississippi. American Emery asserted that under state common law as declared by the Mississippi Supreme Court nearly 30 years earlier, privity of contract was necessary in a products liability case and no privity existed here. The district court agreed and granted summary judgment to American.

Issue: What is the role of a diversity court when state common law governs a substantive issue, but the relevant ruling by the state supreme court is outdated and has lost its vitality?

Rule: Where the federal district court sitting in diversity determines that the relevant state supreme court ruling has lost its vitality, it must divine how that state court would presently resolve the issue. Since there had been a major change in products liability law in other jurisdictions over the ensuing 30 years, it was unlikely that the Mississippi Supreme Court would adhere to its earlier ruling, particularly since there is dicta in one of its recent rulings indicating dissatisfaction with the earlier precedent. Remand for reconsideration of that state law by the trial judge.

Clearfield Trust Co. v. United States (S. Ct. 1943)

Facts: Clearfield Trust cashed a federal government-issued check that had been forged by an unknown third party. Clearfield also guaranteed all prior endorsements on the check. The United States sued Clearfield Trust in Pennsylvania federal court for the repayment of the value of the cashed check. The trial court applied Pennsylvania state law, which barred recovery.

Issue: Must a federal court sitting in diversity apply state or federal law to a claim brought by the federal government that concerns commercial paper that was issued by the federal government?

Rule: Federal law. Where strong federal interests are at stake (as here, where the United States is a party), the federal interest in preserving a national law mandates that the state law be inapplicable. In the absence of an applicable federal statute, the federal courts must fashion the governing rule of law in order to have a uniform rule.

Miree v. DeKalb County (S. Ct. 1977)

Facts: After a plane crashed at the DeKalb-Peachtree Airport, the survivors brought a breach of contract claim against the county in a federal diversity action in Georgia, alleging that the county's negligent maintenance of a landfill adjacent to the airport breached its contractual obligation with the federal government (through the FAA) to use the land in a manner compatible with airport operations and, in fact, caused the crash. Although state law gave the survivors standing to sue based on the contract, federal common law regarding the FAA did not. The trial court applied state law and dismissed the action. The Fifth Circuit reversed, ruling that federal law applied because the federal government was a party to the contract.

Issue: In a breach of contract case, must the federal court sitting in diversity apply federal law simply because one of the parties to that contract is the federal government?

Rule: No. The fact that the federal government is one of the contracting parties is a factor to consider, but does not *per se* mandate the application of federal law to a claim alleging breach of that contract. State law applies to this substantive issue unless there is a significant federal interest at stake that makes a uniform standard desirable. Since the dispute involves only the rights of private litigants, and not the federal government, there is an insufficient federal interest to justify the application of federal common law. Thus, the trial court was correct in applying state law and so the circuit court's ruling is reversed.

Boyle v. United Technologies Corp. (S. Ct. 1988)

Facts: Boyle, the father of a Marine helicopter pilot, brought a diversity tort claim in federal court against United Technologies, the manufacturer of component parts, after the son died when the helicopter crashed into a body of water and the son was trapped inside the helicopter and drowned. The plaintiff based all of its theories on state tort law. The trial court upheld the jury award in the plaintiff's favor, but the federal appellate court reversed recovery on one of the plaintiff's state law tort theories on the ground that under federal law the defendant was immune from liability as a federal military contractor.

Issue: Can a diversity court employ federal immunity doctrine with respect to a products liability claim brought against a federal military contractor?

Rule: Yes. A federal military contractor is immune from liability for design defects under state law because the federal interest preempts state law in a case, such as this, involving the contractual obligations of the federal government and the imposition of civil liability on federal employees for actions taken in the scope of their employment and where, as here, there is a significant conflict between the state law (which imposes liability) and the federal interest (the Federal Tort Claims Act exempts claims for damages based on discretionary decisions). Thus, federal law should apply.

DelCostello v. International Brotherhood of Teamsters (S. Ct. 1983)

Facts: Several employees brought an action alleging that their employer had breached a provision of the collective bargaining agreement and that their union had breached its duty of fair representation. Under a related state statute of limitations, the suit was time barred. But under a related federal statute of limitations, the suit could proceed.

Issue: Should a federal court apply an analogous federal statute of limitations or a related state statute of limitations?

Rule: Although it is standard practice for a federal court to "borrow" a suitable state statute of limitations for a federal cause of action, if the state statute of limitations does not adequately protect federal policies, the court should apply an analogous federal statute of limitations instead.

Dissent: (Stevens, J.) The Rules of Decisions Act mandates federal courts to "borrow" the appropriate state statute of limitations, rather than the analogous federal statute. Nothing in the Constitution, statutes, or treaties mandates a different result.

Dice v. Akron, Canton & Youngstown Railroad Co. (S. Ct. 1952)

Facts: Dice, a railroad employee, sued the railroad when he was injured. He brought a negligence claim in Ohio state court under the Federal Employers' Liability Act. The railroad asserted that Dice had signed a release of liability, but Dice maintained that he had signed it under false pretenses. The jury issued a verdict for Dice, but the trial court granted a motion for judgment notwithstanding the verdict based on state law concerning the enforceability of releases. The state appellate court reversed on the ground that federal law (recognizing a fraud exception to enforceability of releases) should have been applied. The Ohio Supreme Court reversed the appellate court and reinstated the trial court judgment for the defendant.

Issue: Where an action brought in a state court arises under a federal statute, can the state court apply state law?

Rule: No. Where a state court suit is based on a federal claim in which the state courts have concurrent jurisdiction, state laws do not control the enforcement of that federal right. Here, the Seventh Amendment right to a jury trial on an issue under federal law must control and the state trial judge could not take the fraud issue determination away from the jury.

Dissent: (Frankfurter, J.) Imposing the federal requirement of a jury determination on the fraud issue unconstitutionally invaded the state's power to allocate the division of decision-making authority between judge and jury.

Burlington Northern Railroad Co. v. Woods (S. Ct. 1987)

Facts: Woods sued Burlington Railroad for negligence in Alabama state court. Burlington removed to federal court based on diversity. After losing the suit, Burlington stayed judgment and then unsuccessfully appealed the holding. Alabama state law imposed penalties on appellants who stay judgment pending an unsuccessful appeal. FRCP 38 authorizes penalties at the court's discretion only for frivolous appeals.

Issue: Should a federal court sitting in diversity apply a state statute or federal statute that authorizes penalties?

Rule: Since the federal and state rules conflict, under *Hanna v. Plumer* the federal rule must control unless it is unconstitutional, or, if passed pursuant to the Rules Enabling Act, if it abridges, enlarges or modifies any substantive right. However, rules located in the FRCP are presumptively valid. The federal rule here is valid and should control.

CHAPTER 4

Pleadings

I. INTRODUCTION

A. Generally

The purpose of pleadings under the Federal Rules is to give each party sufficient notice about a lawsuit. Under the Federal Rules, pleading the facts that serve as the basis for the complaint are not needed; a claimant's verified impression of a fact will suffice.

B. Pleading Stages

There are three pleading stages under the Federal Rules:

1. Complaint

Informs the defendant of the charges against him.

2. Answer

Alerts the plaintiff to the allegations in the complaint the defendant will contest, as well as any existing counterclaims and affirmative defenses.

3. Reply

In the event of a counterclaim, serves the same function as the answer to the complaint.

II. THE DEVELOPMENT OF MODERN PLEADING

A. Historical Survey

1. At the time of the Norman Conquest (1066) and for a century afterward, suitors resorted not to royal courts but to local and feudal courts. Royal courts handled offenses against the King's laws and did not interfere with the other courts.

2. Increasingly, people would seek justice from the King.

a. A writ issued by the King was required for this.

b. At first, the King drew each writ to fit a particular case.

c. Patterns emerged and writs became standardized.

d. By the twelfth century, a party could have justice done by the King if his case fit within the fixed formula of an existing writ.

3. Each writ came to embody a form of action that controlled
   a. The manner in which a suit was commenced.
   b. The substantive requirements of the case.
   c. The procedure of the trial.
   d. The remedies available.
4. Forms of Action
   a. Trespass
      A means of seeking damages from a party who had done violence to land, body, and/or property.
   b. Case
      Some trespass actions did not involve the direct application of unlawful force and evolved into an action on the "case."
      i. The law of negligence unfolded within this form of action.
      ii. Sometimes the line between trespass and case was not clear. One of the rules employed was that a trespass action was maintainable if an "immediate injury" resulted from the action.
   c. Other forms of action included debt, detinue, replevin, covenant, account, assumpsit, and trover.

B. Common Law Pleading
1. Objective
   To present a single issue for trial.
2. Highly Technical System
   Required each pleading to be designed in accordance with a form of action that bound the party to one theory of substantive recovery.
3. No Amendments
   Therefore an error in the pleadings would prove fatal to a complainant's case.
4. Only Pretrial Procedure
   This necessitated the use of numerous pleadings and responses, which wasted judicial time (now we have summary judgment, pretrial conferences, discovery, etc.).

C. Rise of Equity
1. The Chancellor at the head of the Chancery drew up the writs for common law actions.
2. By the fourteenth century, the Chancery was also granting remedies in equitable proceedings.
3. Equity courts were entirely distinct from the common law courts and developed their own procedural methods and remedies.
4. Equitable relief was available if there was no adequate remedy at law. The court would be reluctant to fashion an equitable remedy if it was difficult to enforce or if it required detailed supervision.
5. Specific relief was obtainable through equity.

6. Equity courts could allow defenses or actions based on fraud, grant injunctions, or require specific performance. This was different from the common law courts, which usually granted money damages.

7. Equity acted against the person so that a failure to satisfy a judgment could be enforced by fines and imprisonment. Since common law did not act against the person, the plaintiff would have to resort to additional measures if the defendant failed to satisfy a common law judgment.

D. Code Pleading

Modern pleading originated with the 1848 New York Code of Civil Procedure, referred to as the "Field Code." The Code altered the old pleading structure in many ways:

1. Abolished forms of action so that the plaintiff could recover under any legal theory.

2. Merged law and equity.
   a. All civil courts could grant legal and equitable relief.
   b. The same procedure was to be used in all civil actions.

3. Emphasized factual pleadings
   a. The pleadings were to include only "ultimate facts" and not evidentiary facts or conclusions of law.
   b. The difficulty in determining whether or not a pleading contained "ultimate facts" was the cause of much litigation.

4. Limited the pleadings to a complaint, answer, reply, and demurrers.

5. Required liberal construction of the pleadings so that cases would not be decided for technical reasons.

E. Theory of Pleadings

Many judges in Code states were reluctant to pull too far away from the rigidity of forms of action.

1. Required the judge to determine the single legal theory upon which the party relied.

2. If the facts pleaded did not support the legal theory, the cause of action could not be maintained and the party usually could not shift reliance to another legal theory of recovery.

3. Therefore, even in Code states cases were still being decided for technical reasons.

F. Federal Rules of Civil Procedure

1. The Federal Rules of Civil Procedure were introduced in 1938.

2. The principal purpose of pleadings under the Federal Rules is to give notice to the other party of the nature of the lawsuit.

3. Formal pleading requirements have been eliminated. Much reliance is placed on pretrial discovery to develop the issues of the case.

4. Many states have modeled their codes after the Federal Rules.

III. THE COMPLAINT

The complaint, when filed by the plaintiff, commences a lawsuit.
A. Requirements
   A valid complaint should include the proper:
   1. Elements
      a. Jurisdictional basis for the claim.
      b. A statement of the claim.
      c. The relief sought.
   2. Language
      The complaint need not be overly specific but should contain
      plain language (i.e., plaintiff need not specify which codes or
      statutes defendant allegedly violated). Thus, the defendant can-
      not say that the allegations were not technical enough or that he
      could not understand certain allegations.
B. Code Requirements
   To be valid, a complaint must allege the material and ultimate
   facts upon which plaintiff's right of action is based.
C. Federal Rules Requirements
   Under FRCP 8(a) a complaint must contain the following:
   1. A short and plain statement of the grounds upon which the
      court's jurisdiction depends.
   2. A short and plain statement of the claim showing the pleader is
      entitled to relief.
   3. A demand for judgment for the relief the pleader seeks.
D. The Right to Relief
   Under FRCP 8(a)(2), the pleader must show that he is entitled to
   relief. A complaint lacking a material element should not be dismissed if the plaintiff can prove the material element at trial.
E. Alternative and Inconsistent Allegations
   FRCP 8(e)(2) permits alternate pleadings even when they are
   inconsistent. In the past, courts have held that pleadings containing inconsistent allegations are defective if they appear in a
   single cause of action or defense, but they have approved such
   inconsistent allegations when listed in separate causes of action
   or separate defenses. Most jurisdictions now permit inconsistent allegations whether or not separately stated. Several states
   have modified their pleading rules to permit inconsistent
   allegations.
F. Damages
   FRCP 9(g) requires that special damages must be specifically stated.
   Moreover, special damages must be pleaded before evidence relating to such damages is introduced.

G. Relief

FRCP 8(a)(3) states that a complaint that claims a relief must contain a demand for judgment for the said relief. FRCP 54(c) states that a judgment by default shall not be different from or exceed the demand for the judgment. However, some courts have held that a claimant may be awarded damages in excess of those demanded in his pleadings if he is entitled to those damages under the evidence.

IV. RESPONSE TO THE COMPLAINT

A. The Time to Respond

FRCP 12(a) requires that most defendants respond to a complaint within 20 days. The United States government has 60 days to respond, 10 days for motions.

B. Motions Against the Complaint

The following technicalities can invalidate a complaint and serve the function of alerting the plaintiff or the plaintiff's attorney drafting the complaint to write precisely. If a motion to dismiss under FRCP 12(b)(6) is granted by the court, the plaintiff can choose between two avenues: abandon the action or appeal (i.e., the plaintiff is not "locked-in" if a motion to dismiss is granted and can still appeal).

1. Lack of subject matter jurisdiction;
2. Lack of in personam jurisdiction;
3. Improper venue;
4. Insufficiency of process;
5. Insufficiency of service of process;
6. Failure to state a claim upon which relief can be granted; and
7. Failure to join a necessary party.

C. Motion to Dismiss

1. Background

The motion to dismiss finds its roots in the common law demurrer. Under the common law, a party could either answer the complaint or demur. If the defendant demurred, and the demurrer was overruled, he was not allowed to contest the facts of the complaint. Moreover, if the demurrer was sustained, the plaintiff had no right to replead or amend the complaint. These austere requirements were later dropped, allowing a defendant to proceed to the merits if the demurrer was overruled and to allow the plaintiff to amend the complaint if the demurrer was sustained.

2. Motion to Dismiss for Failure to State a Claim

The federal system's counterpart to the common law demurrer is FRCP 12(b)(6), motion to dismiss for failure to state a claim upon which relief can be granted. FRCP 12(b)(6) must be viewed in light of other rules, such as FRCP 8.

3. Motion for More Definite Statement

Under FRCP 12(b)(6) a cause of action does not fail if a plaintiff does not set forth the allegations of his complaint with particularity. Instead of moving to dismiss the complaint, the defendant should move for a more definite statement under FRCP 12(e).

4. Motion to Strike

Under FRCP 12(f) a party may motion to strike his opponent's pleadings when they contain scandalous, impertinent, and irrelevant information. To strike material as scandalous it must be obviously false and unrelated to the subject matter of the action. Even when allegations are not related to the subject matter of the case, in most cases they will not be stricken from a complaint unless their presence will prejudice the adverse party. Prejudice to the adverse party turns on whether the contents of the pleadings will be disclosed to the jury.

5. Motion to Strike the Pleading

This motion challenges the entire pleading because it was filed too late, necessary court approval had not been obtained, or other rules of order had not been satisfied.

V. ANSWERING THE COMPLAINT

A. Generally

The answer serves a notice function. The court has to know the defendant's reply to the complaint. Under FRCP 15, pleadings can be liberally amended. This rule serves as a consideration both to the plaintiff and to the plaintiff's attorney (i.e., if the plaintiff misunderstood some fact and included this error in the pleading or the plaintiff's attorney failed to carefully and thoroughly research a point of law, the plaintiff will not suffer a loss as a result). Therefore, the rules favor a very liberal amendment policy.

B. Requirements of an Answer

Under FRCP 8 a defendant must do one of three things to the paragraphs of plaintiff's complaint:

1. Defendant may deny the allegations.
2. Defendant may admit the allegations.
3. Defendant may plead insufficient information in response to each allegation.

C. Failure to Answer

If defendant fails to specifically respond to an averment he is deemed to have admitted it. As a safeguard against inadvertent admission, defendants usually add an all-inclusive paragraph denying each and every averment unless otherwise admitted.

D. General Denials

General denials of the entire complaint are permitted under FRCP 8 and under most state rules. This is very risky. If a court rules that a general denial does not meet the substance of the denied averments, the defendant may be deemed to have admitted the plaintiff's specific averments. Moreover, general denials do not put into issue matters that under FRCP 9 must be specifically challenged.

E. Affirmative Defenses

FRCP 8(c) enumerates 19 affirmative defenses that must be specifically raised. Generally, defendants are required to raise such affirmative defenses that do not logically flow from plaintiff's complaint. In deciding whether a defense must be raised affirmatively, courts generally look to statutes in federal questions and to state practice in diversity actions.

VI. THE REPLY

FRCP 7(a) permits a reply to a counterclaim and allows courts to order plaintiff to reply to allegations other than counterclaims. According to FRCP 8(d), allegations to which a reply is neither required nor permitted are considered denied or avoided, and plaintiff may contest them at trial. Under FRCP 8(d) allegations requiring responsive pleadings are deemed admitted if not denied in the reply.

VII. AMENDMENTS

A. Generally

1. Before a Reply

FRCP 15(a) allows a party to amend its pleading once before a responsive pleading is served, or if no responsive pleading is permitted and the action has not been placed on the trial calendar, 20 days after service.

2. Three-Strike Rule

A party may otherwise amend its pleading with the written consent of the adverse party or by leave of court, which shall be freely given when justice so requires. Most courts follow an unofficial three-strike rule, which gives a party three chances to correct defects in its pleadings, after which the court will find that justice no longer requires another opportunity. A party must amend a pleading within the response time to the original pleading or ten days after service of the amended pleading, whichever period may be longer, unless the court orders otherwise.

B. Amendments to Conform to the Evidence

FRCP 15(b) states that issues not raised by the pleadings when tried by the consent of the parties shall be treated as if raised in the pleadings. This motion can be made at anytime, even after judgment.

C. Relating Back Amendments

FRCP 15(c) states that when a claim or defense asserted in an amended pleading arose out of the conduct, transaction, or occurrence set forth or attempted to be set forth in the original pleading, the amendment relates back to the date of the original pleading for purposes of statutes of limitations.

D. Supplemental Pleadings (FRCP 15(d))

Where relevant activity occurs after the pleadings have been filed, the court has discretion to allow the parties to file supplemental pleadings to reflect the new circumstances.

CASE CLIPS

Veale v. Warner (Eng. 1670)

Facts: Warner tricked Veale in the pleading by omitting part of the arbitration award.
Issue: May a party use deception when crafting the pleadings?
Rule: A party who uses a trick in the pleadings may not receive a favorable judgment even if the court agrees with his position.

Scott v. Shepherd (The Squib Case) (Eng. 1773)

Facts: Scott brought a trespass action when his eye was put out by a lighted squib made of gunpowder that had originally been lighted by Shepherd. But in the moments between the lighting and the explosion, the squib had been thrown about by several others to avoid injury. Shepherd pleaded that the case should be dismissed as the plaintiff pled the wrong cause of action, asserting action in trespass when it should have been brought on the case.
Issue: Is an action in trespass available for a claimed injury resulting from a wrongful act?
Rule: Yes. Two theories are advocated by the four judges: (1) A trespass action is maintainable if the injury is caused by an illegal act; and (2) A trespass action is maintainable if an injury is the immediate result of an action. There is difficulty in deciding whether an injury is "immediate" or "consequential."

Bushel v. Miller (Eng. 1718)

Facts: The defendant had removed some of the plaintiff's goods that were blocking the path to his assigned area of a storage hut. The plaintiff brought an action in trover against the defendant when the goods were lost.
Issue: May an action in trover be brought against a party who has lost goods but not through conversion?
Rule: An action in trover may only be used when there has been a conversion. Although the defendant moved the plaintiff's goods and that led to their loss, the defendant never exercised dominion or control over them and thus his actions did not amount to conversion.

Gordon v. Harper (Eng. 1796)

Facts: Harper, a sheriff, seized and later sold furniture that was in a home owned by Gordon while the home was under lease to someone else. The seizure was made in execution of a judgment against yet another party. Gordon sued Harper in trover to recover the value of the furniture.

Issue: Will trover to recover the value of goods lie where the plaintiff had neither the actual possession of the goods taken nor the right of possession?

Rule: No. In order to recover the value of property in an action of trover, a party must have had both actual possession and a right to possession of the goods taken.

Slade's Case (Eng. 1602)

Facts: Slade brought an action on the case against Morley for nonpayment of grains sold to Morley by Slade.

Issue: Does an action on the case lie for alleged nonpayment of money?

Rule: Yes. When someone agrees to sell something to another who agrees to pay upon delivery, both parties have an action for debt or an action on the case on assumpsit, at their choice.

Lamine v. Dorrell (Eng. 1705)

Facts: The defendant, pretending to be J.S.'s administrator, sold debentures from the estate as one that claimed a title and interest in them. The rightful administrator brought an action on indebitatus assumpsit for money received by the defendant.

Issue: May a party maintain an action on indebitatus assumpsit if the defendant did not receive the money at issue for the use of the plaintiff?

Rule: Yes. Although an action may be maintained for detinue or trover, a party may bring an action on indebitatus assumpsit even if the defendant did not receive the money at issue for the use of the plaintiff.

Jones v. Winsor (S.D. Sup. Ct. 1908)

Facts: The plaintiffs brought actions against their attorney both in assumpsit for money he wrongfully accepted from them and also for fraudulent conversion of that money. The South Dakota Code had abolished the common law pleadings, requiring only that the facts be established in a plain and concise manner. The court overruled the defendant's demurrer to the complaint.

Issue: Since the Code has abolished forms of pleading, may two theories of recovery be united in one cause of action?

Rule: Although the Code has abolished forms of pleading, distinctions between forms of actions as they formerly existed cannot be totally ignored. These two theories of recovery may not be united in one cause of action. The trial court erred in overruling the demurrer.

Garrity v. State Board of Administration
(Kan. Sup. Ct. 1917)

Facts: Garrity claimed that a university official came onto his land and wrongfully removed a fossil. The state board claimed that Garrity's petition, asserting that the state board unlawfully converted Garrity's valuable fossil, was subject to a demurrer because the tort claim of conversion was barred by the statute of limitations. Garrity claimed the right to waive the tort claim and to seek recovery upon an implied promise to pay the value of the fossil, which was subject to a longer limitations period.

Issue: If a petition stated a cause of action, may a party waive the theory of recovery asserted in the petition and recover upon another theory?

Rule: Yes. The complaint stated a valid cause of action and there were sufficient allegations to authorize the plaintiff to waive the theory of recovery asserted in the petition and recover upon another theory.

Gillispie v. Goodyear Service Stores (N.C. Sup. Ct. 1963)

Facts: Gillispie alleged that she was assaulted and humiliated by Goodyear's employees when they trespassed upon her residence. Gillispie further alleged that the employees' actions were both malicious and intentional. Goodyear demurred to the complaint on the ground that it did not state facts sufficient to support a cause of action.

Issue: Is a complaint that alleges only conclusions of law, but not facts, sufficient to constitute a proper cause of action?

Rule: No. To be valid, a complaint must allege the material, essential, and ultimate facts upon which plaintiff's right of action is based. When a defendant demurs to the complaint, the court must assume as admitted only the facts alleged, and not the pleader's conclusions, in determining if the complaint states a claim. In this manner, the defendants may ascertain the charges against them and react accordingly.

Dioguardi v. Durning (2d Cir. 1944)

Facts: Dioguardi drafted his own complaint in federal court stating ambiguously that Durning, the Collector of Customs, had converted two cases of bottles belonging to him and that Durning had illegally sold items at a public auction in violation of a federal statute. Durning moved to dismiss for failure to state facts sufficient to constitute a cause of action. The trial court dismissed the complaint.

Issue: Can a complaint that states facts that put the defendant on notice of the claim, but does not offer a legal basis for relief, satisfy the pleading requirements in federal court?

Rule: Yes. Under FRCP, it is sufficient for the complaint only to contain sufficient information to put the adverse party on notice of the claim against him. It need not contain an explanation of legal theory. The FRCP intended to move away from formal requirements of code pleading and focus on providing notice rather than on the quality of the pleading.

Swierkiewicz v. Sorema N.A. (S. Ct. 2002)

Facts: Swierkiewicz brought an action in federal court alleging a violation of the two federal statutes against Sorema, his former employer, alleging discriminatory discharge on the basis of national origin and age. The federal court of appeals upheld the trial court's dismissal of the complaint on the grounds that Swierkiewicz had failed to allege facts concerning all the elements of a prima facie claim of discrimination under the applicable substantive law.

Issue: Do federal pleading rules require a civil rights plaintiff to allege specific facts relevant to all elements of the prima facie claim?

Rule: No. Per FRCP 8(a)(2), the plaintiff need only provide a short and plain statement of the claim showing that it is entitled to relief. The elements of the prima facie claim constitute an evidentiary, and not a pleading, standard. These requirements do not apply to a challenge to pleading sufficiency. A trial court should dismiss a complaint only if it is clear that no relief could be granted under any set of facts that could be proved consistent with the allegations. This standard was met here because the complaint put the defendant on notice of the factual and legal basis of the plaintiff's claims. Thus, the courts below erred in dismissing the complaint.

Bell Atlantic Corp. v. Twombly (S. Ct. 2007)

Facts: Customers filed a class action in federal court against major telephone companies alleging that the companies engaged in monopolistic and anticompetitive behavior in violation of the federal antitrust statutes. The trial court dismissed for failure to state a claim under FRCP 12(b)(6) because the complaint did not allege sufficient facts of anticompetitive behavior. The Second Circuit reversed, ruling that the trial judge had erred in holding the plaintiff to this heightened pleading standard.

Issue: To defeat a motion to dismiss on the pleadings, with what level of specificity must a complaint allege facts relevant to the antitrust claim?

Rule: To state an antitrust claim, the complaint must state enough factual matter to suggest that the alleged conspirators entered into an agreement. Since the plaintiff alleged a conspiracy in restraint of trade, the complaint must allege sufficient facts to suggest the existence of an antitrust conspiracy. It is not enough for the claim to be conceivable based on the pleadings; it must be plausible.

Dissent: (Stevens, J.) This is an unwarranted departure from pleading precedent. This ruling substitutes a new standard of plausibility for the former standard of legal sufficiency.

Garcia v. Hilton Hotels International, Inc. (D.P.R. 1951)

Facts: Garcia's defamation claim filed in federal court alleged that Hilton falsely and slanderously accused him of facilitating prostitution, and then fired Garcia from his job. Hilton moved to dismiss on the grounds that Garcia's complaint did not allege publication, which is a necessary element of libel.

Issue: Is a complaint lacking a material allegation that may be proven at trial subject to dismissal?

Rule: No. A complaint lacking a material element should not be dismissed if the plaintiff can prove the material element at trial. On a motion to dismiss for failure to state a claim, the court must construe the complaint in the light most favorable to the plaintiff with all doubts resolved in the plaintiff's favor. Despite the absence of a material allegation, the complaint put Hilton on notice of the charges against it. The complaint will not be dismissed but Hilton's alternative motion for a more definite statement is granted.

Denny v. Carey (E.D. Pa. 1976)

Facts: Denny and other purchasers of First Pennsylvania Corp. brought a class action alleging that the defendants violated state and federal securities laws by issuing false and misleading financial statements about First Pennsylvania Corp.'s financial condition. The defendants moved to dismiss the complaint pursuant to FRCP 12(b)(6), alleging that the plaintiffs' allegations failed to state the circumstances constituting the alleged fraud with sufficient particularity as required by FRCP 9(b).

Issue: Does a complaint that fails to state the particular circumstances constituting fraud, but that sufficiently identifies the general circumstances of the alleged fraud, meet the requirements of FRCP 9(b)?

Rule: Yes. The requirements of FRCP 9(b) are satisfied when there is sufficient identification of the circumstances constituting fraud so that the defendant can answer the allegations.

Tellabs, Inc. v. Makor Issues and Rights, Ltd. (S. Ct. 2007)

Facts: Shareholders brought a securities fraud class action under the Securities Litigation Reform Act (SLRA) against Tellabs and Notebaert, its chief executive officer. The defendants filed a Rule 12(b)(6) motion to dismiss. The trial court dismissed the complaint, reasoning that although the shareholders had sufficiently pleaded that Notebaert's statements were misleading, they had insufficiently alleged that he acted with scienter. The Seventh Circuit agreed with the trial court that the shareholders had pleaded the misleading character of Notebaert's statements with sufficient particularity, but it disagreed with the trial court on the scienter issue, holding that the plaintiffs had sufficiently alleged that Notebaert acted with the requisite state of mind. In judging pleading sufficiency, the appellate court said, district courts should examine all of the complaint's allegations to decide whether collectively they establish an inference of scienter. Under that analysis, a complaint should survive if a reasonable person could infer from the complaint's allegations that the defendant acted with the requisite state of mind.

Issue: In determining whether a securities fraud complaint alleges facts sufficient to establish a strong inference that the defendant acted with the intent to deceive that is required by the SLRA, must the trial court consider competing inferences of an innocent mental state that could be drawn from the same facts?

Rule: Yes. Under these circumstances the court must consider competing inferences of intent and decide whether a reasonable person would consider the inference of unlawful intent to be at least as strong as any opposing inference.

Ziervogel v. Royal Packing Co. (Mo. Ct. App. 1949)

Facts: In a tort case filed in state court, Ziervogel was awarded $2,000 for injuries suffered in a collision with Royal Packing Co.'s truck. Royal Packing objected to introduction of evidence at trial showing that Ziervogel's blood pressure increased and her shoulder was injured as a result of the accident on the ground that those injuries had not been alleged in the complaint. The plaintiff maintained that through discovery procedures Royal Packing had notice of Ziervogel's claim of those injuries. The trial court overruled the objection and the jury issued a verdict for the plaintiff.

Issue: Can a party plead general damages in her complaint, and then introduce evidence at trial to recover for special damages or must the special damages be specifically pleaded?

Rule: Under the governing state statute, special damages that include a specific personal injury must be pleaded before evidence relating to such damage can be introduced.

Bail v. Cunningham Brothers, Inc. (7th Cir. 1971)

Facts: Bail sued Cunningham Brothers, Inc. alleging damages of $100,000. At trial, Bail moved to amend the complaint, increasing the amount to $250,000. The court denied Bail's motion. After the jury returned a verdict for $150,000, Bail was granted leave to amend his complaint to $150,000 in a post-trial motion.

Issue: Can a claimant be awarded damages in excess of those demanded in his pleadings?

Rule: Yes. A claimant may be awarded damages in excess of those demanded in his pleadings if he is entitled to those damages under the evidence.

American Nurses' Association v. Illinois (7th Cir. 1986)

Facts: The American Nurses Association brought a class action suit in federal court against the state of Illinois, alleging that wages in predominantly male job categories were substantially higher than those wages paid in predominantly female job categories. The trial court granted the defense motion to dismiss under FRCP 12(b)(6) on the grounds that such a claim for comparable worth was not cognizable under the governing federal antidiscrimination law.

Issue: Should a federal court dismiss a complaint under FRCP 12(b)(6) if it appears that the plaintiff could prove facts that would support a broad interpretation of that claim for relief?

Rule: No. Unless the plaintiff can prove no set of facts in support of a claim that would entitle the pleader to relief, the complaint should not be dismissed. This complaint should not be construed to allege that comparable worth was the sole basis for relief. It could be construed to allege a claim upon which relief could be granted.

Zielinski v. Philadelphia Piers, Inc. (E.D. Pa. 1956)

Facts: Zielinski was injured in an accident by a forklift driven by Johnson. Zielinski sued his employer, Philadelphia Piers, in federal court based on diversity. Although Johnson previously had worked for Philadelphia Piers, he was not its employee at the time of the accident, although he was not aware of the fact that he was then an employee of the company that leased the forklift from Philadelphia Piers. Philadelphia Piers officers were present at a deposition where Johnson said he worked for Philadelphia Piers. Philadelphia Piers did not respond then, but later denied that it employed Johnson.

Issue: Is a defendant that knowingly allows a plaintiff to rely on erroneous facts in the complaint estopped from denying the facts alleged in the complaint at trial?

Rule: Yes. A defendant who knowingly makes false statements upon which a plaintiff relies will be estopped from denying such statements at trial. The defendant made a general denial of that part of the complaint alleging that Johnson was its agent and had driven the forklift but it was clear that the defendant knew otherwise. It should have made a specific denial of those parts of the complaint it believed and knew to be false and admitted the parts it knew to be true so that the plaintiff could have known that he was suing the wrong party. The defendant will be estopped from denying Johnson's agency and its ownership of the forklift.

Ingraham v. United States (5th Cir. 1987)

Facts: Ingraham and the Bonds alleged in two separate actions in federal court that they were negligently injured as a result of medical malpractice by the Air Force physicians. In both cases, the plaintiffs were awarded damages. On appeal, the air force raised for the first time a state statutory limitation on recovery in malpractice cases.

Issue: Is a statutory cap on damage recovery a waiveable affirmative defense?

Rule: Yes. A statutory damage cap is an affirmative defense that must be timely pleaded or it is considered waived under FRCP 8(c).

Beeck v. Aquaslide 'N' Dive Corp. (8th Cir. 1977)

Facts: Beeck was injured while using a water slide. Aquaslide 'N' Dive Corp. initially admitted in its answer it was the slide's manufacturer, but later moved to amend its answer to deny manufacturing the slide. The motion was granted.

Issue: When may a court grant a motion to amend an answer?

Rule: A court may grant a motion to amend an answer unless the opposing party can show he would be prejudiced if the motion is granted.

Worthington v. Wilson (C.D. Ill. 1992)

Facts: After Worthington had been arrested by two police officers, he filed a civil rights complaint in state court against the police department and "three unknown named police officers" for using excessive force during his arrest. The defendants removed the case. More than two years after the arrest, Worthington filed an amended complaint naming the actual officers involved in the arrest. The officers moved for dismissal, claiming that the two-year statute of limitations had run before the amended complaint was filed. The plaintiff argued that the amended complaint related back to the time of the filing of the original complaint.

Issue 1: May an amended complaint that names persons referred to as "unknown" in the original complaint relate back to the time of filing of that pleading for the purposes of the statute of limitations pursuant to FRCP 15(c)?

Rule 1: No. Under FRCP 15(c), relation back of an amended complaint can occur when a defendant had actual notice that he was mistakenly omitted from a complaint (e.g., through misidentification), but identifying a defendant as "unknown" is not such a mistake so there is no relation back. The motion to dismiss, therefore, is granted.

Surowitz v. Hilton Hotels Corp. (S. Ct. 1966)

Facts: Surowitz brought a shareholder derivative action against the officers and directors of Hilton Hotels Corp. for allegedly defrauding the corporation of several million dollars. In an oral examination, Surowitz revealed that although she had verified her complaint, as required by FRCP 23(b), she did not understand it at all, and had relied mainly on information given to her by her son-in-law in proceeding with the suit.

Issue: Does a party who verifies a complaint in a derivative suit have to possess full understanding of the complaint to satisfy the requirements of FRCP 23.1?

Rule: No. A party who verifies a complaint in a derivative suit pursuant to FRCP 23.1 may do so based on the advice of a competent and trustworthy person, and not necessarily based on the party's personal knowledge. The complaint had been verified by the plaintiff's attorney and explained to her by her son-in-law so she did believe the allegations to be true. Since she had competent advice from a trustworthy source, her verification was proper.

Concurrence: (Harlan, J.) FRCP 23.1 requires verification, but that need not come from the actual party. Verification may also come from party's counsel.

Hadges v. Yonkers Racing Corp. (2d Cir. 1995)

Facts: Hadges filed a motion under FRCP 60(b) asking the federal district court to reconsider its dismissal of his due process claim against Yonkers that challenged its decision to bar him from working at its raceway. In the motion papers, Hadges and counsel signed affidavits containing false information and failed to inform the court of a pending state court action. The court denied the motion and granted Yonkers' FRCP 11 motion for sanctions against Hadges and his counsel.

Issue: Before issuing sanctions under FRCP 11, must the trial court provide the target with adequate notice and opportunity to appear?

Rule: Yes. Those facing sanctions under FRCP 11 are entitled to receive adequate notice and the opportunity to respond. Additionally, a FRCP 11 request for sanctions must be made separately from any other motion and the allegedly offending party must be served in a timely fashion. Yonkers did none of these things and so the imposition of sanctions is reversed.

Business Guides, Inc. v. Chromatic Communications Enterprises, Inc. (S. Ct. 1991)

Facts: Business Guides published various trade directories. The directories contained "seeds," which were deliberate errors planted to provide evidence of copyright infringement if they turned up in competitors' directories. Business Guides sought a temporary restraining order against Chromatic Communications, alleging that its directory contained ten seeds. A one-hour investigation by a law clerk revealed that nine of the ten were actually legitimate listings. Chromatic Communications sought Rule 11 sanctions against Business Guides and their attorneys, Finley, Kumble. Because Finley, Kumble was in bankruptcy, the motion was only pursued against Chromatic Communications, which was held liable for $13,866.

Issue 1: What is the standard of care imposed by Rule 11?

Rule 1: Any party who signs a pleading, motion or other paper has an affirmative duty to conduct a reasonable inquiry into the facts and the law before filing. The applicable standard is reasonableness under the circumstances.

Issue 2: To whom does Rule 11 apply?

Rule 2: Rule 11 applies to those whose signatures are present on court papers, whether an attorney or a party, and whether or not their signatures were required.

Dissent: (Kennedy, J.) The purpose of Rule 11 is to control the practice of attorneys or those who act as their own attorneys. It is an abuse of discretion to sanction a represented litigant who acts in good faith but errs as to the facts.

David v. Crompton & Knowles Corp. (E.D. Pa. 1973)

Facts: David was injured by an allegedly defective machine manufactured by Hunter, predecessor to Crompton & Knowles, and filed a tort action against Crompton & Knowles. In its answer, Crompton denied the allegation of having manufactured the machine on lack of information but later moved to amend its answer to deny that allegation once it discovered that its purchase agreement disclaimed assumption of liabilities.

Issue: Will a denial based on lack of information be deemed an admission if the pleader knows or has control of the facts relevant to that issue? When may a defendant, who avers that it is without sufficient knowledge and information to admit or deny plaintiff's allegations, be estopped from amending its response to deny those allegations?

Rule: Yes. Where a defendant avers that it is without sufficient knowledge and information to admit or deny plaintiff's allegations, that will be deemed an admission if the defendant is actually in possession of such information or the relevant facts are within its control. Consequently, it will be estopped from amending its pleadings and the plaintiff's allegations will be deemed admitted.

Gomez v. Toledo (S. Ct. 1980)

Facts: In a civil rights suit brought in federal court under 42 U.S.C. §1983, Gomez alleged that in dismissing him from the Puerto Rican Police Force, the city of Toledo violated the principles of procedural due process. Gomez neglected to allege that the city had acted in bad faith, and the city could dismiss Gomez in good faith.

Issue: Is it necessary for a plaintiff to allege that an official acted in bad faith to state a claim against a public official under 42 U.S.C. §1983?

Rule: In an action against a public official whose position might entitle him to immunity if he acted in good faith, a plaintiff need not allege bad faith on the part of the official in order to state a claim for relief under 42 U.S.C. §1983.

Leatherman v. Tarrant County Narcotics Intelligence and Coordination Unit (S. Ct. 1993)

Facts: Plaintiffs sued several municipal bodies for civil rights damages under 42 U.S.C. §1983 in federal district court located within the U.S. Fifth Circuit. Because municipalities are generally immune from respondeat superior liability under §1983, Fifth Circuit doctrine required plaintiffs suing municipalities under the statute to plead with specificity why the defendant municipalities were not immune from liability.

Issue: May a federal court in a civil rights case alleging municipal liability impose a higher pleading standard than that required by FRCP 8 and FRCP 9?

Rule: No. A federal court may not impose a higher pleading standard than that required by Rules 8 and 9 of the FRCP. To permit the federal circuit courts to raise the pleading standards and require greater specificity in pleading would interfere with the primary purpose of "notice pleading" under the FRCP, which is merely to provide the defendant with fair notice of what the plaintiff's claim is and the grounds upon which it rests.

Connecticut v. Doehr (S. Ct. 1991)

Facts: In connection with a tort suit, DiGiovanni submitted an ex parte request in Connecticut state court for prejudgment attachment of Doehr's home. The relevant state statute provided for ex parte prejudgment attachments of real property upon verification that there was probable cause to sustain the plaintiff's claim, but did not require a demonstration of extraordinary circumstances justifying prejudgment attachment. Based on the ex parte application, i.e., without notice to the property holder, the attachment order was issued by the state court. Thereafter, Doehr filed suit in federal court claiming that the ex parte attachment statute violated the Due Process Clause of the Fourteenth Amendment.

Issue: Does a state statute that allows prejudgment attachments of real estate without prior notice or hearing in the absence of a showing of exigent circumstances violate the Due Process Clause of the Fourteenth Amendment?

Rule: Yes. There can be no prejudgment attachment of realty without notice and hearing absent a showing of exigent circumstances. A prejudgment remedy statute that concerns deprivation of real property must satisfy a three-part inquiry: (1) consideration of the private interest affected by the measure; (2) examination of the risk of erroneous deprivations of that private interest; and (3) assessment of the interest of the party seeking the remedy. Property owners have obvious interests in continuous possession of their property and attachment severely limits the owner's opportunity to alienate or encumber it. Ex parte proceedings present serious risks of erroneous deprivations of property and absent exigent circumstances, the plaintiff has no compelling interest in controlling the property pending receipt of a judgment.

Evans v. Jeff D. (S. Ct. 1986)

Facts: Jeff D. and other children suffering mental and emotional handicaps sued the governor and several state officials of Idaho on both federal and state constitutional grounds seeking injunctive relief to improve their treatment. The Idaho Legal Aid Society represented the children and instructed its employee, attorney Johnston, to reject any settlement offer conditioned on a waiver of fees or costs. Nevertheless, Johnston accepted a settlement offer that included generous injunctive relief for the plaintiffs but conditioned this on a waiver of statutorily authorized attorneys' fees. Subsequently, Johnston filed a motion, based on the Civil Rights Attorney's Fee Awards Act (CRAFAA) of 1976, with the district court, requesting that the court reject settlement portions dealing with waiver of attorneys' fees. The court denied the motion. On appeal, Legal Aid argued that Johnson had been compelled to accept the settlement offer consistent with his ethical obligation to obtain the most favorable relief for his clients, but that the trial court had abused its discretion in accepting the settlement conditioned on the attorneys' fee waiver and, instead, had a duty to reject such a settlement.

Issue: Can a court accept a settlement agreement that contains a waiver of statutorily authorized attorneys' fees?

Rule: Yes. The law guaranteeing attorneys' fees was not intended to stand in the way of settlements that include a waiver of that right. Courts can assess the reasonableness of settlement offers that deny statutorily authorized fees.

CHAPTER 5

Joinder

I. ABILITY TO SUE

A. Justiciability

   1. The Supreme Court and lower federal courts will only hear justiciable cases, i.e., cases appropriate for federal adjudication on the merits.

   2. Sources of Justiciability Standards

     The conditions necessary for justiciability are derived either from interpretations of the Article III, §2 requirement that there be a "case or controversy," or from general Supreme Court policies developed apart from the Constitution.

   3. Requirements for Justiciability

     A suit is justiciable when certain conditions are present. Mnemonic: **SCRIMPS**

     a. **S**tanding

       A plaintiff must have standing to invoke the adjudicatory power of the federal courts. Standing is created when the plaintiff has a personal stake in the suit's outcome. The "personal stake" requirement is met where:

         i. There is distinct and palpable (not speculative) injury to the plaintiff;

         ii. A fairly traceable causal connection exists between the claimed injury and the challenged conduct; and

         iii. There is a substantial likelihood that the relief requested will prevent or redress the claimed injury.

         iv. Taxpayer Standing

           A taxpayer will have standing to challenge a congressional expenditure only if it meets the dual-nexus test established in *Flast v. Cohen.*

           (1) The expenditure must be an exercise of power under the Taxing and Spending Clause.

(2) The expenditure must violate a specific constitutional provision that limits the taxing and spending power, such as the prohibition against an established religion. In reviewing a suit that requests more than one type of relief, the Supreme Court will impose a separate standing test for each.

b. **Case or Controversy**

The issues must arise out of an actual and current case or controversy between adverse litigants. Adjudication of hypothetical or removed disputes would result in advisory opinions — something federal courts may not issue.

c. **Ripeness**

The case must be ripe for review, i.e., the issues must be fully crystallized and the controversy concrete. Ripeness is established when litigants claim actual interference with their rights. Hypothetical threats to those rights do not invoke federal adjudicatory power.

d. **Mootness** (*DeFunis v. Odegaard*)

A federal case must involve controversies that are active and ongoing at the time of adjudication. A case becomes moot, and thus ineligible for judgment on the merits, once the controversy between the parties ceases to be definite and concrete and when a court's decision would no longer affect the litigants' rights.

e. **Political Questions**

A suit is nonjusticiable as a political question if:

   i. The issues involve resolution of questions committed by the Constitution's text to a coordinate governmental branch;

   ii. There is a lack of judicially discoverable and manageable standards for resolving the case, or if a decision would require a policy determination clearly outside judicial discretion; and

   iii. Judicial intervention would produce an embarrassing diversity of pronouncements on the issue by various governmental departments.

f. **Self-restraint/Discretion**

There must not be a risk that federal adjudication would breach principles of judicial self-restraint and discretion. For example, federal courts and the Supreme Court avoid suits that would entail interfering with:

   i. State courts' ability to resolve federal question cases;

   ii. Pending state court proceedings; or

   iii. Execution of state court judgments.

       iv. Judicial self-restraint recognizes the importance of preserving the balance between state and federal interests. Such restraint also prevents the unwarranted federal constitutional decisions that may result when federal courts interpret state statutes.

  4. The Problem of "Jus Tertii"

The Supreme Court and lower federal courts will not recognize the standing of a plaintiff who represents the constitutional rights of third parties ("jus tertii"), i.e., those not parties to the case. This rule is not constitutionally based; it is founded on policies of judicial self-restraint.

    a. The Court hesitates to permit assertions of "jus tertii" (third-party rights) because:

      i. Nonparties may not want to assert their own rights;

      ii. Nonparty rights may be unaffected by the litigation's outcome; and

      iii. Third parties are often the best proponents of their own interests.

    b. Federal courts may recognize "jus tertii" standing when:

      i. The nonparties' rights are inextricably bound up with the activity the litigant wishes to pursue;

      ii. The plaintiff is no less effective a proponent of third-party rights than the third parties themselves; and

      iii. There is a genuine obstacle to the nonparties representing their own interests.

B. Real Party in Interest (FRCP 17(a))

  1. Defined

Every action shall be prosecuted in the name of the real party in interest (RPI). The RPI is the individual or individuals who will be directly affected by the action at hand.

  2. Insurers

An insurer that has fully paid a claim to an insured individual would be the RPI in any action to recover damages, since the insured has already been compensated. Had the claim been only partially paid, however, both the insured and the insurer could be real parties in interest.

C. Capacity to Sue and Be Sued (FRCP 17(b))

  1. Defined

States sometimes condition some groups' ability to enforce rights and obligations. For instance, minors and mental incompetents often cannot sue or be sued, except in specific cases.

  2. Individuals

The ability of an individual to enforce rights or duties against others is determined by the state in which the person is domiciled.

3. Corporations
   A corporation's capacity to sue or be sued is determined by the law of the state under which the corporation is incorporated.
4. Unincorporated Associations
   Even if state law does not grant unincorporated associations the capacity to sue or be sued, FRCP 17 grants such capacity to these groups where federal or constitutional rights or obligations are at stake.

II. JOINDER OF CLAIMS

A. Multiple Claims by One Party Against One Adverse Party (FRCP 18)
   One party may join an unlimited number of additional causes of action against another party as long as one claim against that party is otherwise joinable.
B. Counterclaims (FRCP 13)
   All counterclaims are joinable, without restriction. Some are joinable at the pleader's option; others must be pled if they are transactionally related to the opposing party's claim against it.
C. Compulsory Counterclaims (FRCP 13(a))
   FECP 13(a) requires all transactionally related counterclaims to be brought by the defendant. A compulsory counterclaim that has not been asserted cannot be raised in a subsequent lawsuit in federal court and those states with an analogous compulsory counterclaim rule.
D. Cross-Claims (FRCP 13(g))
   Parties to a lawsuit (either plaintiffs or defendants) can assert cross-claims against their co-parties (co-plaintiffs or co-defendants, respectively) only if the claims arise out of the same transaction as the case at hand.
E. Third-Party Claims (FRCP 14(a))
   A defending party can bring a claim against a party not previously named in the complaint (third party) only if that claim is for contribution or indemnity.

III. JOINDER OF PARTIES

A. Permissive Joinder (FRCP 20)
   Parties can join as plaintiffs if they assert claims that are transactionally related to claims of all other plaintiffs and that raise at least one question of either law or fact common to the claims of all plaintiffs. Defendants can be joined as long as the claim against them is transactionally related to the claims against the other

defendants and raises at least one question of either law or fact common to the claims against all defendants.

B. Necessary Parties (FRCP 19(a))
  1. Generally
     Necessary parties to an action must be joined if possible, but their nonjoinder will not result in dismissal. A court will deem a party to be necessary if:
     a. The party's absence will preclude complete relief to present parties;
     b. The party's absence will preclude complete relief to that party in a subsequent suit; or
     c. The party's absence may subject a present party to multiple liabilities.
  2. Involuntary Necessary Party
     A necessary party who does not consent to joinder may be made a defendant or an involuntary third-party plaintiff upon order of the court. However, if the court does not have proper jurisdiction over the party, or if venue is improper, the court may continue the action without this "necessary" party.

C. Indispensable Parties (FRCP 19(b))
  1. Generally
     Indispensable parties are those whose presence at trial is so necessary that their joinder will be compelled, even at the cost of dismissing the action, if that party cannot be joined.
  2. Factors
     A court may deem a necessary party to be indispensable by weighing how that party's absence will affect the following factors:
     a. Prejudice to parties present as well as the necessary party;
     b. Judicial options that may alleviate that prejudice;
     c. Adequacy of the judgment without the party; and
     d. Alternative remedies for the plaintiff in case of dismissal.

D. Consolidation (FRCP 42)
  1. Consolidating Cases
     Where several transactionally related actions are before the same court, the judge may order all of those actions to be consolidated in one suit.
  2. Policy
     Combined discovery, shared costs, and general reduction in delay.
  3. Separation
     Alternatively, where consolidation actually hinders speedy adjudication of the suits, the judge may also order separation.
  4. Multidistrict Litigation (28 U.S.C. §1407)

Transactionally related claims occurring in separate federal courts may be consolidated for concurrent discovery and other pretrial procedures upon a proper determination by a judicial panel on multidistrict litigation. This measure has been used frequently with asbestos liability and other mass tort litigation.

E. Impleader (FRCP 14)

1. Generally

   Impleader is a device by which the defendant joins a third party to a suit asserting a claim for indemnity or contribution.

2. Policy

   a. Judicial efficiency

   b. Prevents multiple liability, or windfall decisions. Prevents a plaintiff from first suing the defendant and then the third party, recovering twice from both.

3. Jurisdiction

   The court must have personal jurisdiction over the impleaded party and subject matter jurisdiction (original or supplemental) over the claim.

F. Intervention (FRCP 24)

1. Generally

   Intervention allows a third party to join an action, even if neither the plaintiffs nor the defendants request that party's presence. The intervenor may present both new claims and defenses to charges.

2. Permissive Intervention (FRCP 24(b))

   Courts have the discretion to allow a petitioner to intervene if either:

   a. A federal statute confers such a right to intervene; or

   b. The petitioner's claim or defense is transactionally related to the main action.

3. Intervention as of Right

   The court must allow a petitioner to intervene if either:

   a. A federal statute confers such an absolute right; or

   b. The petitioner presents:

      i. A transactionally related claim or defense;

      ii. Without adjudication, the petitioner's rights would be impaired or impeded; and

      iii. Existing parties would not adequately represent the petitioner's interests.

   c. Courts will generally use the same analysis in determining whether a petitioner may intervene as of right as it does when determining whether a party is indispensable under FRCP 19.

G. Interpleader
1. Generally
Interpleader allows one party to join various adverse claimants who each have separate claims to a single piece of property or fund, where that property cannot be split among the adverse claimants to the satisfaction of all the claims. This procedure is used most often by insurance companies who must pay out a limited fund to several parties.
2. Rule Interpleader (FRCP 22)
As long as general jurisdictional requirements are met, and none of the interpleaded parties ruin the requirement of complete diversity, FRCP 22 allows the debtor to join all the parties. Diversity in this context means that none of the claimants may be from the same state as the debtor.
3. Statutory Interpleader (28 U.S.C. §1335)
Since most interpleaders will not satisfy the traditional elements of diversity jurisdiction, Congress enacted a second interpleader statute. This statute differs from rule interpleader in several respects.
a. The amount in controversy need be only $500, as opposed to the $75,000 normally required for diversity jurisdiction.
b. Minimum, not complete diversity is required. So long as any two claimants are diverse regarding one another, diversity is satisfied.
c. The property being disputed must be deposited with the court throughout the proceedings.

CASE CLIPS

Harris v. Avery (Kan. Sup. Ct. 1869)

Facts: Harris called Avery a thief and confined him to a county jail. Avery's petition alleged two causes of action: false imprisonment and slander. Harris demurred, stating that the two issues were improperly joined.

Issue: Can two causes of action be joined in a single petition when they arise out of the same event or transaction?

Rule: Yes. The governing state code of civil procedure provides that a petition may unite several causes of action where they arise out of the same transaction. The old common law rule was different; under it, plaintiffs could join multiple claims only if they could all be sued in an action on the case, regardless of whether the claims were or were not transactionally related.

M.K. v. Tenet (D.D.C. 2002)

Facts: In a federal court action, six former CIA agents filed an amended complaint that added many new plaintiffs and defendants as well as new claims by the six original plaintiffs. The CIA moved to sever the original claims of the originally named plaintiffs.

Issue: Does FRCP 18 permit a plaintiff to join additional claims against an existing party that are unrelated to the existing claims?

Rule: Yes. If a party has a validly joined claim against another party, it can join an unlimited number of additional claims against that party regardless of whether these new claims are related to the originally filed claims. FRCP 18 permits joinder of all claims one party has against another party. Motion to sever is denied.

United States v. Heyward-Robinson (2d Cir. 1970)

Facts: Heyward-Robinson entered into subcontracts with D'Agostino for construction of a naval base and for another, nonfederal project. D'Agostino sued Heyward-Robinson for nonpayment for work performed on the naval job to which Heyward-Robinson asserted a counterclaim alleging overpayment for work performed by D'Agostino on both projects. D'Agostino interposed a reply counterclaim for monies due on the non-federal job. Since no diversity of citizenship existed, subject matter jurisdiction existed only with respect to claims relating to the federal job.

Issue: When is a counterclaim deemed compulsory within the meaning of FRCP 13(a)?

Rule: Under FRCP 13(a), a counterclaim will be deemed compulsory if it bears a logical relationship to one of the plaintiff's claims. There does not have to be absolute factual identity; it is sufficient if they arise out of the same transaction or series of transactions.

Plant v. Blazer Financial Services (5th Cir. 1979)

Facts: Plant executed a note in favor of Blazer. Plant brought suit under the federal Truth in Lending Act for failure to make required disclosures. The defendant brought a counterclaim on the underlying debt. There was no independent jurisdictional basis for the federal court to adjudicate the counterclaim (i.e., federal question or diversity jurisdiction), such that the court could only hear the counterclaim if it was compulsory under its supplemental jurisdiction.

Issue: When is a counterclaim compulsory?

Rule: A counterclaim is compulsory when there is a logical relationship between the claim and the counterclaim that indicates that they arose from the same aggregate of operative facts. Because both actions in this suit arose from a single loan transaction and depend on overlapping evidence, the court held that the action on the underlying debt was a compulsory counterclaim to the truth-in-lending action.

Lasa Per L'Industria del Marmo Societa Per Azioni v. Alexander (6th Cir. 1969)

Facts: Lasa brought suit in federal district court based on diversity against Alexander, Southern Builders, and Contract Casualty for nonpayment on a construction contract. Both Alexander and Southern Builders filed counterclaims, and Alexander filed cross-claims against both Southern Builders and Contract Casualty.

Issue: When may a party assert a cross-claim against a co-party or a third-party claim?

Rule: FRCP 13 and 14 (governing cross-claims and third-party claims) are intended to "dispose of the entire subject matter arising from one set of facts in one action," thus allowing several claims to be tried at the same time. But cross-claims can only be joined under FRCP 13(g) if they are transactionally related to the original action or a counterclaim. And a third-party claim is joinable under FRCP 14 only if it is for indemnity or contribution.

Ellis Canning Co. v. International Harvester Co. (Kan. Sup. Ct. 1953)

Facts: Ellis Canning alleged that International Harvester negligently started a fire on its tractor while servicing it. Ellis Canning had been paid in full for the damage by its insurance company, but under an agreement with the insurance company, brought suit against International Harvester to recover the insurance company's loss.

Issue: Is an insured, after having been paid for his loss, legally entitled to maintain an action in his own name for the benefit of the insurer?

Rule: No. Where the insured has been fully paid for the damages sustained, it is the insurance company that is the real party in interest and therefore must maintain its own action for reimbursement.

Ryder v. Jefferson Hotel (S.C. Sup. Ct. 1922)

Facts: The Ryders, husband and wife, were forced to leave the Jefferson Hotel due to an employee's rudeness and insults. The Ryders suffered injury individually, yet the state court suit was brought in a single action containing claims on behalf of each spouse. The court overruled the defense demurrer based on alleged misjoinder.
Issue: Can several plaintiffs, each alleging individual personal torts arising out of the same occurrence, join in a single action?
Rule: No. Two plaintiffs alleging separate tortious conduct, even arising out of a common occurrence, must try their actions separately. To maintain a joint action, the alleged tortious conduct must produce common damage to all the plaintiffs. This married couple's claims do not affect their legal relationship and so there is no joint cause of action and neither has the right to sue for the benefit of the other. The trial court's decision is reversed.

M.K. v. Tenet (D.D.C. 2002)

Facts: In a federal court action, six former CIA agents filed an amended complaint that added many new plaintiffs and defendants as well as new claims by the six original plaintiffs. The original claims all related to alleged acts of employment discrimination and retaliation. Among the newly added claims was an allegation that the defendant CIA had denied all plaintiffs and their counsel access to CIA employment-related files. The CIA moved to sever the original claims of the originally named plaintiffs.
Issue: Does FRCP 20(a) permit the joinder of plaintiffs who allege a pattern of obstruction of counsel by the defendant?
Rule: Yes. An alleged pattern of obstruction of counsel satisfies the transactional relatedness and common question requirements of FRCP 20(a). The defendant's alleged repeated efforts to shield files from the plaintiffs and their counsel constitutes a "series of transactions or occurrences" within the meaning of the Rule.

Mosley v. General Motors Corp. (8th Cir. 1974)

Facts: Mosley and nine others jointly filed suit alleging that General Motors discriminated against them on the basis of race and/or sex. FRCP 20(a) provides that all persons may join in one action as plaintiffs if they assert any right to relief arising out of the same transaction(s) and if any questions of law or fact are common to all. The district court severed the action and required each plaintiff to bring a separate suit, finding that the joinder requirements of FRCP 20(a) had not been met as the plaintiffs' claims did not arise out of a common transaction or series of transactions and did not contain a common question of law or fact.

Issue: Does a Title VII action brought by several plaintiffs who allege discrimination by a common employer satisfy the FRCP 20(a) joinder requirements?

Rule: Parties may join as plaintiffs in a suit brought on the basis of a company-wide policy of discrimination because it arises out of the same series of transactions and depends on similar questions of law and fact, even if the actual effects of the policy (i.e., damages) vary throughout the class.

Tanbro Fabrics Corp. v. Beaunit Mills, Inc. (N.Y. App. Div. 1957)

Facts: Three lawsuits arose out of a single business dispute concerning the sale of fabrics between Beaunit, Tanbro, and another party, Amity. Beaunit sued Tanbro first, seeking to recover the price of cloth it had sold to Tanbro. Tanbro counterclaimed, alleging that Beaunit's cloth had been defective. Tanbro then sued Amity in a separate action, seeking to recover the cloth it had sent to Amity. Amity counterclaimed for its contract price. Tanbro then tried to sue both Beaunit and Amity on a theory of alternative liability. Beaunit and Amity moved separately to dismiss Tanbro's last suit on the ground that there were prior actions pending between the parties with respect to the same cause of action.

Issue: What factors are necessary to permit consolidation of several actions?

Rule: To consolidate actions, it is no longer necessary that there be an identity of duty or contract between the parties. It is necessary that the alternative liability arise out of a common transaction or occurrence involving common questions of law and fact.

Bank of California National Association v. Superior Court (Cal. Sup. Ct. 1940)

Facts: Sara Boyd died testate, naming Bank of California as her executor. Her will named several legatees. Bertha Smedley, one of the legatees, brought an action to enforce an alleged contract between her and Boyd by which she was to receive the entire estate. Although the complaint named the Bank of California and all the beneficiaries, only the Bank of California and the residuary legatee had been served with process. No other legatees had been notified, nor did they appear in court.

Issue: Are legatees named in a will indispensable parties to an action filed against the executor and one legatee where the complaint alleges that the decedent contracted to leave the entirety of the estate to the plaintiff?

Rule: No. Necessary, but not indispensable, parties are those who are so interested in the dispute that they should be made parties to enable the court to do justice to the entirety of the dispute but whose interests are separable so that the court can proceed to judgment without prejudicing their interests or the interests of named parties. Indispensable parties are those without whom the court cannot proceed (i.e., complete relief cannot be awarded in their absence as a judgment would affect their interests). Where absent parties are deemed to be indispensable, the court has the option of dismissing the case or staying it until the indispensable parties are joined. In the instant case, each missing legatee has his or her individual claim to the estate and none is interested in the granting or denial of relief to others. Consequently, although they are necessary parties in the sense that the validity of the will cannot be finally adjudicated without an adjudication of the interests of every claimed legatee, they are not indispensable because the plaintiff can bring separate actions against the unnamed legatees in a subsequent action while obtaining a judgment in the instant case that binds only the named defendants, i.e., the executor and the residuary legatee. The absent legatees will not be bound by this judgment and so their property will not be affected.

Helzberg's Diamond Shops v. Valley West Des Moines Shopping Center (8th Cir. 1977)

Facts: Helzberg entered into a lease agreement with Valley West that provided that Valley West would not lease space to more than two additional jewelry stores. Valley West leased space to a third jewelry store, Lord's. Helzberg sued Valley West, seeking injunctive relief. Lord could not be joined as a party to the action because it was not subject to personal jurisdiction. Valley West moved to dismiss for failure to join an indispensable party.
Issue: When should a suit be dismissed for failure to join an indispensable party?
Rule: A suit should be dismissed for failure to join an indispensable party if a judgment rendered in the party's absence would be prejudicial to that party or another defendant. A party is not indispensable to an action to determine rights under a contract simply because that party's rights or obligations under an entirely separate contract will be affected by the result.

Provident Tradesmens Bank & Trust Co. v. Patterson (S. Ct. 1968)

Facts: A car owned by Dutcher and driven by Cionci got into an accident with a truck driven by Smith. Cionci, Lynch (a passenger), and Smith were killed, and Harris (another passenger) was injured. Provident, the administrator of Lynch's estate, settled with Cionci's estate for $50,000, but Cionci had no money to pay. Actions against Dutcher by Smith's estate and by Harris had yet to go to trial. Dutcher had an insurance policy with Lumbermens Mutual Casualty Company worth $100,000 that Lynch's estate wanted to use to recover the value of its settlement with Cionci. Lynch's estate could only recover if it was proven that Cionci had Dutcher's permission to drive his car. Lynch's estate sued Cionci and Lumbermens in federal court to collect the $50,000 settlement out of Dutcher's policy, but did not join Dutcher as a defendant because that would have destroyed diversity.

Issue: In the absence of a party who cannot be joined, how does a court decide whether to dismiss the entire case or proceed without the non-joined party?

Rule: FRCP 19(b) states that a court must assess whether in "equity and good conscience" it can proceed without an absent party. Four "interests" should be weighed in determining whether the court should proceed: (1) the plaintiff's interest in selecting the forum, including the possibility of a satisfactory alternative remedy if the action is dismissed; (2) the defendant's interest in avoiding multiple litigations; (3) the absent party's interest in being present when his interests may be affected (even if the case would have no res judicata effects on him); and (4) the court's interest in complete, consistent, and efficient settlement of controversies. The court should strive to shape relief to accommodate these interests. Further, some interests might have greater or lesser weight if the issue is raised at trial or on appeal.

Republic of the Philippines v. Pimentel (S. Ct. 2008)

Facts: Merrill Lynch filed an interpleader action when faced with conflicting claims to property it possessed that had formerly been owned by former President Ferdinand Marcos of the Philippines. Among the named interpleader defendants (i.e., the claimants) were the Republic of the Philippines and a Philippine commission set up to recover property of Marcos, both of whom claimed that the property was stolen. Another claimant consisted of a class of approximately 10,000 persons who had obtained a large money judgment against Marcos for violations of their human rights. In the lower courts, the Commission and the Republic moved for dismissal of the proceedings under Rule 19(b), on the grounds that they were required parties under Rule 19(a), but that their joinder was not feasible because they were entitled to sovereign immunity. Although the Republic and the Commission were dismissed as parties, the trial court ultimately allowed the interpleader action to proceed against the remaining claimants. The district court then ruled that the disputed property be awarded to the class of human rights victims. The Ninth Circuit eventually affirmed the district court's decision to go forward with the interpleader proceedings without the Republic and the Commission. It concluded that, under Rule 19(b), the action could properly proceed in their absence, primarily based on its conclusion that the Republic and the Commission had little chance of recovery on the merits, owing to statute of limitations problems.

Issue: When will non-joinder of a necessary party not result in dismissal?

Rule: FRCP 19(b) sets forth a nonexclusive list of factors to consider in determining whether or not to dismiss an action for failure to join a necessary party. Here, the court of appeals gave too little weight to the sovereignty interests that would be prejudiced in the absence of the Republic and the Commission, whose claims were nonfrivolous. In addition. there was no possible way to avoid the prejudice to those sovereign interests. Nor would a judgment in their absence have been "adequate" because that consideration focuses not on the satisfaction of the claims of the victims of human rights violations, but on the "public stake in settling disputes by wholes, whenever possible." On the question whether the plaintiff would have an adequate alternative forum if the interpleader proceeding was dismissed, the court indicated that the focus should not be solely on the "defendant" human rights claimants, but also on the "plaintiff" Merrill Lynch, who might be prejudiced in the absence of a judgment involving all potential claimants.

Jeub v. B/G Foods (D. Minn. 1942)

Facts: Jeub brought suit in state court against B/G Foods for injuries sustained by eating contaminated ham. B/G Foods interposed a third-party complaint against Swift Premium, the canner, seeking indemnity for any recovery that Jeub might recover against B/G. Swift moved to dismiss the third-party complaint on the ground that governing state law did not provide a right to indemnification until after liability had been assessed and damages had been paid.

Issue: May a defendant implead a third party for indemnification when governing state law does not permit indemnification until after the defendant has been compelled to pay damages?

Rule: Yes. The purpose of FRCP 14 is to provide an efficient means of determining all parties' rights in a single proceeding. FRCP permits the joinder of a claim for indemnity or contribution by a party who is or "may be" liable. Thus, if a third party is or may be liable to a defendant for any damages sustained, there is no reason a defendant shouldn't avail himself of the ability to implead such third party in the action in which initial liability is sought.

Too, Inc. v. Kohl's Department Stores, Inc. (S.D.N.Y. 2003)

Facts: Too brought a copyright and trademark infringement action against Windstar in federal court. Windstar tried to implead two employees for their role in the alleged violations.
Issue: Is a third-party complaint for contribution or indemnity joinable when the third-party allegations are facially meritless?
Rule: No. A third-party complaint for indemnity or contribution is joinable under FRCP 14(a) unless it is facially without merit. The contribution claim is not facially meritless and is, therefore, joinable. But governing state law prohibits indemnification if the party seeking it bore some fault for the alleged wrongdoing, which is the case here. So this indemnity claim is facially meritless and should not be joined.

Hancock Oil Co. v. Independent Distributing Co. (Cal. Sup. Ct. 1944)

Facts: Hopkins leased land to Hancock Oil for which he was to receive owner's royalties. Independent Distributing Co. subsequently claimed it owned the land. Hancock brought suit against Hopkins and Independent to determine to whom the royalties were owed.
Issue: When may a debtor interplead several claimants to a debt?
Rule: Common law interpleader has four elements: (1) the same debt must be claimed by both/all parties; (2) all claims must arise from a common source; (3) the party seeking relief must have no claim or interest in the subject matter; and (4) the party owing the debt must not have incurred independent liability to any claimant. All four requirements were met here even though the debtor/tenant interpleaded his landlord as the fourth common law requirement has been relaxed to permit tenants to invoke interpleaders.

New York Life Insurance Co. v. Dunlevy (S. Ct. 1916)

Facts: A judgment creditor of Dunlevy brought a garnishment proceeding in Pennsylvania on money due to Dunlevy from a fund set up by Gould, Dunlevy's father, through New York Life. New York Life admitted its indebtedness, but both Dunlevy and Gould had claims to the fund. New York Life interpleaded Dunlevy. Dunlevy was given notice in California but never appeared. After the Pennsylvania court awarded the insurance claim to Gould, Dunlevy brought an action in California against New York Life to recover the value of the policy. She claimed that the Pennsylvania court had no jurisdiction over her as she was a resident of California and had no contacts with Pennsylvania.

Issue: Where a party is interpleaded to determine an interest in property, must the court have personal jurisdiction over the interpleaded party?
Rule: Yes. Interpleader actions bring about a final and conclusive adjudication of personal rights; consequently, a court must have personal jurisdiction over the parties.

Pan American Fire & Casualty Co. v. Revere (E.D. La. 1960)

Facts: The Pan American Fire & Casualty Company sought to interplead all present and potential claimants involved with a multi-vehicle accident. Several suits already had commenced and numerous other claims had been made as Pan American was the insurer of the tractor-trailer that had collided with a school bus and two cars that had been following the bus. It deposited a bond in the amount of the policy limits, alleged that it was a "disinterested stakeholder," and denied all liability. Pan American also sought to enjoin all parties from initiating other suits and directing them to assert their claims in the instant action.
Issue: Is interpleader available to an insurer in the federal courts even though the insurer claims that the proceeds should go to none of the claimants but should remain with the insurance company itself?
Rule: Yes. The common law rule of interpleader no longer applies. FRCP 22 only requires that the claims be such that plaintiff is, or might be, exposed to multiple liability. It does not matter that the insurer itself has a claim to the money. FRCP 22 eliminated the common law distinction between a strict interpleader (involving a disinterested stakeholder) and a bill in the nature of interpleader (where the plaintiff denies the validity of some or all of the claims to the funds at issue).

State Farm Fire & Casualty Co. v. Tashire (S. Ct. 1967)

Facts: State Farm brought an action in federal court in the nature of impleader because it was the insurer for the driver of the truck that had collided with a Greyhound bus, killing some bus passengers, and injuring other bus passengers, the truck driver, and the truck passenger. State Farm alleged that already filed claims exceeded its policy limits. State Farm deposited the amount of the policy limit with the court and asked the court to issue an injunction requiring all prospective claimants to pursue their claim against the truck driver in this interpleader proceeding. The court granted State Farm's requested order. The Ninth Circuit reversed on the grounds that an insurance company could not invoke federal interpleader jurisdiction until all claims against it had been reduced to judgment.
Issue: Is a federal interpleader action appropriate before all claims to that fund have been adjudicated?

Rule: Yes. Insurance companies can interplead prospective claimants prior to judgment being rendered; however, a plaintiff is not entitled to enjoin prospective claimants from bringing suit outside the jurisdiction of the interpleader action. The trial court's injunction prohibiting the bringing of claims associated with this accident in any court outside of this interpleader proceeding is dissolved. However, the trial court injunction can properly preclude claimants from seeking to enforce against State Farm any judgment obtained against its insured that were received outside of this interpleader proceeding.

Smuck v. Hobson (D.C. Cir. 1969)

Facts: In a prior class action suit between parents of minority children and the board of education, the court held that the children had been denied the right to equal educational opportunities. When the board chose not to appeal, the superintendent and several nonminority parents filed motions to intervene to challenge on appeal the trial court's findings that the board of education had violated the Constitution in administering the schools under its jurisdiction.

Issue: Under what circumstances will a federal court allow nonparties to intervene in a pending case?

Rule: Federal courts will grant a petition for intervention when (1) the party has an interest to be protected; (2) denying the petition to intervene would prohibit the petitioners' ability to protect their interests; and (3) the petitioners are not effectively represented by parties in the litigation.

Natural Resources Defense Council v. United States Nuclear Regulatory Comm'n (10th Cir. 1978)

Facts: The Natural Resources Defense Council sought an injunction to prevent the U.S. Nuclear Regulatory Commission and the New Mexico Environmental Improvement Agency from issuing licenses to uranium mills without first preparing environmental impact statements. Kerr-McGee, a potential license recipient, moved to intervene in the suit, pursuant to FRCP 24. The trial court denied the motion on the grounds that the movant's interests were well represented by other parties. FRCP 24(a)(2) provides that one can intervene in an action if he has an *interest* relating to the subject of the action and is so situated that the disposition of the action may *impair* his ability to protect that interest, unless the interest is *adequately represented* by existing parties.

Issue: When does a party have a sufficient interest in an action to intervene under FRCP 24(a)(2)?

Rule: A party has a sufficient interest in an action when there is a genuine threat to a substantial degree. A general interest in the public welfare is not a sufficient interest. Any significant legal effect in the applicant's interest satisfies the impairment requirement. The interest is not adequately protected by existing parties if there is even a small possibility that their interests will diverge. The impact upon the movant's right does not have to rise to a preclusive (res judicata) effect. The proposed intervenors have rights that will be affected and not protected by other parties to the litigation so they must be allowed to intervene. Judgment reversed.

CHAPTER 6

Class Actions

I. GENERALLY

A. Defined

Class actions are lawsuits brought (or defended) by several representative members on behalf of all group members, pursuant to FRCP 23.

B. Jurisdiction

The class representative must satisfy the requirements of subject matter jurisdiction, personal jurisdiction, and venue.

II. PREREQUISITES (FRCP 23(A))

A. Policy

Before certifying a class, the judge must determine that certain prerequisites have been met. The prerequisites for a class action mandate the principle that one cannot automatically file a class action unless there is a definable class with specific interests at issue in the controversy.

B. Elements

FRCP 23(a) requires that four conditions be satisfied before there is any possibility of a class action:

Mnemonic: **CAN'T**

1. **C**ommonality

The class must present common questions of law and fact.

2. **A**dequacy

The representatives must fairly and adequately represent the interests of the class.

3. **N**umerosity

The size of the class must be very large so that joinder is not possible (i.e., people are from different jurisdictions or cannot afford to join).

4. **T**ypicality

The representatives must present claims and defenses typical of those of the class.

III. NAMED REPRESENTATIVE

  A. Policy

    After certifying the class, the court will seek out an individual who will represent that class. Every class of litigants is represented by what is known as a named plaintiff. This is generally the individual who initially files the class action.

  B. Elements

    1. Satisfy Requirements

      Named representatives must satisfy the four requirements pursuant to FRCP 23.

    2. Common Injury

      Named representatives filing a class action must show a common injury.

    3. Common Claims

      Named representatives must be suing on similar legal grounds.

  C. Headless Class Actions

    In cases of class action defendants, or where the original class action plaintiff withdraws from the litigation or is disqualified, there may be a situation where a valid class action exists without a named representative. These are so-called headless class actions. A court then has several options:

    1. Voluntary Replacement

      The court may allow the attorneys for a disqualified named representative to locate a new individual, who fulfills all of the qualifications for named representative, to voluntarily pick up where the disqualified representative left off.

    2. Assigned Representative

      For class action defendants, and some class action plaintiffs, a court may simply assign a named representative to prevent dismissal of an action.

    3. Retained Representative

      The court may decide to maintain the original named representative despite a technical disqualification, such as mootness (as regarding the individual named plaintiff). But the court must be sure that the named individual will proceed in the best interests of the class.

IV. CERTIFICATION

  A. Policy

    Having certified the class and located a named representative (i.e., having already determined that the prerequisites set forth in FRCP 23(a) have been satisfied), a judge must then decide what type of class action will proceed. FRCP 23(b) sets out three types of class actions. These classifications are not mutually exclusive, and a single class action may be certified under more than one classification. Further, some issues may be certified under one classification, while other issues in the same class action may be certified under others.

B. Types of Class Action
   1. Legal Class Action (FRCP 23(b)(1))
      The most common type of class action occurs if either of two criteria is present:
      a. Inconsistent Results
         Often there is a danger that, if litigated separately, severe injustice could accrue to one or more of the class members. Examples are where substantive rights are at issue that might determine future conduct (e.g., patent infringement); or
      b. Dispositive Adjudication
         Occasionally, one litigation could effectively litigate a claim of a party not present. For instance in mass tort litigation, were suits to be brought individually a defendant may go bankrupt paying out large claims (or simply by defending individual suits) to the first few plaintiffs, before others, who may be even more seriously injured, get a chance to even litigate. This class action would allow all injured parties to at least get partial adjudication.
   2. Injunctive Relief (FRCP 23(b)(2))
      Class actions will be certified under FRCP 23(b)(2) where the class opponent acted or refused to act on grounds that apply generally to the class so that injunctive or declaratory relief is appropriate for the entire class as a whole.
   3. Predominating Issues of Law or Fact (FRCP 23(b)(3))
      Class actions will be certified under FRCP 23(b)(3) if the court finds that the issues of law or fact, common to all class members, predominate and that a class action is superior to alternative methods of adjudicating the dispute. In making this assessment, a court will look at the following factors: Mnemonic: **COIL**
      a. **C**oncentration
         Desirability of concentrating litigation in one forum, where the class members may be from many different jurisdictions, and subject to different laws.
      b. **O**versight
         Difficulties in managing a class action with many different claims and parties who may have different interests.

   c. Individual Control
      Interest of individuals in controlling their own suits, as
      opposed to being thrown into a class-driven suit, where
      their individual concerns may not be as adequately addressed.
   d. Litigation
      Extent of litigation already started by other class members
      that may be impeded by the onset of a class action.
C. Amending Certification (FRCP 23(c)(1)(C))
   A certification order may be altered or amended to reflect a change
   in circumstances (i.e., a court determines a certain subclass should
   be decertified, or the class should be expanded, or the case requires
   injunctive relief, etc.) before final judgment.

V. NOTICE

A. Policy
   It normally is not possible to individually notify all the class members because they are too numerous, or because not all the members
   can be positively identified. FRCP 23(c)(2) and 23(c)(3) require
   different notice depending on the type of class action certified.
B. Requirements for FRCP 23(b)(3) Class Actions (FRCP 23(c)(2))
   1. Best Notice Practicable
      The court must notify FRCP 23(b)(3) class members in the best
      practicable way, including individual notice to all members who
      can be identified through reasonable effort.
   2. Opt-Out Provisions
      Notice to FRCP 23(b)(3) members must include notification that
      individuals may be able to "opt out" of the class. If they opt out, an
      adverse judgment will not be binding on them, but neither will
      they receive any benefit of a favorable judgment. If they neglect to
      opt out (even if they do not actively opt in) any judgment will be
      binding, whether or not they participate actively.
C. Requirements for FRCP 23(b)(1) and 23(b)(2) Class Actions (FRCP
   23(c)(3))
   1. Judicial Discretion
      Courts have wide discretion in notifying class members under
      FRCP 23(b)(1) and 23(b)(2). This may include individual notice
      or notice by publication. Some courts have gone so far as to
      require the named representative to take out large newspaper,
      magazine, and television advertising to contact as many potential
      class members as possible.
   2. No Opt-Out
      Individual class members may not opt out of FRCP 23(b)(1) and
      23(b)(2) class actions. That is why notice requirements are not as

stringent. However, this means that a class member may become bound by a suit to which the member neither had notice nor input.

D. Costs of Notice

Often, the named representative must bear the cost of notice. However, if the individual defendant (or plaintiff) can afford to notify the class members less expensively, a court may require that defendant to notify all class members, with a reimbursement by the named representative if the costs are substantial.

VI. JUDGMENTS

A. Preclusive Effect

Class actions have the same preclusive effect on all class members as any other suit may have. (See Chapter 11.) A judgment in a class action is binding on all members of the class unless there is an opportunity to opt out of the class and the class member takes advantage of that opportunity.

B. Attorneys' Fees

The court's award of attorneys' fees is separate from the plaintiff's award. This is unusual because in most cases attorneys' fees are paid by the plaintiff out of whatever award is granted (if any).

C. Settlements (FRCP 23(e))

Class actions may be settled by agreement between the named representative and the individual defendant (or plaintiff), as long as:

1. Notice is provided to members of the class, and
2. The settlement is approved by the court.

CASE CLIPS

Castano v. American Tobacco Co. (5th Cir. 1996)

Facts: Castano sought class certification in a federal court action under FRCP 23(b)(3) for the class of nicotine-dependent individuals. The trial court granted conditional certification on the issues of liability and punitive damages.

Issue: Must the requirements of predominance and superiority be established before a court can certify a class action under FRCP 23(b)(3)?

Rule: Yes. The plaintiff did not consider the impact of variation in state law on predominance and superiority and so court did not weigh whether such variations would make a class action unmanageable or whether individual issues would predominate over common ones. Thus, class certification is reversed.

Hansberry v. Lee (S. Ct. 1940)

Facts: Hansberry, a male African American, purchased land that may have been subject to a racially restrictive covenant. Lee, an owner of land who had signed that covenant, sought to enforce the restriction against Hansberry. According to the covenant, the restriction would only be valid if signed by 95 percent of the landowners. In a prior case involving the class of landowners, to which neither Lee nor Hansberry had been a party, a state judge had held that 95 percent of the landowners had signed.

Issue: Can an individual be bound by a prior judgment in a class action suit?

Rule: Yes, but due process requires that members of a class not present as parties to an action be bound by the judgment only if they were adequately represented by the parties present. Such members are also bound if they participate in the litigation, if they have joint interests, or if a legal relationship exists between the parties present and those absent such as to entitle the former to stand in judgment for the latter. None of these criteria was present in this case. Hansberry, the party sought to be bound by the prior judgment in the class action, was not adequately represented by the class of landowners in that case. He could not even have been a member of that class as his interests were too different from theirs. So the prior judgment is not binding upon Hansberry.

Phillips Petroleum Co. v. Shutts (S. Ct. 1985)

Facts: Shutts brought a class action suit in Kansas state court on behalf of royalty owners possessing rights to leases with Phillips Petroleum. The members of the class resided throughout the world. The class was certified and notice was sent by first class mail to each plaintiff, informing the recipients that they would be bound by the judgment unless they opted out of the class suit. Almost all of the leases and class members had no connection with Kansas. The defense maintained that the Due Process Clause precluded the Kansas court from exercising personal jurisdiction over those 97 percent of members who had no contacts with the forum state.

Issue: Can a court exercise jurisdiction over members of a class whose contacts with the forum state are not sufficient individually to confer personal jurisdiction over that individual?

Rule: Yes. A forum state may exercise jurisdiction over the claim of an absent class action plaintiff who lacks "minimum contacts" with the forum. Class action plaintiffs are treated differently from individuals in non-class actions because the perils of exercising jurisdiction are not as great in terms of inconvenience. However, the court must provide minimal due process protections, including reasonable notice, opportunity to be heard as well as participate in the litigation, an "opt out" provision, and adequate representation.

Communities for Equity v. Michigan High School Athletic Ass'n (W.D. Mich. 1999)

Facts: Communities filed a class action alleging that the defendant had denied girls equal treatment in interscholastic athletics. The class proposed to include all present and future female students enrolled in MHSAA schools who participate or are deterred from participating in athletics.

Issue: How carefully must the trial court apply the Rule 23(a) prerequisites to certifying a class action?

Rule: The court must apply all FRCP 23(a) prerequisites "rigorously" and not certify the class merely because the complaint parrots the formal requirements of FRCP 23(a). The court must go beyond the pleadings and assess whether the requirements have been satisfied.

Amchem Products, Inc. v. Windsor (S. Ct. 1997)

Facts: All pending federal court asbestos exposure cases were consolidated and transferred to a single district for pretrial. A global settlement was reached purporting to include future claimants who had not been injured by exposure or who had not filed a claim, and provided for specified damages to be paid based on the nature of injuries. The trial court approved the settlement and certified the class solely for settlement purposes. The circuit court separated out the issues of settlement and class certification, ruling that settlement should not affect the certification assessment and reversed the certification.

Issue: Where certification is for settlement purposes only, must the proposed class still meet the FRCP 23 requirements?
Rule: Yes. The predominance of common questions of law and fact and superiority to other methods of adjudication requirements of FRCP 23 must be met even if certification is only for settlement purposes. Predominance goes to those issues that existed prior to settlement and not with respect to the terms of the settlement. Also it appears that the entire class of future claimants is not adequately represented by the named plaintiffs as named plaintiffs have an interest in immediacy of payment while future claimants may be concerned about inflation protection for the fund. Certification was in error and appellate court judgment affirmed.

Cooper v. Federal Reserve Bank of Richmond (S. Ct. 1984)

Facts: The bank was sued in federal court by a class of former and current employees alleging employment discrimination. Cooper and some other class members also filed separate suits. The district court ruled in favor of the bank in the class action suit after trial. The bank moved to dismiss the individual actions on the grounds of claim preclusion (res judicata). The trial court denied the motion, but was reversed by the appellate court.
Issue: Does a class action judgment preclude a class member from maintaining a subsequent civil action on the same issue?
Rule: No. Claim and issue preclusion only apply when the claim or issue previously adjudicated is the same as the one sought to be precluded. The issues litigated in a class action discrimination suit are not the same as those in individual suits. A class action involves a finding of a pattern of discrimination while an individual suit involves discrimination against an individual or individuals. So appellate court dismissal on preclusion grounds is reversed and the case remanded for further proceedings in line with the trial court decision.

Gonzales v. Cassidy (5th Cir. 1973)

Facts: Gonzales sought to represent a class in a federal court action that had already been litigated in a prior lawsuit involving the same class, the same defendant, and the same issues. The previous class representative, Gaytan, did not appeal an order that granted relief for himself but not for the class.
Issue: Will the failure of a class representative to appeal an order denying relief to everyone in the class except for the class representative preclude any res judicata effect?
Rule: A class action judgment will bind only those members of the class whose interests have been adequately represented by parties to the litigation. A class representative who obtained relief only for himself and failed

to prosecute an appeal on behalf of the other class members inadequately represented the class.

General Telephone Co. v. Falcon (S. Ct. 1982)

Facts: Falcon, a Mexican American, brought a class action suit against his employer, General Telephone Co., claiming illegal discrimination in its promotion policies. Falcon then sought to maintain a discrimination class action based on General Telephone's hiring policies.

Issue: Can a plaintiff maintain a class action on behalf of a class to which he is not a member, but which is factually related to issues relating to his class action suit?

Rule: The type of injury claimed by the plaintiff must be the same as that type of injury claimed by the class purported to be represented. That all the class members share a common bond (such as race) is not necessarily enough. Nor is it enough that all class members claim discrimination. The type of discrimination must have affected the named plaintiff as well as the class members.

Heaven v. Trust Company Bank (11th Cir. 1997)

Facts: Heaven leased a car from Trust but claimed that the preprinted lease form failed to comply with disclosure requirements set forth in the federal Consumer Leasing Act. Heaven filed an action in federal court seeking to certify a class under Rule 23(b)(3). Trust counterclaimed that individual defendants had defaulted on the lease agreement and falsified their lease applications. The trial court found that although Heaven established all FRCP 23(a) requirements, it had to deny certification because the counterclaims would involve defenses that would raise issues that precluded certification under FRCP 23(b).

Issue: Can certification under FRCP 23(b)(3) be denied on the basis of counterclaims?

Rule: Yes. The presence of counterclaims can be the basis for denying certification under FRCP 23(b)(3). This case involved compulsory counterclaims within the meaning of FRCP 13(a) and since individual defenses to the counterclaims would require separate factual determination vis-à-vis each plaintiff, the trial court properly considered this as a factor in denying certification. It was a close call, but denying certification was within the trial court's discretion and so its ruling is affirmed.

Eisen v. Carlisle & Jacquelin (S. Ct. 1974)

Facts: Eisen filed an antitrust and securities class action. The trial court determined that of the six million members in the class, only 7,000 members would be notified personally of the lawsuit. Notice to the other class members would be accomplished by publication. The cost of notice would be distributed between both plaintiffs and defendants after a hearing on the merits.

Issue 1: Is publication sufficient notice for known members of a large class on grounds that personal notice would be too costly?

Rule 1: Due process requires that notice be made in the best method possible under the circumstances, including individual notice to all known members.

Issue 2: Can a court hold a preliminary hearing on the merits in order to determine who should pay for notice?

Rule 2: A preliminary hearing on the merits of a class action may prejudice the defendant. The plaintiff must therefore bear the cost of notice to the class except where a fiduciary duty preexisted between plaintiff and defendant.

Oppenheimer Fund, Inc. v. Sanders (S. Ct. 1978)

Facts: Representatives of the Oppenheimer Fund, in a class action suit brought under FRCP 23(b)(3), requested that Sanders help compile a list of the names and addresses of the members of the plaintiff class so that individual notice required by FRCP 23(c)(2) could be sent.

Issue 1: Can a court require a defendant to send notice to all plaintiffs in a class action?

Rule 1: Generally, the representative plaintiff should finance his own lawsuit. But a court can shift the responsibility of performing tasks necessary for sending notice to a defendant, such as providing its business records to the plaintiff, if the defendant could perform the tasks with less difficulty or at a lesser expense than the plaintiff.

Issue 2: Can a court require a defendant to pay for the cost of sending notice to all plaintiffs in a class action?

Rule 2: If an expense necessary for sending notice to the plaintiff class is substantial, it must be borne by the plaintiff. Only if the expense involved is minimal may such an expense be shifted to the defendant.

CHAPTER 7

Pretrial

I. DISCOVERY

Discovery is the obtaining of information, prior to trial, from opponents and witnesses regarding matters that are relevant to the cause of action.

A. Policies
1. Goals
   a. Preserve evidence when a witness will not be available for trial.
   b. Narrow the issues that will be introduced at trial.
   c. Control the course of the trial and prevent trial delays and surprises.
   d. Promote just and informed settlements.
2. Concerns
   a. Control costs of discovery
   b. Prevent use of discovery as a method of one party imposing unreasonable costs on another.
   c. Prevent discovery as a method of harassing the other party.
   d. Prevent parties from gaining evidence through the hard work of others.

B. Scope of Discovery
1. Relevancy
   The information must be reasonably calculated to lead to the discovery of admissible evidence.
   a. Discovery may not be used as a "fishing expedition."
   b. Discovery may not be used to determine an adversary's legal analysis or strategy.
   c. Nonparties may not be deposed more than 100 miles from where they reside, are employed, or regularly transact business in person. FRCP 45(c)(3).
   d. Depositions may not be used against a party without notice of the deposition. FRCP 32(a).

2. Discovery Scope and Limits (FRCP 26(b))
   a. Scope in General (FRCP 26(b)(1))
      Parties can obtain discovery regarding non-privileged matter
      that is relevant to a claim or defense. Relevant information
      need not be admissible at trial if discovery appears reasonably
      calculated to lead to discovery of evidence that would be
      admissible at trial.
   b. Limitations on Electronically Stored Information
      Discovery need not be provided of electronically stored infor-
      mation from sources that the party asked to provide the infor-
      mation determines are not reasonably accessible based on
      burden or cost.
   c. Mandatory Limitation (FRCP 26(b)(2)(C)):
      On motion or on its own, the court must limit the frequency or
      extent of otherwise allowable discovery if it determines that:
      i. It is unreasonably duplicative, or cumulative, or can more
         conveniently or less expensively be obtained elsewhere;
      ii. The party seeking discovery already had ample opportunity
          to obtain the information through discovery; or
      iii. The burden or expense of the proposed discovery out-
           weighs its likely benefits.
   d. Materials Used in Trial Preparation (FRCP 26(b)(3))
      Only discoverable if there is a substantial need and the party
      cannot, without undue hardship, obtain the information or
      equivalent by other means.
   e. Experts (FRCP 26(b)(4))
      i. Experts Who May Testify at Trial (FRCP 26(b)(4)(A))
         A party can depose someone identified as an expert whose
         opinion may be presented at trial
      ii. Experts Retained by Counsel but Will Not Testify (FRCP
          26(b)(4)(B))
          No discovery of expert retained only for trial preparation
          and who is not expected to testify as a witness at trial unless
          it is impracticable to get the information by other means.
          There is no discovery of experts consulted but not retained.
      iii. Fees (FRCP 26(b)(4)(C))
           The discovering party must pay experts a reasonable fee for
           time spent in responding to discovery.
           Where discovery is permitted under FRCP 26(b)(4)(B) with
           respect to an expert employed only for trial preparation, the
           party seeking discovery must pay the other party a fair
           portion of the fees and expenses it reasonably incurred in
           obtaining the expert's information. FRCP 26(b)(4)(C)(ii).

3. Protective Orders (FRCP 26(c))
   The court may, upon a showing of good cause, prevent or restrict discovery to protect a party from annoyance, embarrassment, oppression, or undue burden or expense. The court can also tailor discovery to prevent prejudice.
4. Sequence and Timing of Discovery (FRCP 26(d))
   A court may order discovery in a certain order at its discretion.
5. Supplementation of Responses (FRCP 26(e))
   A party who made a disclosure has the duty to supplement or correct its disclosure or response in a timely manner if it learns that the disclosure or response is incomplete or incorrect and that additional information has not otherwise been made known to other parties during discovery or in writing.
6. Verifications and Sanctions (FRCP 26(g))
   a. Documentation must be signed by an attorney or an unrepresented party.
   b. There must be a good faith belief after reasonable inquiry that information:
      i. Is consistent with the rules and warranted by existing law or a good faith extension, modification, or reversal of the law;
      ii. Is not interposed for an improper purpose such as harassment or delay; and
      iii. Is not unduly burdensome or costly given the stakes.
7. Privilege
   Unless the privilege is waived, privileged matters are not discoverable. Examples include information involving:
   a. The lawyer-client relationship.
   b. The doctor-patient relationship.
   c. Husband-wife (i.e., marital confidences). Some jurisdictions limit the knowledge protected to that gained after the wedding, some jurisdictions protect only information gained before divorce, some protect only information between those two points, and some jurisdictions may not have it at all.
   d. Self-incrimination.
   e. Priest-penitent.
8. The Work-Product Doctrine (FRCP 26(b)(3) and 26(b)(4))
   Ordinarily, information obtained by an attorney (or other agent such as consultant, surety, etc.) while preparing for litigation is not discoverable.
   a. Examples include:
      i. Mental impressions
      ii. Conclusions

           iii. Opinions

           iv. Legal theories

    b. Purpose

        To promote full investigation of a case.

    c. Exceptions

        i. Any party can obtain his or her own statement.

        ii. The doctrine cannot be used to hide evidence or to severely prejudice a party.

C. Mechanics of Discovery

  1. Requests to Perpetuate Testimony (FRCP 27)

    a. Before Action Is Filed (FRCP 27(a))

        A court order allows parties to depose for the purpose of perpetuating testimony in preparation for a yet unfiled suit. The potential adverse parties must be named, and the subject matter of the deposition must be disclosed.

    b. Pending Appeal (FRCP 27(b))

        Such court orders are infrequent, and good cause must first be shown.

  2. Authorization of Person Taking Deposition (FRCP 28)

    All depositions must take place before a person authorized by the government to take depositions.

  3. Oral Depositions (FRCP 30)

    a. Once an action has been filed, no court order is required unless

        i. In absence of a stipulation, if party wants to take more than ten depositions.

        ii. In absence of a stipulation, where the deponent already has been deposed in the case.

        iii. If the deponent is in prison.

    b. Corporation as Party (FRCP 30(b)(6))

        The corporation will supply appropriate experts, so that the expert is considered a party whose deposition may be used in the witness's absence.

    c. Motion to Limit (FRCP 30(d)(3))

        Depositions will be limited or terminated if they were conducted in bad faith or in a manner calculated to harass the deponent or party.

  4. Written Depositions (FRCP 31)

    a. No court order is needed unless

        i. In absence of stipulation, this would be more than the tenth deposition;

        ii. In absence of stipulation, the deponent already has been deposed in the case; or

        iii. The deponent is in prison.

5. Interrogatories (FRCP 33)
   a. Number (FRCP 33(a)(1))
      Absent stipulation or court order, more than 25 written interrogatories cannot be served, including discrete subparts.
   b. Time to Respond (FRCP 33(b)(2))
      Submit answers and objections within 30 days after service of interrogatories absent stipulation or court order.
   c. Documents (FRCP 33(d))
      Businesses may provide documents as an answer, but only if the burden is the same for the deponent or the deposing parties to find the answer within the documents.
6. Requests for Evidence (FRCP 34)
   Parties may request production of documents or the right to inspect, copy, or test the following items in another's possession, custody, or control:
   a. Electronically stored data.
   b. Tangible things.
   c. Producing the Documents or Electronically Stored Information
      i. Documents must be produced as kept in usual course of business or they must be organized and labeled to correspond to requested categories.
      ii. If request does not specify form for producing electronically stored data, it must be produced in a form in which it is ordinarily maintained or a reasonably useful form and the party need only produce it in one form.
7. Physical and Mental Examinations (FRCP 35)
   a. Only enforceable against parties.
   b. Court will try to protect the person's privacy as much as possible.
      i. The health of the party must be in controversy.
      ii. The scope of the examination must be specifically stated.
      iii. Court order is required and will only be granted if good cause is shown.
   c. Failure to comply will bring sanctions, but generally not contempt. Sanction can include excluding testimony at trial by examiner.
8. Requests for Admissions (FRCP 36)
   a. A party may request another to admit a matter presently at issue.
   b. The failure to admit or deny an issue is an admission.
   c. If a party denies an issue that has already been proven, forcing the other party to reprove it at trial, sanctions may be imposed.
   d. An admission may be retracted at the court's discretion.

     9. Nonparty Documents (FRCP 45(b))
       Are only accessible if a court issues a subpoena duces tecum.
  D. Sanctions for Noncompliance (FRCP 37)
    1. Motions to Compel Discovery (FRCP 37(a))
    2. Sanctions for Failure to Obey Granted Motion
      The refusing party must pay reasonable expenses incurred in obtaining a court order if refusal was without sufficient justification.
    3. Failure to Comply with Court Order (FRCP 37(b))
      a. Opposing party can be held in contempt of court.
      b. Failure to respond to requests could be deemed admission of the facts.

II. PRETRIAL CONFERENCE

  A. Purposes
    A pretrial conference is used for trial preparation to:
    1. Clarify issues.
    2. Amend pleadings.
    3. Identify witnesses and documents.
    4. Discuss settlement or extrajudicial procedures (i.e., alternate dispute resolutions, special proceedings).
  B. Scheduling
    In most cases, a judge is required to issue a scheduling order within 120 days after the complaint is filed.
  C. Limits
    A pretrial conference may not be used to:
    1. Serve as a substitute for trial.
    2. Steal opponent's trial preparation.

III. PRETRIAL ORDER

  A. Purposes
    A pretrial order serves to:
    1. Document the issues agreed upon at the pretrial conference.
    2. Control the parties' courses of action.
  B. Effects
    Failure to comply with the pretrial order can result in:
    1. Striking of pleadings or defenses.
    2. Exclusion of evidence at trial.
    3. Dismissal of action.
    4. Mistrial.
    5. Attorneys' fees.

CASE CLIPS

In Re Petition of Sheila Roberts Ford (M.D. Ala. 1997)

Facts: Daughter of father killed by police officers did not know which offers to sue or whether the shooting was justified. Instead of filing suit, she filed motion under FRCP 27 to depose the sheriff, alleging that she needed to depose him before filing suit to identify the officers involved and to ensure that the sheriff's trial testimony would remain accurate.

Issue: Can a federal court order a pre-complaint deposition under FRCP 27 absent any showing that the deposition is necessary to perpetuate the deponent/potential witness's testimony at trial?

Rule: No. Under FRCP 27, there must be a showing that the deposition is necessary for the perpetuation of the witness's testimony. The plaintiff's claim that she needed the deposition to ensure the truthfulness of the sheriff's trial testimony is insufficient, as is the contention that the deposition was needed to comply with the FRCP 11 requirement that the plaintiff have some evidentiary basis for filing suit.

Kelly v. Nationwide Mutual Insurance Co. (Ohio Ct. Com Pl. 1963)

Facts: Kelly sued for damages. Kelly answered all of Nationwide's interrogatories, but Nationwide moved to require more complete answers.

Issue: In answering interrogatories, must the plaintiff reveal what it hopes to prove in support of its case?

Rule: No. Interrogatories may discover information that is not privileged, that would be admissible as evidence in the action, and that is relevant to an issue in the action. But they may not seek to discover the manner by which the opponent's case is to be established, including to what his witnesses will testify.

Marrese v. American Academy of Orthopaedic Surgeons (S. Ct. 1985)

Facts: The American Academy of Orthopaedic Surgeons (Academy) refused to admit two surgeons who had applied for membership. The surgeons filed suit in federal court, alleging violations of antitrust laws by the academy. The academy then refused to produce confidential membership applications requested during discovery. The trial court ordered the production of the files plus a protective order requiring the plaintiff to keep the information confidential. The academy refused to comply and was held in contempt and fined.

Issue: Should a motion under FRCP 26(c) to limit discovery be granted when the party seeking discovery would incur hardship without the sought information and the party asked to supply it would suffer hardship if forced to produce it?

Rule: No. Although both sides would suffer hardship, the trial court could have mitigated the burdens of compelling disclosure by using various methods such as in camera review or the supply of redacted versions of the files.

Seattle Times Co. v. Rhinehart (S. Ct. 1984)

Facts: Rhinehart, the leader of a religious group called the Aquarian Foundation, brought a state action in Washington against the Seattle Times, alleging defamation of character and invasion of privacy. In response to the Times' request, the trial court ordered Rhinehart to provide a list of society members, subject to a protective order prohibiting the Seattle Times from publishing the information.

Issue: Can a protective order directing a newspaper not to publish discovered information violate the First Amendment?

Rule: No. If a protective order, limited to pretrial civil discovery, is granted on a showing of good cause, the First Amendment is not violated when the protective order does not restrict dissemination of the protected information if gained from other sources.

Cummings v. General Motors Corp. (10th Cir. 2004)

Facts: A passenger injured in a GM car driven by her husband brought suit in federal court alleging liability based on a design defect in the seat. The trial court denied various motions to compel discovery filed by the plaintiff and granted several defense motions for protective orders. The jury returned a defense verdict. After the plaintiff filed her appeal, she learned that GM recently had produced videos of tests involving seats for an unrelated case and she alleged that her discovery motions had included these videos.

Issue: Does FRCP 26 require a party to disclose relevant evidence that it does not intend to use at trial?

Rule: No. FRCP 26 does not require disclosure of relevant evidence that the party in possession of it does not intend to use at trial. GM did not intend to use these videos at the plaintiff's trial and so disclosure was not mandatory and, therefore, failure to disclose does not support relief for misconduct under FRCP 60(b)(3).

Davis v. Precoat Metals (N.D. Ill. 2002)

Facts: Davis and other plaintiffs sued Precoat in federal court alleging racial and national origin-based harassment by supervisors. Davis sought

discovery of other complaints against Precoat made by other non-clerical/
non-administrative employees working at the same plant.

Issue: What is the standard of relevance for discoverable material?

Rule: This information is discoverable because the plaintiffs limited their
request to complaints within the time period of the alleged discrimination
by employees at the same plant relating to the same type of discrimination
alleged in the complaint. Motion to compel discovery is granted.

Stalnaker v. Kmart Corp. (D. Kan. 1996)

Facts: Stalnaker brought a sexual harassment suit against Kmart in federal court and sought to discover information concerning the voluntary
romantic conduct of four other employees, none of whom were parties to
this suit. Kmart moved for a protective order against this discovery.

Issue: When is a protective order appropriate to preclude discovery?

Rule: Protective orders are appropriate to preclude discovery of irrelevant
and private information. Courts have discretion to protect individuals
from annoyance, embarrassment, oppression, or undue burden, and the
party seeking the protective order must shoulder the burden of establishing good cause. Information about voluntary romantic and sexual activities of other employees is irrelevant to the plaintiff's claim of unwelcomed
sexual harassment by a co-employee. The only possibly relevant information is the alleged harasser's relationship with nonparty witnesses and so a
protective order is granted except as to questions concerning whether
the nonparty witnesses had romantic contact with alleged harassing
co-employee.

Steffan v. Cheney (D.C. Cir. 1990)

Facts: Steffan "resigned" from the U.S. Naval Academy after admitting he
was gay and appearing before an administrative board. He was not charged
with actual homosexual conduct. Steffan filed a subsequent action in
federal court challenging the constitutionality of the naval regulations.
During discovery, he invoked his Fifth Amendment privilege against
self-incrimination and refused to answer deposition questions directed
to whether he had engaged in homosexual conduct during his tenure.
He also contended that the questions were irrelevant to the legality of
his separation. After warning Steffan, the trial judge dismissed the suit
for failure to comply with discovery orders. And though the court also
found that Steffan had not been discharged based on his statements, but
because of conduct, the judge nevertheless determined that the questions
were relevant.

Issue: Can a party obtain discovery of evidence that is irrelevant to the
issue in the case?

Rule: No. Only relevant evidence can be discovered and judicial review is limited to the grounds upon which the cause of action was based. Since the suit here challenged the plaintiff's involuntary separation and that separation was based on engaging in homosexual conduct, then the questions about statements made in response to a supervisory inquiry are irrelevant to whether or not he engaged in particular conduct. Thus, the area was not discoverable.

Polycast Technology Corp. v. Uniroyal, Inc. (S.D.N.Y. 1990)

Facts: Polycast sued Uniroyal in federal court, alleging that it provided misleading financial information to induce Polycast to purchase one of Uniroyal's subsidiary companies. Uniroyal proposed deposing an auditor who had been in charge of auditing Uniroyal's subsidiary after it had been purchased by Polycast.

Issue: Should the deposition of a nonparty witness be ordered when that information is relevant and not duplicative of the testimony of other witnesses?

Rule: Yes. A nonparty witness should be ordered to be deposed if that testimony is relevant and not duplicative of the testimony of other witnesses. Other witnesses could not recall key facts about the relevant information on the financial performance of the subsidiary at the time of sale. Motion to bar the deposition is denied but the deposition is limited to one full day.

Wilson v. Olathe Bank (D. Kan. 1999)

Facts: [Facts not included in casebook's edited version of case.]

Issue: Can the party conducting a deposition choose to record it by videotape?

Rule: Yes. FRCP 30(b)(2) permits recording a deposition by videotape. The choice of means of recording a deposition resides with the party taking the deposition. Although the opposing party could have objected on the grounds of annoyance, embarrassment, oppression, or undue burden or expense, it has the burden of proving this and did not meet its burden here.

In re Auction Houses Antitrust Litigation (S.D.N.Y. 2000)

Facts: In a class action suit brought in federal court against several auction houses alleging antitrust violations, one defendant served interrogatories on another defendant asking for detailed information about notes written by the latter defendant's former CEO. The defendant who had been asked to produce declined on the grounds that the CEO no longer worked for it. The requesting defendant moved for an order compelling answers since the answering defendant still owed its former CEO millions under his termination agreement and, therefore, had significant leverage over him.

Issue: Must a company answer interrogatories despite its claim that the sought-after information is outside of its control if that company has methods for acquiring the information and if the factors that compel discovery are present?

Rule: Yes. If the company has methods for acquiring the requested information, it must produce it despite its claim that the information is outside of its control when other factors argue, as here, for production. There are no particular governmental interests arguing against production nor would the burden on the providing company be more than minimal. Motion to compel answers is granted.

In re Convergent Technologies Securities Litigation (N.D. Cal. 1985)

Facts: The defense filed a motion to compel answers to over 1,000 interrogatories.

Issue: What factors should a court consider in ruling on a motion to compel answers to a huge number of interrogatories?

Rule: Discovery should be compelled only when it is reasonably calculated to lead to the discovery of admissible and useful evidence and does not unduly burden the serving and responding parties. The court found that most of the interrogatories were premature and compelled answers to a small minority.

Zubulake v. UBS Warburg LLC (S.D.N.Y. 2003)

Facts: Zubulake filed an employment discrimination case against her former employer and sought access to UBS's email records that existed on archived media. UBS agreed voluntarily to produce emails from five employees and no more, citing excessive expense. Zubulake filed a motion to compel production of the email records with the defendant to bear the cost of production.

Issue: Where email records are relatively accessible and inexpensive to produce, should the possessor of extensive relevant email records be ordered to produce them at its own expense?

Rule: Yes. A company with extensive relevant email records should be ordered to produce them at its own expense if they are relatively accessible and inexpensive to produce. If producing places an undue burden or expense on the producing party, the Rules permit shifting the cost to the requesting party. Deciding whether to shift requires review of eight factors: (1) specificity of the request; (2) likelihood of success on the request; (3) availability of information from other sources; (4) reason for the requested information; (5) how the information benefits each party; (6) cost of production; (7) each party's ability and incentive to control costs of disclosing that information; and (8) each party's resources.

Schlagenhauf v. Holder (S. Ct. 1964)

Facts: Holder and other bus passengers involved in a collision between a Greyhound bus and a tractor trailer sued Schlagenhauf (the bus driver), Greyhound (the bus line), Contract Carriers (the tractor owner), McCorkhill (the truck driver), and National Lead (the trailer owner). Contract Carriers and National Lead claimed the accident was due to Schlagenhauf's negligence and requested, pursuant to FRCP 35(a), that Schlagenhauf submit to four physical and mental examinations. The trial judge granted the motion.

Issue: Under what circumstances may a court order a defendant to submit to mental and physical exams pursuant to FRCP 35?

Rule: FRCP 35 providing for physical and mental examinations of parties applies to defendants as well as to plaintiffs. Although the person being examined must be a party, that party need not be adverse to the party requesting the examination. But the Rule also requires an affirmative showing that each condition to which an examination is sought is really and genuinely in controversy and that good cause exists for ordering each particular exam.

Concurrence: (Black, J.) Where allegations of a party put another party's health "in controversy," an examination may be made pursuant to FRCP 35.

Dissent: (Douglas, J.) Ordering defendants to submit to physical examination must be very limited. In an examination there is no judge present to ensure that a doctor's probing is limited only to what is relevant to the case. The right to keep one's person inviolate should not be affected simply because one has been sued.

Battle v. Memorial Hospital at Gulfport (5th Cir. 2000)

Facts: Infant and parents sued Hospital and some staff members for malpractice in federal court. The plaintiffs offered experts to testify that the injuries were the result of unreasonable delay in administering a drug. One of the plaintiffs' experts was deposed pretrial by the defendants. It was recorded by video while attorneys for the defendants were present and asked questions. This expert was unavailable to testify at trial. The plaintiffs offered the video deposition as evidence at trial, but it was excluded by the trial judge on the grounds that a discovery deposition was solely for deposition purposes and not for admission as evidence at trial. A second plaintiffs' witness had a videotaped deposition before trial because he stated he would be unavailable on the trial date. He was cross-examined at the deposition by defense counsel. When the trial date was continued, the trial judge refused to allow the plaintiffs to call the second expert on the grounds that the defendants had cross-examined him at the deposition on the theory that he would be unavailable for trial and to allow him to testify would reveal the hospital's cross-examination strategy, which was on the videotape. The jury issued a verdict for the defendants.

Issue 1: Should a videotaped deposition be admitted into evidence where the witness is unavailable and the party objecting to the introduction of the video had the same motive for cross-examining the witness at the deposition that it had at trial?

Rule 1: Yes. Depositions are fully admissible at trial under the discovery rules if the witness is unavailable and the party objecting to the video had the same motive for questioning during the deposition as at trial, particularly when offered against the parties who conducted them.

Issue 2: Should the trial court preclude a witness whose deposition had been videotaped from testifying at trial if the offering party's conduct caused the other side to incur the expense of the witness's videotaped deposition?

Rule 2: Yes. The trial court has discretion to prohibit live testimony in favor of videotaped deposition testimony where the witness is unavailable and the offering party's own conduct caused the other side to incur the expense of videotaping the deposition.

Hickman v. Taylor (S. Ct. 1947)

Facts: Taylor, the owner of a tugboat that sank, had obtained statements from survivors and crew members. Hickman, representing the deceased, requested copies of the statements but Taylor refused on the grounds that the information was protected by attorney-client privilege.

Issue: What does a party have to establish to obtain statements, reports, records, or other memoranda prepared by opposing counsel in preparation for possible litigation?

Rule: This material is not protected by the attorney-client privilege. Nevertheless, it does constitute the attorney's work product and so the party seeking work product material has a burden to show reasons that justify its production. When it is relevant and non-privileged, work product can be discovered only upon a showing of necessity or undue prejudice. No such showing was made here as the witnesses who made the statements were known and available to opposing counsel and no reasons were offered to justify production. Merely stating that one wants the material to help prepare for trial is insufficient to invade the privacy of an attorney's professional activities.

Concurrence: Discovery should not be allowed to enable counsel to perform its functions on wits borrowed from its adversary. To rule otherwise would be to force attorneys to tell their opponent everything they have learned via their own hard work.

Upjohn Co. v. United States (S. Ct. 1981)

Facts: Upjohn lawyers conducted an internal investigation to determine whether illegal bribes had been made to foreign governments by the company's subsidiaries. The lawyers interviewed employees and made notes and memos about the investigation. The government sought discovery of the notes and memos to aid in its prosecution in federal court of Upjohn for those same alleged offenses. The trial court rejected Upjohn's claims of attorney-client privilege and work product and ordered disclosure. The Sixth Circuit affirmed.

Issue: What documents produced by attorneys are protected by the attorney-client privilege and the work product rule?

Rule: The attorney-client privilege extends to communications between corporate counsel and non-managerial employees. FRCP 26(b)(3) protects the notes made of interviews of witnesses. An attorney's notes and memos are protected by the work product rule codified in FRCP 26(b)(3) and, therefore, are not subject to discovery when they reveal the attorney's mental processes in evaluating attorney-client communications. To overcome the protection of work product, the requesting party must show substantial need and no such showing was made. Reverse the rulings ordering production.

Krisa v. Equitable Life Assurance Society (M.D. Pa. 2000)

Facts: Krisa brought an action in federal court after Equitable denied her application for disability benefits under her policy. Equitable refused Krisa's request for production of preliminary reports and other documents created by Equitable's experts in connection with litigation on the grounds they were protected work product.

Issue: Is work product that is prepared by an attorney still protected from discovery after it has been disclosed to an expert and is part of an expert's report?

Rule: Yes. The work product rule should be expansive and product documents prepared by experts that relied on the attorney's work product.

Thompson v. The Haskell Co. (M.D. Fla. 1994)

Facts: Thompson filed a sexual harassment claim against Haskell in federal court. Thompson's former counsel hired a psychologist to examine

Thompson. Thompson sought a court order to protect the report prepared and possessed by the doctor.

Issue: Can a party discover information prepared by an opponent's expert who was retained in anticipation of litigation and is not intended to be called as a witness?

Rule: Yes. A party can obtain information prepared by an opponent's expert who is not called as a witness but was retained in anticipation of litigation, but only under exceptional circumstances. This is one of those exceptional circumstances. The doctor's report is the only evidence probative of Thompson's emotional state at the relevant time and so the motion to preclude discovery is denied.

Chiquita International Ltd. v. M/V Bolero Reefer (S.D.N.Y. 1994)

Facts: Chiquita sued a cargo carrier in federal court for cargo loss and damage based on its negligent loading of bananas. The defendant moved for an order compelling discovery from a marine surveyor (via deposition) who had been employed by Chiquita to inspect the carrier upon its arrival at the destination, arguing that the surveyor was a fact witness and not an expert and that even if he was an expert, he was a non-testifying expert whose information could be discovered under exceptional circumstances such as these.

Issue: Can a non-testifying expert be subject to discovery?

Rule: Yes, but only under exceptional circumstances. The general answer is no. A fact witness is one whose information was obtained in the normal course of business. This surveyor was an expert hired to make an evaluation in anticipation of litigation. The defendant could have hired its own expert to examine the carrier and so no exceptional circumstances exist here. Application for deposition of surveyor is denied.

Cine Forty-Second Street Theatre Corp. v. Allied Artists Pictures Corp. (2d Cir. 1979)

Facts: The Cine Forty-Second Street Theatre Corporation (Cine) sued Allied Artists Pictures Corporation (Allied) and other competing movie theaters in federal court, alleging a conspiracy to block its access to certain films in violation of federal antitrust laws. Allied served Cine with detailed interrogatories. Cine then failed to obey two court orders requiring more specific answers to Allied's requests for discovery. The magistrate ruled that Cine willfully failed to comply with court discovery orders relative to the issue of damages and precluded it from introducing evidence on the issue of damages, leaving only the claim for injunctive relief in the case. The district judge concluded that Cine had only been grossly negligent and not willful and that the severe sanction imposed by the magistrate judge was inappropriate under FRCP 37 and certified an interlocutory appeal on this question.

Issue: Is gross negligence in failing to abide by discovery orders sufficient to justify the harshest disciplinary measures available under FRCP 37?

Rule: Yes. Grossly negligent failure to obey discovery orders is sufficient to justify the harshest sanctions available under FRCP 37. Gross professional incompetence is as responsible for the delays plaguing modern litigation as willful disobedience.

Silvestri v. General Motors Corp. (4th Cir. 2001)

Facts: Silvestri sued GM in federal court for injuries caused by the failure of his airbag to deploy. Before suit was filed and while Silvestri was in the hospital, his attorney retained experts to examine the car and they concluded that the airbag was defective. But neither Silvestri nor the lawyer took steps to preserve the car or to notify GM of the existence of the car until nearly three years later when Silvestri filed suit. The trial court dismissed the case for spoliation of evidence.

Issue: Does a party's duty to preserve relevant real evidence extend to the period prior to the filing of a complaint when that party reasonably should know that the evidence might be relevant to anticipated litigation and, therefore, the object of discovery?

Rule: Yes. The duty to preserve extends to the period prior to litigation when a party reasonably should know that evidence may be relevant to anticipated litigation. Silvestri knew he would be suing GM while he retained possession of the car and also knew that GM would want to inspect the car. Although dismissal is a severe sanction, it is appropriate and necessary here because the prejudice caused by the spoliation was irreparable. The trial court's dismissal is affirmed.

National Hockey League v. Metropolitan Hockey Club, Inc. (S. Ct. 1976)

Facts: As a result of Metropolitan failing to obey a court order requiring it to provide the National Hockey League with answers to certain interrogatories, Metropolitan's antitrust suit was dismissed.

Issue: Can a complaint be dismissed on the grounds that a party failed to respond to discovery orders?

Rule: (Per Curiam) FRCP 37 permits a complaint or portions of pleadings to be dismissed if, in bad faith, a party fails to comply with discovery orders.

Coca-Cola Bottling Co. v. Coca-Cola Co. (D. Del. 1986)

Facts: In a suit between the manufacturer of Coca-Cola and some of its bottlers over the division of profits, the distributors requested, during discovery, the formula for Coca-Cola. The manufacturer refused to disclose the formula, even under a strict protective court order. The manufacturer acknowledged that it could be sanctioned for its noncompliance. The bottlers moved for default judgment under FRCP 37(b), on the basis of the manufacturer's noncompliance. The trial judge refused to enter default judgment but issued an order saying it would instruct the jury to infer that the formulas of Coke and Diet Coke were identical and order the defense to pay attorneys' fees and costs on the motion to compel, though not the costs associated with its original refusal to produce.

Issue: Under FRCP 37(b), when will noncompliance with a discovery order warrant entry of a default judgment?

Rule: A court should consider six factors: (1) the extent of the party's personal responsibility; (2) the prejudice to the adversary caused by the failure to meet scheduling orders and respond to discovery; (3) a history of dilatoriness; (4) whether the conduct of the party or the attorney was willful or in bad faith; (5) the effectiveness of sanctions other than dismissal, including alternative sanctions; and (6) the merit of the claim or defense.

Velez v. Awning Windows, Inc. (1st Cir. 2004)

Facts: Velez sued Awning in federal court for employment discrimination under federal and state antidiscrimination laws. Velez obtained a default judgment after the defendants failed to answer the complaint and engaged in other dilatory action. The judge later set aside the default; defendants continued to fail to comply with the court's pretrial orders concerning filing deadlines for motions and oppositions to motions. As sanction for untimely filed opposition to plaintiff's motion for summary judgment on liability, the trial court deemed the motion unopposed and entered judgment on liability for plaintiff. It also sanctioned the defendants by denying their request to dismiss some claims and let the issue of damages go to the jury, which returned an award of $740,000 for the plaintiff.

Issue: Does a federal judge's case management authority under FRCP 16 authorize severe sanctions such as entry of judgment and refusal to dismiss claims for repeated failure to comply with court-ordered pretrial filing deadlines?

Rule: Yes. The FRCP 16 case management authority does authorize such drastic sanctions for repeated failure to comply with court-ordered pretrial filing deadlines. The defendants' failure to excuse their repeated late filings provided the court with the discretion to impose these sanctions.

G. Heileman Brewing Co. v. Joseph Oat Corp. (7th Cir. 1989)

Facts: A federal magistrate ordered Joseph Oat to send a corporate representative with the authority to make a full settlement to a pretrial conference, but Oat did not comply. The court determined this omission to be a violation of the court order, and imposed a sanction pursuant to FRCP 16(f). Joseph Oat appealed the sanction, contending that the silence of FRCP 16(a)(5) as to a court's authority to compel a personal appearance by a party who is represented by counsel prohibited the court from making such an order.

Issue: May a federal court order litigants already represented by counsel to appear before it in person at a pretrial conference for the purpose of discussing settlement of the case?

Rule: Yes. The absence of specific language in FRCP 16 authorizing a court to compel a represented defendant to appear at a pretrial conference does not signify that the power to do so is prohibited. FRCP 16 is intended to allow courts to actively manage and prepare cases for trial, and should therefore not be construed as a device to limit the authority of the district judge in the conduct of pretrial conferences.

Payne v. S.S. Nabob (3d Cir. 1962)

Facts: In an admiralty action filed in federal court, the trial judge, per FRCP 16 authority, requested that both parties submit pretrial reports including a list of anticipated witnesses. At trial, Payne attempted to call witnesses not included in the report and the court did not allow them to testify. Payne maintained that since no pretrial order had been issued, it was not bound by the pretrial report.

Issue: Can a federal district judge exclude a witness whose name is not contained in a pretrial report in the absence of a pretrial order?

Rule: Yes. Even if no pretrial order is made, the trial judge can exclude a witness not named in a pretrial report. The parties have a duty to make accurate pretrial reports regardless of whether a pretrial order is issued. The trial judge's exclusion of the witness is affirmed.

McKey v. Fairbairn (D.C. Cir. 1965)

Facts: Water leaked into the house McKey rented from Fairbairn, allegedly causing McKey's mother-in-law to slip and fall. The pretrial order in the federal action set forth an allegation of negligence for failure to repair and eliminate a dangerous condition after receiving notice. During the trial, McKey sought to amend the pretrial order to permit him to introduce local housing regulations that required roofs and walls to be leak-proof.

Although the landlord was aware of these regulations, the trial court did not permit the plaintiff to change recovery theories.

Issue: May a plaintiff depart from a pretrial order and present a new theory of recovery at trial?

Rule: Where a plaintiff has not presented a particular theory of recovery until trial, refusing to permit the appellant to change her theory is within the judge's discretion.

Dissent: Whether a plaintiff should be permitted to establish a new theory of recovery during trial is determined by balancing the possible prejudice to the defendant against the injustice that would be prevented by permitting the modification. Because the defendants in this case knew of the regulations, their disadvantage would be small in comparison with the injustice the plaintiff would suffer if relevant evidence is precluded.

Nick v. Morgan's Foods, Inc. (8th Cir. 2001)

Facts: Nick sued his employer, Morgan's, alleging employment discrimination in violation of Title VII. The parties agreed to pretrial mediation and the trial judge issued a referral order imposing a set of requirements on the parties during the mediation. Morgan's failed to supply required memoranda to the mediator and no one with settlement authority appeared at the mediation, in violation of the court's order. Nick made offers at the mediation but Morgan's rejected them without making any counteroffer. Morgan's admitted that it violated the referral order and said that this order constituted only a set of nonbinding guidelines. The trial judge sanctioned Morgan's by ordering it to pay mediation and attorneys' fees, a fine payable to the clerk of court, and Nick's expenses incurred in attending the mediation. It subsequently sanctioned Morgan's for filing a frivolous motion to reconsider the sanctions decision. Morgan's appealed only the sanction of the fine payable to the clerk of court.

Issue: Does FRCP 16(f) authorize a district judge to impose sanctions for failure to comply with orders on pretrial conferences?

Rule: Yes. FRCP 16 (f) authorizes "any other sanction" beyond reasonable attorneys' fees and expenses for failure to comply with orders on pretrial conferences including mediation and that includes the authority to order fines payable to the clerk or court. Although the misconduct was solely the fault of counsel, a party may be held liable for its counsel's actions. Trial judge's order is upheld.

CHAPTER 8

Adjudication Without Trial

I. INTRODUCTION

Despite the constitutional right to trial by jury, a suit may very well be dismissed before opening arguments. Courts have several means for disposing of a suit before trial. Given the enormous costs of litigation, as well as the increasing delay brought about by overcrowded court dockets, it is not surprising that the law is more tolerant of pretrial resolution of disputes, especially if voluntary or if the suit is essentially frivolous.

II. SUMMARY JUDGMENT (FRCP 56)

A. Purposes
   Summary judgment serves to:
   1. Determine if a dispute exists.
   2. Avoid useless trials.
   3. Achieve a final determination on the merits.
   4. Eliminate certain issues or claims from trial.
B. Standards and Burdens of Proof
   1. Summary judgment may be granted only if:
      a. There is no genuine issue of relevant (material) fact; and
      b. The moving party (the party who wants summary judgment) is entitled to judgment as a matter of law (i.e., must have a valid legal claim).
   2. The moving party has the initial burden of establishing that there is no factual dispute regarding the matter upon which summary judgment is sought.
   3. All doubts will be resolved against the moving party.

4. A judge will award summary judgment where a reasonable jury could not possibly decide against the moving party according to the appropriate standard the jury would be asked to apply (preponderance of the evidence, clear and convincing evidence, or beyond a reasonable doubt).

5. No summary judgments may be entered against criminal defendants.

C. Partial Summary Judgment

A court need not dismiss the entire case. If several issues are present, but one of the issues has no genuine issue of fact, the court may summarily dismiss that claim while allowing the rest to go to trial.

III. DISMISSAL OF ACTIONS (FRCP 41)

A. Voluntary (FRCP 41(a)(1))

1. The plaintiff can voluntarily dismiss an action by filing a notice of dismissal before the defendant has served an answer.

2. The plaintiff can voluntarily dismiss an action after the defendant has answered by a stipulation signed by all parties or by leave of court.

3. The first voluntary dismissal is without prejudice to the plaintiff. This means it is not precluded from bringing the claim again later.

4. After the second voluntary dismissal, the plaintiff will be precluded from bringing another action on the same claim.

B. Involuntary (FRCP 41(b))

1. Upon motion by the defendant, a court can order dismissal of the plaintiff's action for:

   a. Failure to prosecute, or

   b. Failure to comply with the FRCP.

2. An involuntary dismissal usually constitutes a judgment on the merits, except when the court dismisses without prejudice or the grounds for dismissal are:

   a. Improper venue,

   b. Lack of jurisdiction, or

   c. Failure to join an indispensable party under FRCP 19.

IV. DEFAULT JUDGMENTS (FRCP 55)

A. Entry of Default

1. The clerk enters a default judgment if the defendant:

   a. Does not answer the plaintiff's complaint,

   b. Fails to appear at trial, or

   c. Fails to comply with the FRCP.

   2. If money is allegedly due, the clerk can enter a default judgment for that sum.
B. Default Judgment
   1. A subsequent hearing may still be held to determine:
      a. Damages, or
      b. Whether the default judgment should be vacated because the defendant had a:
         i. Valid excuse, and
         ii. A meritorious defense to the action.
   2. A motion to set aside a default judgment should be made within one year after entry.

CASE CLIPS

Lundeen v. Cordner (8th Cir. 1966)

Facts: Lundeen, on behalf of Maureen and Michael Cordner, sued Metropolitan Life Insurance to recover on a life insurance policy held by Lundeen's ex-husband, Joseph Cordner, which named Maureen and Michael as beneficiaries. Joseph's second wife, France Cordner, intervened on behalf of herself and her child. France introduced evidence that Joseph had completed all the necessary paperwork designating France and her child as the new beneficiaries, and then moved for summary judgment on the grounds that Lundeen had not introduced any controverting evidence. Lundeen contended that the evidence would emerge during cross-examination of an insurance agent and asked for the case to be sent to the jury.

Issue: Is summary judgment permissible when the opposing party claims that cross-examination of a witness will provide information that would aid its cause?

Rule: Yes. Summary judgment is appropriate when all evidence relevant to a summary judgment motion indicates that no issue of material fact exists between the parties, even if the opposing party contends that cross-examination is essential but fails to show how the testimony would be impeached or how additional testimony will be adduced.

Cross v. United States (2d Cir. 1964)

Facts: Cross, a foreign language professor, tried to get a tax refund for the expense of attending a European seminar. The Internal Revenue Service unsuccessfully opposed Cross's motion for summary judgment. The IRS claimed there was a dispute as to the nature of the trip — information it could only get from Cross.

Issue: Is summary judgment appropriate even though the opposing party claims its only counter-evidence will come out during cross-examination?

Rule: No. Summary judgment is inappropriate where the inferences the parties seek to draw deal with motive, intent, and subjective feelings and reactions.

Adickes v. S. H. Kress & Co. (S. Ct. 1970)

Facts: Adickes, a white schoolteacher, and her six African-American students entered S. H. Kress & Co. (Kress) for lunch. Kress served the children, but not Adickes. Adickes then brought suit, claiming that the community's custom of segregated restaurants violated her Fourteenth Amendment Equal Protection Clause guarantees. To win her case, Adickes would have to prove a specific custom. Adickes did not offer any evidence of any custom in her complaint. S. H. Kress then moved for summary judgment.

Issue: When may a court grant a motion for summary judgment?

Rule: A court may only grant a motion for summary judgment when the party requesting summary judgment has shown the absence of a genuine issue of material fact.

Celotex Corp. v. Catrett (S. Ct. 1986)

Facts: Catrett alleged that her husband died as a result of exposure to asbestos manufactured by Celotex. Catrett sued in state court for negligence, breach of warranty, and strict liability. Celotex moved for summary judgment under FRCP 56 on the grounds that Catrett had not offered any evidence to support the allegation that her husband had been exposed to Celotex products. Catrett argued that Celotex had to produce evidence negating the allegation that her husband had been exposed. The trial court granted the motion, but the state court of appeals reversed, holding that the movant had not offered sufficient evidence to rebut the plaintiff's allegations.

Issue: Must summary judgment be granted against a party who does not meet its burden of proof on an essential element of its claim?

Rule: Yes. The court must enter summary judgment against a party if that party fails to establish the existence of an essential element of its case as to which it bears the burden of persuasion. The plaintiff bore the burden of persuasion on the issue of exposure and failed to meet that burden. Thus, the plaintiff did not establish a genuine issue of material on that issue. Thus, summary judgment was appropriate.

Scott v. Harris (S. Ct. 2007)

Facts: Harris was injured during a police car chase and brought suit in federal court against Scott, the police officer, for using excessive force in violation of Harris's Fourth Amendment rights. Scott moved for summary judgment on the basis of qualified immunity. The trial judge denied the motion and the circuit court affirmed that ruling.

Issue: Must all facts be viewed in the light most favorable to the nonmoving party in ruling on a motion for summary judgment?

Rule: At summary judgment, facts must be viewed in the light most favorable to the nonmoving party only if there is a genuine dispute as to those facts. The nonmoving party must offer some basis for concluding that there is a doubt as to the material facts. When no reasonable jury could believe the opponent's allegedly contradictory evidence, the court should not adopt the version of the facts favorable to the opponent. The plaintiff here did not offer any believable evidence to create a genuine issue of fact and so the defendant is entitled to summary judgment.

Anderson v. Liberty Lobby, Inc. (S. Ct. 1986)

Facts: Liberty Lobby sued Anderson for publishing allegedly libelous articles about it. In support of his summary judgment motion, Anderson asserted that Liberty Lobby couldn't prove actual malice (the standard required for libel suits) by "clear and convincing evidence."

Issue: What standard must be applied to determine whether a motion for summary judgment should be granted?

Rule: In determining whether to grant a summary judgment motion, a judge must decide whether a reasonable jury could possibly find in favor of the party opposing summary judgment according to the standard the jury will ultimately use. In making this determination, the judge should resolve all issues of credibility in favor of the party opposing summary judgment.

Arnstein v. Porter (1946)

Facts: Arnstein sued Cole Porter for copyright infringement of Arnstein's songs. The trial judge granted Porter's motion for summary judgment on grounds of vexatiousness and the fact that Arnstein previously had brought five similar and unsuccessful suits against others.

Issue: Can summary judgment be granted when credibility of the parties is crucial to resolving the case?

Rule: No. When there exists even a slight doubt regarding material facts, summary judgment is improper, and summary judgment is particularly improper when the parties' credibility is in issue.

Coulas v. Smith (Ariz. Sup. Ct. 1964)

Facts: Smith sued Bray on a promissory note in state court. Bray then cross-claimed against co-defendant Coulas on the grounds that Coulas was the party who really owed the debt to Smith. Coulas answered both the cross-claim and complaint but failed to attend the trial. Smith received a judgment on the merits against Bray and against Coulas who, two years later, moved to have the judgment vacated on the grounds that he did not receive the three days' notice of the default judgment required by FRCP 55.

Issue: Can a court issue a default judgment when the defendant has answered but does not appear at trial?

Rule: No. Once a party files pleadings or answers in response to any of the claims against him, a default judgment cannot be entered. Even if the defendant does not appear at trial, the court must examine the sufficiency of the plaintiff's proof to determine the validity of the cause of action. Since the court did not enter a default judgment here, the defendant was not entitled to the applicable three-day statutory notice requirement.

Peralta v. Heights Medical Center (S. Ct. 1988)

Facts: Heights Medical Center sued Peralta in state court alleging that he had guaranteed to pay the medical expenses of one of his employees. Peralta did not appear or answer, claiming that he was not properly served with process. A default judgment was entered against him and a lien was placed on his real property, which fetched a deflated price at auction. Peralta filed an action to void the sale and to set aside the default judgment on the grounds that service had been invalidly made. The Texas court dismissed this second action, holding that Peralta had to show something about his defense on the merits of the underlying claim, which he could not do, and this was affirmed by the state appellate court.

Issue: May a state require that an appellant who seeks to set aside a default judgment entered after improper service show that he had a meritorious defense to the original claim?

Rule: No. A meritorious defense is not required to set aside a default judgment based on improper service. To require an appellant who has been deprived of property in a manner contrary to due process to show that he had a meritorious defense to the original action violates the Due Process Clause of the Fourteenth Amendment.

Matsushita Elec. Industrial Co. v. Epstein (S. Ct. 1996)

Facts: A class action suit was filed in Delaware state court against the directors of a Delaware corporation for failing to maximize shareholder value after a tender offer had been made for the corporation. While this suit was pending, another suit was filed against those defendants in federal court for securities act violations, over which the federal court had exclusive subject matter jurisdiction. The federal district court refused to certify the class and the plaintiffs appealed. Pending appeal, the state court suit was settled, which settlement included a global release of all claims arising out of the acquisition. The defendants in the federal suit then asserted that the settlement of the state court action mandated the dismissal of the federal case. The Ninth Circuit rejected this argument, holding that the settlement did not preclude claims that fell within the federal court's exclusive subject matter jurisdiction.

Issue: Can a settlement of class action suits in state court release exclusively federal claims that are pending in federal court?

Rule: Yes. Settlement of state class action suits can release exclusively federal claims pending in federal court. The Full Faith and Credit Act mandates that state court proceedings have the same credit in every federal court that they are accorded in state court and federal courts must accept state rules concerning the effect of state court judgments. Delaware courts decided that a global release of claims precludes subsequent federal court litigation of released claims and so the federal court must give the release full effect. The Ninth Circuit's judgment is reversed.

Kalinauskas v. Wong (D. Nev. 1993)

Facts: Kalinauskas brought a sexual discrimination suit against her employer, Desert Palace, in federal court. She sought to depose a former employee of Caesar's Palace who had sued Caesar's for sexual harassment and subsequently settled the claim. That settlement contained a confidentiality agreement that precluded the employee from discussing all aspects of her employment with Caesar's. Caesar's sought a protective order to enforce the confidentiality agreement to bar Kalinauskas from taking that employee's deposition.

Issue: Can a confidentiality agreement be modified to place private litigants in a position they would otherwise reach only after repetition of another's discovery if modification would not tangibly prejudice substantial rights of the party opposing modification?

Rule: Yes. A confidentiality agreement can be modified to place private litigants in a position they would otherwise reach only after repetition of another's discovery if modification would not tangibly prejudice substantial rights of the party opposing modification. Kalinauskas's claim duplicates the proposed witness's claim and so to force Kalinauskas to duplicate all of that employee's work would be wasteful. The protective order is granted only to the extent that during the deposition of that Caesar's employee no information concerning the settlement itself can be disclosed. Otherwise, the deposition is ordered and the protective order is denied.

Ferguson v. Countrywide Credit Industries, Inc. (9th Cir. 2002)

Facts: After Ferguson brought suit in federal court alleging sexual harassment, Countrywide moved to compel arbitration pursuant to an arbitration agreement in Ferguson's employment contract. The district court refused to compel arbitration on the grounds that the arbitration agreement was unenforceable for unconscionability.

Issue: Is an arbitration agreement in an employment contract unenforceable when it is a prerequisite to employment, one sided, and otherwise unconscionable?

Rule: Yes. An arbitration agreement, like any other contract, can be denied enforcement on the grounds of unconscionability. There are two possible bases: procedural unconscionability and substantive unconscionability. Procedural unconscionability existed here because that goes to the manner in which the agreement was drafted and entered into. Here, it was drafted solely by the employer, was not subject to negotiation or modification by the employee, and agreement to it was a prerequisite to employment. This provision was also substantively unconscionable because of the nature of its terms as it mandated arbitration only of claims by employees and not by the employer and assigned the costs of arbitration to the employee and those costs could exceed the costs of litigation.

CHAPTER 9

Trials and Judgments

I. BURDEN OF PROOF

A. Burden of Production
   Each party must produce sufficient evidence to prevent a directed verdict.
   1. The plaintiff bears the initial burden, then the defendant must rebut the plaintiff's evidence.
   2. The defendant submitting affirmative defenses bears the burden of proving those defenses, but the plaintiff may then rebut.
B. Burden of Persuasion
   1. The plaintiff (or the defendant asserting an affirmative defense) must persuade the jury (or judge) of the existence of the facts claimed.
   2. Generally, the burden is met where a party establishes by a preponderance of evidence (i.e., more likely than not) that the events occurred as claimed.
   3. However, stronger burdens may be applied in certain cases.
      a. Clear and Convincing
         This stricter standard is most often used where personal reputation is at stake, such as libel and slander cases. This standard also applies to many aspects of family law as well as probate litigation.
      b. Beyond a Reasonable Doubt
         This standard is rarely used in civil cases, since it is the highest burden available at law. It is typically used in criminal cases.
C. Presumptions
   1. A presumption is a rule of law holding that when a basic fact is found, another fact is presumed to exist, absent rebuttal.
   2. Various types of presumptions exist. Some may be used to satisfy burdens of production; others may not. Some may be used to satisfy burdens of persuasion; others may not.

3. Two Types
   a. Rebuttable presumptions are ones where the party opposing the presumption is given the opportunity to offer evidence to rebut (destroy) the otherwise mandatory link between the proven and presumed fact.
   b. Irrebuttable presumptions are ones where the party opposing the presumption is not permitted to offer evidence that would destroy the link between the proven and presumed fact.

II. JURY TRIAL

A. Demand for Jury Trial (FRCP 38)
   Must be served on all parties not later than ten days after service of last pleading.
B. Jury Selection
   1. Voir Dire
      a. Each party's counsel questions potential jurors to discover possible bias.
      b. Judge may also pose questions.
   2. Juror Dismissal
      a. Provided dismissal does not violate Fourteenth Amendment (i.e., solely motivated by racial consideration, etc.), each side's lawyer has unlimited challenges for cause (i.e., bias) to juror's suitability to hear case.
      b. Each litigant gets three peremptory challenges (i.e., cause need not be shown).
C. Jury's Role
   Juries decide factual issues only.
   1. Basic Facts
      The occurrence or nonoccurrence of a fact that does not itself prove one of the necessary elements of the claim or defense.
   2. Ultimate Fact
      Established basic facts that prove a party's claim.
D. Jury Charge
   1. Judge instructs jury as to the doctrine relevant to a party's claim and its application to factual findings.
   2. Each party may submit to the judge instructions the party wants read to the jury.
   3. Judge's failure to submit correct instruction is reversible error if it prejudices verdict.
E. Unanimity (FRCP 48)
   The verdict must be unanimous unless parties stipulate that a stated majority shall deliver the verdict.

F. Right to Jury Trial
  1. Seventh Amendment
     a. Guarantees jury trial in actions triable at law.
     b. Nonjury cases
        i. Actions in equity and cases where a jury is waived are tried before a judge.
        ii. Trial judge must make specific factual findings and legal conclusions, clearly and distinctly stating both.
  2. Mixed Legal and Equitable Claims
     a. In federal court, where legal issues are incidental to equitable issues, a right to jury trial for legal issues exists (most state courts hold jury trial waived in this situation).
     b. In federal court, where legal issues are not incidental to the equitable issue, the legal issue is tried before a jury (preferably prior to the equitable issue), and the equitable issue is tried before a judge.
  3. Statutory Actions and Administrative Proceedings
     a. Congress has broad power to create a statutory right to jury trial where none existed in common law.
     b. A right to jury trial does not extend to administrative proceedings.
  4. State Law Right to Jury Trial
     a. Diversity cases
        If state law disallows jury trials where federal law would permit them, federal law controls.
     b. Federal issues in state courts
        A party pressing a federal issue in state court is entitled to a jury if federal law mandates a jury trial.

III. DISPOSITION

A. Nonsuit
   If after the plaintiff presents its case, it fails to show a right to relief, its case is dismissed. (The test is the same as for directed verdicts.)
B. Judgment as a Matter of Law (FRCP 50)
   Judgment as a matter of law encompasses the motions previously known as directed verdict and judgment notwithstanding the verdict (JNOV).
   1. Directed Verdict
      a. Takes case away from jury.
      b. The defendant may move for a directed verdict at the close of the plaintiff's case-in-chief; either party may move for a directed verdict when all the evidence is in.
      c. Judge views the evidence in the most favorable light to whoever opposes the directed verdict.

        d. The motion will be granted where:
           i. There exists insufficient evidence to go to the jury; or
          ii. The evidence is such that reasonable people could not differ as to the result.
    2. Judgment Notwithstanding the Verdict (JNOV) (Renewed Motion for Judgment as a Matter of Law)
      a. The judge substitutes his verdict for that of the jury.
      b. A party must move for a directed verdict before a motion for a JNOV is submitted.
      c. The same standard is applied as with the directed verdict.
  C. Motion for a New Trial

Courts have broad discretion in ordering new trials; they may be granted based on either questions of law or fact.

    1. Grounds
      a. Misconduct of judge or lawyers.
      b. Juror discovered evidence.
      c. Newly discovered evidence.
      d. Insufficient evidence to support judgment or verdict.
      e. Error in law (e.g., evidentiary rulings, erroneous jury charge).
    2. Partial New Trial

Where liability is clearly established, courts can order new trials regarding a damage award that is considered inappropriate.

  D. Motion for Relief from Judgment (FRCP 60)
    1. Defined

A motion granted where a party is prevented from presenting a full case.

    2. Grounds for Reopening a Case
      a. Mistake or excusable neglect.
      b. Newly discovered evidence.
      c. Judgment satisfied or underlying prior judgment is void, reversed, or vacated.
      d. Fraud or misrepresentation of a litigant.
      e. Any other reason advancing the interests of justice.
    3. Other Considerations
      a. The motion will be granted only where a substantial right is prejudiced.
      b. The court may correct errors made by a clerk entering judgment.

IV. VERDICTS

  A. General Verdict
    1. The jury finds for a party and grants relief without articulating specific factual findings.

2. The implication is that all essential issues were found in favor of the prevailing party.
3. There exists the potential to conceal the jury's misunderstandings of fact, etc.

B. General Verdict with Interrogatories
   1. Jury is instructed to deliver a general verdict as well as answers to questions regarding essential factual findings and issues.
   2. Purpose
      a. Ensures that the jury considered essential facts and issues.
      b. Permits the court to verify the accuracy of verdict by comparing the verdict with the jury's answers to see if they are consistent.
   3. Generally, if the answers to the interrogatory are consistent with each other but inconsistent with the general verdict, the answers control (court may also grant new trial or direct the jury to deliberate further).
   4. If the answers are inconsistent among themselves and some are inconsistent with the verdict, a new trial results.
   5. The court must try to harmonize the general verdict with the jury's answers.

C. Special Verdicts (FRCP 49(a))
   1. Juries make factual findings only.
   2. Judges apply the law to the juries' factual findings and render a verdict.

D. Erroneous Verdicts
   1. Failure by a jury to follow instructions may be grounds to set the verdict aside (e.g., a compromise verdict is erroneous).
   2. An internally inconsistent verdict results when jury findings are inconsistent and irreconcilable (e.g., jury holds employer liable under respondeat superior, yet finds employee acted with due care).
   3. If an erroneous verdict is correctable, a court abuses its discretion if, upon motion, it fails to direct further jury deliberations.
   4. Errors are waived unless the prejudiced party timely objects; errors that do not prejudice a substantial right are held harmless.

E. Contempt Orders
   1. The property of the judgment debtor is seized.
   2. Only that amount of property sufficient to cover the judgment may be levied.
   3. Civil Contempt of Court
      a. A party returns to court to show the other party's noncompliance with the judgment.
      b. A noncomplying party held in contempt may be fined, imprisoned, or both until compliance results.

CASE CLIPS

Sioux City & Pacific Railroad Co. v. Stout (S. Ct. 1873)

Facts: At trial, the judge charged the jury with instructions on determining whether the railroad was negligent. The jury then found for Stout.

Issue: May a judge charge a jury with determining whether a party was negligent?

Rule: The question of negligence is one properly charged to the jury, and if it is reasonable that the jury could find negligence, the decision must stand.

Beacon Theatres, Inc. v. Westover (S. Ct. 1959)

Facts: Fox West Coast Theatres, Inc. sued Beacon Theatres, Inc., asking for a declaratory statement that it was not violating antitrust laws, and an injunction stopping Beacon from bringing an antitrust suit against Fox. Beacon filed a counterclaim against Fox alleging that Fox had violated the antitrust laws, for which it sought damages. It asked for a jury trial on those issues. The trial court ruled that Fox's declaratory and injunctive claims were both in equity, and would be tried by the court without a jury before the jury determined the validity of Beacon's counterclaim.

Issue: Where the plaintiff's complaint seeks only equitable relief, are issues relative to that claim barred from jury consideration as they arise in a counterclaim for legal relief (damages)?

Rule: No. Regarding issues common to the plaintiff's equitable claim and the defense's counterclaim for damages, in light of the FRCP and the Declaratory Judgment Act, a trial court would not be justified in denying a defendant a jury trial on all issues relative to the (legal) claim for damages. Only under the most imperative circumstances can the right to jury trial of legal issues be forfeited through prior determination of equitable claims.

Dairy Queen, Inc. v. Wood (S. Ct. 1962)

Facts: Dairy Queen moved to strike Wood's demand for a jury trial on the grounds that Dairy Queen's action was either purely equitable or, alternatively, that any legal issues raised (i.e., the plaintiff's claim for a money judgment) were merely incidental to the equitable issues.

Issue: Does a party lose its right to a jury trial if the legal issues are incidental to the equitable issues?

Rule: A claim for a money judgment is a claim wholly legal in its nature regardless of how the complaint is framed. Therefore, a damages claim is severable from any equitable issues and shall be tried by a jury if a jury is demanded.

Ross v. Bernhard (S. Ct. 1970)

Facts: Ross and other shareholders sued Bernhard and other directors of the Lehman Corp. alleging that its brokerage firm, Lehman Bros., controlled the corporation illegally. Ross demanded a jury trial on his claims against the corporation.

Issue: Does the Seventh Amendment right to a jury trial extend to stockholders' derivative actions?

Rule: The right to a jury trial attaches to those issues in derivative actions in which the corporation would have been entitled to a jury trial had it been suing in its own right.

Curtis v. Loether (S. Ct. 1974)

Facts: Curtis brought suit in federal court alleging that Loether refused to rent an apartment to her because she was black. Following a preliminary injunction, the Title VIII suit went to trial to determine damages. Loether's request for a jury trial was denied on the grounds that it was authorized by neither Title VIII nor the Seventh Amendment. The circuit court reversed, finding that a jury trial was guaranteed by the Seventh Amendment.

Issue: Is an action for damages an action to enforce "legal rights," thus allowing a Seventh Amendment right to a jury trial?

Rule: Yes. The Seventh Amendment right to jury trials extends beyond those common law actions in existence when the amendment was ratified. The Seventh Amendment applies to subsequently created statutory rights. Therefore, a jury trial must be available if a Title VIII suit involves rights and remedies typically enforced in an action at law.

Tull v. United States (S. Ct. 1987)

Facts: The government sued Tull for dumping waste on wetlands in violation of the Clean Water Act. The suit included requests for an injunction (equity) as well as for damages (law). Tull sought a jury trial.

Issue: Does the Seventh Amendment guarantee a right to a jury trial for both legal and equitable issues?

Rule: The Seventh Amendment requires that a jury trial demand be granted to determine legal issues, but not equitable issues. The plaintiff has a constitutional right to jury trial on the request for a civil penalty as that was a remedy enforced by the law courts.

Reid v. San Pedro, Los Angeles & Salt Lake Railroad (Utah 1911)

Facts: Reid brought an action in state court when his cow was injured by one of the defendant's trains. Reid offered no direct evidence of causation. The jury rendered a verdict for Reid.

Issue: What evidence must the plaintiff have to offer to overcome a defense motion for directed verdict?

Rule: Where the plaintiff's undisputed evidence points equally to two divergent conclusions, one of which supports liability and one which does not, the plaintiff has not sustained its burden of persuading the factfinder more likely than not that the defendant is liable and must suffer a directed verdict. Thus, a directed verdict was appropriate in this case.

Pennsylvania Railroad v. Chamberlain (S. Ct. 1933)

Facts: At trial, the judge directed a verdict for Chamberlain even though the proven facts gave equal support to both the railroad's and Chamberlain's allegations.

Issue: Where the evidence is so insubstantial that if a verdict was rendered for one party the court would have to order a new trial, can the judge direct a verdict to avoid that situation?

Rule: Yes. Where no reasonable jury could find in favor of the party with the burden of persuasion on a claim, then the court should issue a directed verdict. There was insufficient evidence to justify submission to the jury so the trial court's judgment is affirmed.

Amoco Oil Co. v. Torcomian (3d Cir. 1983)

Facts: Amoco brought an ejectment action in federal court against Torcomian, who ran a gas station but never executed a franchise agreement with Amoco. At the beginning of trial, Amoco attempted orally to amend its complaint to delete the request for damages for lost profits as a result of Torcomian's wrongful possession, to preclude a jury trial. Torcomian filed a counterclaim for breach of contract, seeking damages. The trial court refused to order a jury trial.

Issue: Where the plaintiff's claim is in equity but the defendant asserts a legal counterclaim, is the defendant entitled to a jury trial?

Rule: Yes. An equitable main claim cannot preclude jury trial on a legal counterclaim. Joining an equitable to a legal claim does not defeat the Seventh Amendment right to a jury trial. It was error to refuse a jury trial and so judgment is vacated and a new trial is ordered.

Atlas Roofing Co. v. Occupational Safety and Health Review Commission (S. Ct. 1977)

Facts: In 1970, Congress passed the Occupational Safety and Heath Act (OSHA) authorizing the Labor Department to require employers to correct unsafe working conditions, and imposing civil penalties on employers who did not comply. Any disputes were handled before an administrative law judge, and never before a jury.

Issue: May Congress create a cause of action for civil penalties that may be litigated only in an administrative agency that does not provide for a jury trial?

Rule: Yes. The Seventh Amendment applies to all suits "at common law." This does not prevent Congress from assigning suits of the sort normally tried by a jury before an agency instead, if the suit involves new statutes creating "public rights."

Granfinanciera, S.A. v. Nordberg (S. Ct. 1989)

Facts: Nordberg sued Granfinanciera to recover funds transferred to it by a bankruptcy debtor. Granfinanciera was denied a jury trial on the grounds that bankruptcy courts are non-Article III tribunals, which are not governed by the Seventh Amendment.

Issue: Is there a right to a jury trial in cases being adjudicated by non-Article III (e.g., bankruptcy) courts?

Rule: Yes. When sued by the bankruptcy trustee to recover allegedly fraudulent monetary transfers, a person who has not submitted a claim against a bankruptcy estate has a right to a jury trial. If Congress creates new causes of action involving public rights, it may assign their adjudication to tribunals that do not use juries as factfinders. However, Congress may not block application of the Seventh Amendment to private-right cases (e.g., tort, contract, property, and other suits at common law). A bankruptcy trustee's right to recover a fraudulent conveyance most nearly resembles a state law contract claim, which carries with it a right to a jury trial.

Chauffeurs, Teamsters and Helpers Local 391 v. Terry (S. Ct. 1990)

Facts: Workers sued their union in federal court, claiming that the union had breached its duty of fair representation while negotiating collective bargaining agreements. The employees sought relief in the form of back pay and requested a jury trial. The union moved to strike the jury trial request on the grounds that no right to a jury trial exists in a duty of fair representation suit. The trial court denied the motion and this was affirmed on appeal.

Issue: Does the Seventh Amendment right to a jury trial attach to a union member's claim that the union breached its duty of fair representation?

Rule: Yes. A party has a right to a trial by jury under the Seventh Amendment if the action will resolve the legal (rather than equitable) rights of the parties. A two-prong test determines whether the action resolves the legal rights of the parties. First, the court determines whether the issues involved in the action are legal or equitable by determining whether analogous eighteenth century rights were vindicated in a court of law or a court of equity. Second, the court determines whether the remedy sought is legal or equitable. The nature of the remedy sought is a weightier factor than is the nature of the issues involved. In this case, a claim of breach of duty of fair representation is akin to an action for breach of fiduciary duty, which traditionally was an equitable action. However, the action also has elements of breach of contract and so the claim has both equitable and legal issues. But the remedy sought, damages, is wholly legal. So the action is more legal than equitable and thus the right to jury trial attaches. The decisions by the lower courts are upheld.

Concurrence: (Brennan, J.) If the remedy sought in an action is a legal remedy, the parties should have a right to a trial by jury. The historical analysis of issues in the first prong of the Seventh Amendment analysis is outmoded, irrelevant, and unwieldy.

Dissent: (Kennedy, J.) This claim is most analogous to a breach of fiduciary duty claim, which is equitable.

Markman v. Westview Instruments, Inc. (S. Ct. 1996)

Facts: Markman filed a patent infringement suit against its competitor, Westview, in federal court. A key issue was whether the patent's protection of "inventory" referred to cash or clothes. The jury rendered a verdict for Markman but the trial judge granted judgment as a matter of law to the defendant. Markman appealed on the grounds that the patent claim issue was within the jury's exclusive jurisdiction. The appellate court upheld the trial court's judgment.

Issue: Is interpretation of the scope of a patent claim an issue of law subject to judicial determination?

Rule: Yes. Interpretation of the scope of a patent claim is a question of law that should be determined by the judge rather than by the jury. Patent infringement actions are legal in nature and so are tried to a jury but particular issues, issues of law, are reserved to the court. Deciding whether or not an issue is for the judge or the jury also involves a comparative assessment of relative competence. Judges are better suited to construe terms of art.

Dobson v. Masonite Corp. (5th Cir. 1966)

Facts: Dobson orally agreed to clear timber from Masonite's land. Masonite subsequently terminated the agreement and Dobson sued for lost profits.

Issue: Is the meaning of a contract a factual issue for the jury to decide?

Rule: Since interpretation is always a question of fact, a question of contractual meaning must be determined by the trier of fact.

Colgrove v. Battin (S. Ct. 1973)

Facts: A local rule of the district court in Montana stated that the jury for civil trial shall consist of six persons.

Issue: Does a rule requiring a six-member jury violate the Seventh Amendment?

Rule: The Seventh Amendment only applies to cases in which the right to trial by jury was guaranteed at common law, so a six-member jury is not violative except in those cases.

Dissent: (Marshall, J.) It cannot be doubted that the Framers envisioned a jury of 12 when they referred to a trial by jury.

Thiel v. Southern Pacific Co. (S. Ct. 1946)

Facts: After having leapt from the window of one of Southern Pacific's trains, Thiel sued the railroad for damages. After demanding a jury trial, Thiel unsuccessfully moved to strike out the entire jury panel on the grounds that the court clerk had deliberately excluded from the jury lists all people who worked for a daily wage. After the jury had been chosen, Thiel unsuccessfully sought to challenge the individual jurors on the same grounds. The jury eventually found for the defendant.

Issue: Does the deliberate exclusion of a particular segment of the population from a jury list constitute reversible error?

Rule: The general principles underlying jury selection make unlawful the deliberate exclusion from a jury panel of an entire class of potential jurors and, hence, such exclusion constitutes reversible error.

Flowers v. Flowers (Tex. Civ. App. 1965)

Facts: In this action for divorce, Mrs. Flowers's attempt to have a potential juror dismissed for cause was denied. The challenged juror had told another panelist before her selection that she knew Mrs. Flowers had been unfaithful before. The jury returned a verdict for the husband and the wife's motion for a new trial was denied.

Issue: Must a potential juror be dismissed if it appears that she is biased as to any of the parties or the subject matter of the action?

Rule: Yes. If challenged, a potential juror with a bias toward any litigant or the action's subject matter must be disqualified, as a matter of law, when the bias or prejudice is clearly established.

Tanner v. United States (S. Ct. 1987)

Facts: After the jury's verdict and sentencing, a juror informed Tanner's attorney that many jurors had consumed alcohol during the lunch periods and slept throughout afternoon portions of the trial.

Issue: May a juror introduce evidence impeaching the jury upon which he sits?

Rule: Evidence gained from juries during trial is internal to the verdict and therefore is inadmissible.

Dissent: (Marshall, J.) Every defendant is entitled to a trial by competent jurors. Evidence on that point should be admissible or the defendant is denied due process.

Thompson v. Altheimer & Gray (7th Cir. 2003)

Facts: Thompson sued her employer, Altheimer & Gray, in federal court for racial discrimination in violation of federal law. During voir dire, one juror stated a pro-employer prejudice but, in response to a question from the judge, indicated that her past experience would cloud her judgment but that she would do her best. The judge refused to grant Thompson's request to strike the juror for cause and the jury returned a defense verdict.

Issue: Must a juror be excused for cause if he or she holds a belief that would impede his or her ability to give proper weight to the evidence and follow the court's instructions?

Rule: Yes. The issue is not whether a juror has a bias but whether that bias would preclude that juror from giving due weight to the evidence and following the court's instruction. If so, the juror must be excused for cause. Here, the trial judge did not sufficiently question the juror to determine that she was able to perform appropriately, so the decision is reversed.

Edmonson v. Leesville Concrete Co. (S. Ct. 1991)

Facts: The defendant in a federal court negligence action brought by an African American used peremptory challenges to strike prospective African-American jurors. The plaintiff claimed that the defendant's use of peremptory challenges based on race violated the Fifth Amendment's Due Process Clause.

Issue: May a private litigant in a civil case use peremptory challenges to exclude jurors on account of their race?

Rule: No. Peremptory challenges exist only because the government permits them. Peremptory challenges are thus attributable to the government, even when exercised by a private attorney. Therefore, use of peremptory challenges to exclude jurors on account of their race involves state action, thereby invoking the constitutional guarantees of due process and equal protection. Race may not be used as a basis for peremptory challenges.

Dissent: (O'Connor, J.) The state does not significantly participate in the peremptory challenge process, and the exercise of a peremptory challenge is not a traditional government function. Because racially motivated peremptory challenges are not state actions, they do not violate the Fifth Amendment.

Galloway v. United States (S. Ct. 1943)

Facts: Galloway claimed he went insane while fighting in World War I, and sued for disability payments from the Armed Services. The trial court granted the defense motion for directed verdict because Galloway did not offer sufficient evidence of his total disability. Galloway maintained that the court's directed verdict deprived him of his Seventh Amendment right to a jury trial.

Issue: Does a court's power to issue a directed verdict violate the Seventh Amendment right to a jury trial?

Rule: No. When a party's evidence is legally insufficient to sustain a verdict, the court may constitutionally direct a verdict in favor of the other party. The fact that the directed verdict was unknown at the time of the ratification of the Seventh Amendment is not dispositive since the Seventh Amendment preserves only the most fundamental elements of the jury trial that existed at the time of its ratification and not all procedural elements of a jury trial at that time. Plus, there were other procedural mechanisms, such as the demurrer, that would permit a judge to remove a case from jury consideration at the time of the ratification.

Dissent: (Black, J.) This decision erodes a large portion of the Seventh Amendment, which is the mainstay of American jurisprudence. There is sufficient evidence in this case for dispute such that the case should have gone to the jury.

Neely v. Martin K. Eby Construction Co. (S. Ct. 1967)

Facts: Neely won a jury verdict in district court over both motions for directed verdict and for judgment notwithstanding the verdict (JNOV) by Martin K. Eby Construction Co. On appeal, the court reversed the denial of Martin's JNOV motion and dismissed the action.

Issue: When must an appellate court grant a new trial rather than dismiss an action if it determines that the prevailing party's evidence was insufficient to sustain a verdict?

Rule: FRCP 50(d) states that the prevailing party has the right to urge an appellate court to order a new trial rather than set aside a verdict. This rule does not mean, however, that the appellate court must order a new trial in such a case. Hence, appellate courts can enter a JNOV, provided the party prevailing at trial first has an opportunity to establish grounds for a new trial.

Denman v. Spain (Miss. Sup. Ct. 1961)

Facts: Ross's car and Mrs. Eva Denman's car collided, injuring Betty Denman, her daughter. Ross, Mrs. Denman, and a passenger in Ross's car subsequently died. In her personal injury suit, Denman won a jury verdict against Spain, the executrix of Ross's estate. No proof of Ross's negligence was offered except speculative circumstantial evidence. The jury issued a verdict for the plaintiff, but Spain's motion for a judgment notwithstanding the verdict (JNOV) was granted by the state trial judge.
Issue: Can a court overturn a jury verdict based on legally insufficient evidence?
Rule: Yes. A jury verdict can be upheld only if the evidence is legally sufficient to sustain that verdict. The plaintiff had offered evidence that the defendant had driven at an excessive rate of speed, but no evidence that this negligence caused or contributed to the crash. Thus, any finding of causation had to have been based on speculation. Verdicts may not be based on "possibilities." Thus, a court can grant a JNOV motion when evidence is legally insufficient to support the jury's verdict.

Rogers v. Missouri Pacific Railroad (S. Ct. 1957)

Facts: In a suit brought in state court by Rogers under the Federal Employers' Liability Act (FELA), evidence reasonably supported a verdict for either party. The court submitted the liability issue to the jury, who found for Rogers. On appeal, the court reversed, ruling that as a matter of law the plaintiff's conduct was the sole cause of his injury.
Issue: If evidence reasonably supports a verdict for either party, must the court submit the issue to the jury?
Rule: Yes. If probative facts reasonably support a verdict favorable to either party, the decision is exclusively for the jury to make.

Daniel J. Hartwig Associates, Inc. v. Kanner (7th Cir. 1990)

Facts: Hartwig rendered consulting services and expert witness testimony to Kanner, an attorney. Kanner withheld payment, and Hartwig sued to recover payment for the services. Hartwig admitted at trial that he had padded his resume and failed to reveal a conflict of interest. Kanner offered no evidence in his defense. The district judge directed a verdict in favor of Hartwig. Although Kanner did not dispute the amount of the payments owed to Hartwig, he claimed that there was a material issue of fact as to whether the contract was void due to misrepresentation.

Issue: When is it appropriate for a court to grant a directed verdict?

Rule: A court should grant a directed verdict only if there is no credible evidence to sustain a verdict in favor of the party against whom the motion was made. Since the burden of persuasion for the elements of the affirmative defense of misrepresentation, including the fact of misrepresentation, reliance thereupon, and damages, at trial rested on Kanner, his failure to demonstrate any evidence of reliance or damages left the court with no recourse but to find for the plaintiff. Trial court's judgment is affirmed.

Dyer v. MacDougall (2d Cir. 1952)

Facts: Dyer brought slander and libel claims in federal court against MacDougall. MacDougall submitted affidavits of witnesses who denied making the allegedly defamatory utterances. The plaintiff was provided with time to depose these witnesses but did not take their depositions. The trial court granted MacDougall's motion for directed verdict on the grounds that the plaintiff had offered no evidence to support the alleged slanders.

Issue: Can the court grant directed verdict against the plaintiff when all of the plaintiff's witnesses deny the allegations in the complaint?

Rule: Yes. The only basis for a jury verdict in favor of the plaintiff was a finding that the witnesses were not believable, i.e., based on their demeanor at trial. But this is not available for appellate review since it is not on the record. Trial court's judgment is affirmed.

Lind v. Schenley Indus. (3d Cir. 1960)

Facts: After hearing conflicting testimony as to the existence of a contract, a jury found that an oral contract existed and awarded damages. The trial judge did not agree and granted a defense motion for judgment notwithstanding the verdict and, alternatively, for a new trial.

Issue: What is the standard for setting aside a jury's verdict as contrary to the weight of the evidence?

Rule: A trial judge has wide discretion to grant a new trial if a possibly erroneous verdict resulted from circumstances beyond the jury's control (e.g., improperly admitted evidence, prejudicial statements by counsel, or an improper charge). It is an abuse of discretion for a judge to set aside a jury verdict simply because he has reached a different conclusion. The degree of judicial scrutiny should vary with the subject of the litigation. Closer scrutiny of a verdict is warranted when the case deals with complex and specialized subject matter, but the jury's judgment should control on issues such as the veracity of witnesses.

Kennedy v. Southern Cal. Edison Co. (9th Cir. 2000)

Facts: The Kennedy family brought a wrongful death claim in federal court for the death of Mrs. Kennedy as the result of exposure to nuclear radiation from rods manufactured by Southern California Edison. Under governing state law, a jury must be instructed that the plaintiff can meet its burden of proving causation by showing exposure was a substantial factor contributing to the risk of developing cancer. The trial court refused to give this instruction and the jury found for the defendant.

Issue: Where a jury instruction would be helpful to the jury, can the court refuse to give a requested instruction?

Rule: No. Where a jury instruction would be beneficial to the jury's determination, the court cannot refuse a requested instruction. It has a duty to frame and submit a proper instruction to the jury. The refusal to instruct was not harmless error. The trial court's ruling is reversed.

Nollenberger v. United Air Lines, Inc. (S.D. Cal. 1963)

Facts: The Nollenbergers sued and defeated United in a wrongful death action. However, the jury's general award was far less than what was required according to its answer to special interrogatories concerning damages.

Issue: When a general verdict and answers to special interrogatories are irreconcilable, which should control?

Rule: The special verdict answers. When answers to special interrogatories are consistent with each other but irreconcilable with the general verdict, FRCP 49(b) permits the court to either resubmit the matter to the jury for further consideration, grant a new trial, or calculate and enter a judgment in accordance with the special interrogatories' answers. The Rule does not, however, permit additional interrogatories to be submitted after the jury has rendered its general verdict.

Whitlock v. Jackson (S.D. Ind. 1991)

Facts: Whitmore, as estate executor, filed a wrongful death action on behalf of the deceased against the police for using excessive force after an arrest. The jury returned a special verdict finding liability for battery but no civil rights violations and finding that the officers' conduct did not cause the death of the deceased. The jury awarded compensatory and punitive damages of $29,700 collectively against the arresting officers. The executor moved for a new trial on the grounds that the verdict was internally inconsistent since it awarded punitive damages and the law provided that punitive damages were available only upon a finding of a civil rights violation.

Issue: Can a jury's answers to interrogatories be used as a basis for overturning its verdict if there is any means of reconciling the answers with the verdict?

Rule: No. If the answers can be reconciled with the verdict, then the jury's answers to interrogatories cannot be a basis for overturning its verdict. Awarding punitive damages and finding that the officers did not use excessive force in violation of the deceased's civil rights was not inconsistent since punitive damages can be awarded to deter other officers from battering suspects even in the absence of a finding that the officers' conduct in the instant case violated the victim's constitutional rights.

Roberts v. Ross (3d Cir. 1965)

Facts: Roberts sued Ross for breach of contract in federal court. Based solely on the pleadings, the trial judge found for Ross and directed Ross to file his proposed findings of fact, conclusion of law, and draft of judgment. Roberts filed objections, but the court signed the judgment prepared by Ross without change.

Issue: Can a federal trial judge invite counsel for both parties to submit their factual findings and legal conclusions and then order a judgment based on one lawyer's version without making its own factual findings or stating his own legal conclusions?

Rule: No. Although a court may invite both sides to submit their factual and legal conclusions, according to FRCP 52(a), the trial judge must prepare his own specific factual findings and conclusions of law sufficiently to indicate the basis of his decision. The findings and conclusions in this case did not provide a sufficient indication of the bases for the trial judge's decision as required by FRCP 52(a), which is necessary for the appellate court to do its job of properly reviewing the findings of the court below.

Magnani v. Trogi (Ill. App. Ct. 1966)

Facts: Magnani's complaint stated two causes of action, one for wrongful death as administratrix of the decedent, and one for reimbursement in her individual capacity for expenses she incurred as the result of the death. Under the governing law, recovery under the wrongful death claim would be divided between the survivors in the proportion determined by the trial court. No apportionment of recovery would be made under the other claim. No separate verdict forms were submitted by the parties for either claim. Instead, the court submitted a single form of verdict, without objection by either party. The jury returned a single general verdict in favor of Magnani and awarded damages. In response to the defendant's motion for judgment notwithstanding the verdict, the trial court ordered a new trial on the grounds that it was impossible to determine how the damages were to be divided between the two causes of action.

Issue: Does a trial court have the power to grant a new trial in order to correct errors made during the course of the trial?

Rule: Yes. Trial judges have broad discretion to grant new trials to correct errors that they or the jury might have made during the trial. Appellate courts will not disturb a trial court's decision to order a new trial unless a clear abuse of discretion can be shown. Even though the defendant never complained about the verdict form until its post-trial motion, the jury's determination of damages on each claim is unknown because of the general verdict and any conclusion about what it did on each claim would be pure conjecture. No abuse of discretion in awarding a new trial and so that ruling is affirmed.

Robb v. John C. Hickey, Inc. (N.J. Cir. Ct. 1941)

Facts: In this negligence action filed by Robb in state court, the judge instructed the jury that if it found that the plaintiff was negligent, the comparative degrees of negligence of the parties was irrelevant and a verdict should be issued in favor of the defendant. Nevertheless, the jury returned a verdict in favor of Robb after deciding that both Robb and Hickey were negligent, but that Hickey was more negligent. Robb moved to set aside the verdict on the grounds that it was ambiguous, inconsistent, and contrary to the jury charge.

Issue: Can a court substitute its verdict for a jury verdict that is uncertain or ambiguous?

Rule: The verdict here was inconsistent with the jury instruction on the impact of plaintiff negligence. So it was defective in substance. A new trial is ordered because the intent of the jury is not clearly expressed in its verdict.

Peterson v. Wilson (5th Cir. 1998)

Facts: After trial on Peterson's suit in federal court challenging his discharge, the jury awarded damages to Peterson and the defendants moved for a new trial. The judge subsequently granted the motion based on comments made by the jurors after the verdict was rendered that indicated that they had disregarded the judge's instructions.

Issue: Is the admission of juror testimony to impeach a jury verdict prohibited?

Rule: Yes. A jury's verdict can be disregarded if it is against the weight of the evidence but not on the basis of post-verdict comments by jurors to the judge. FRCP 60(b) provides that jurors cannot testify as to statements made in deliberations or about their mental process of decision making other than for outside influences exerted upon them. So the granting of a new trial was clearly erroneous as the jurors' comments were not admissible. Thus, the results of the second trial are vacated and the results of the first trial are reinstated.

People v. Hutchinson (Cal. Sup. Ct. 1969)

Facts: Hutchinson was convicted of drug possession. In support of his new trial motion, Hutchinson produced an affidavit from a juror stating that the bailiff had made remarks that tended to pressure the jury into delivering a guilty verdict. The trial judge refused to consider the affidavit, ruling that juror statements cannot impeach the verdict.
Issue: May jurors offer testimony about objective facts in order to impeach a verdict?
Rule: Yes. When a juror testifies as to a matter of objective verification, that evidence should be admitted to impeach a verdict when the grounds for impeachment are objectively verifiable.

Hukle v. Kimble (Kan. Sup. Ct. 1952)

Facts: In a personal injury suit filed in state court, before deliberating on the issue of the defendant's liability, the jury determined its award by a method known as a quotient verdict. Each juror wrote an amount on a piece of paper; the estimates were then averaged to reach a final amount. The jury awarded that amount. The defendant sought a new trial on the grounds of juror misconduct in calculating damages before deciding the issue of liability.
Issue: Is it jury misconduct to decide the issue of damages via a quotient verdict prior to deliberating and deciding the issue of liability?
Rule: Yes. It is jury misconduct to decide on damages before deliberating and deciding on liability. The trial court erred in not granting a new trial. That motion is granted.

McDonough Power Equipment, Inc. v. Greenwood (S. Ct. 1984)

Facts: Greenwood sued when he was injured while using McDonough Power Equipment's equipment. After a jury verdict for McDonough, Greenwood learned that the jury foreman failed to answer a question during voir dire that may have revealed prejudice.
Issue: Is a party entitled to a new trial because a juror failed to answer a question during voir dire?
Rule: The party seeking a new trial must show that the juror failed to honestly answer a material question during voir dire and that a correct

response would have provided a valid basis for a challenge for cause (the motives for concealing information may vary, but only those reasons that affect a juror's impartiality can truly be said to affect the fairness of a trial).

Aetna Casualty & Surety Co. v. Yeatts (4th Cir. 1941)

Facts: Aetna Casualty sued for a declaratory judgment in federal court that its insured, Yeatts, was not covered for liability resulting from criminally performed abortions. Aetna did not make a motion for directed verdict prior to the verdict. Following a jury verdict for Yeatts, Aetna unsuccessfully moved for a judgment notwithstanding the verdict and for a new trial on the grounds that the verdict was against the weight of the evidence.

Issue: Can a judge set aside a jury verdict and order a new trial even if the weight of the evidence would not have supported a directed verdict?

Rule: Yes. A judge can grant a new trial if the judge determines that the verdict is against the clear weight of the evidence, is based upon evidence that is false, or will result in a miscarriage of justice.

Fisch v. Manger (N.J. Sup. Ct. 1957)

Facts: Fisch was awarded $3,000 in damages that covered his actual loss but not his pain and suffering. Fisch's motion for a new trial was dismissed after Manger agreed, at the trial court's suggestion, to increase the verdict to $7,500.

Issue: Can a trial judge dismiss a party's new trial motion if it is conditioned upon the opposing party's consent to increase or decrease the verdict (additur or remittitur)?

Rule: Yes. A trial court has discretionary power to deny a new trial when denial is conditioned on the other party's consent to either additur or remittitur.

Guenther v. Armstrong Rubber Co. (3d Cir. 1969)

Facts: Guenther filed a negligence action in federal court for injuries sustained when a tire allegedly manufactured by Armstrong exploded. There was conflicting testimony as to the identity of the offending tire. The trial judge entered judgment for the defendant for failure to authenticate the tire.

Issue: Is the authenticity of a highly relevant piece of real evidence a jury question?

Rule: Yes. Authenticity of a piece of real evidence, when that issue is material to the case (as opposed to the authenticity foundation for admission of real evidence), is a jury issue. Judgment reversed and remanded for trial.

Ahern v. Scholz (1st Cir. 1996)

Facts: Scholz, a musician, contracted with Ahern, his manager. Ahern sued Scholz in federal court for breach of contract. The jury issued a verdict for Ahern and awarded damages, attorneys' fees, and costs. The trial judge denied Scholz's motion for a new trial.

Issue: What is the standard of review for a trial judge's denial of a motion for new trial?

Rule: A district court's decision to deny a new trial may be overturned only upon a finding that the trial judge's decision constituted a clear abuse of discretion in determining the jury verdict was not against the great weight of the evidence.

Dimick v. Scheidt (S. Ct. 1935)

Facts: The jury found for Scheidt, but Scheidt claimed that the verdict was contrary to the weight of the evidence and must have been a compromise verdict, based on the amount of the damages. The court then asked Dimick, without first obtaining Scheidt's consent, to increase the damages or go through a new trial. Dimick consented to the damages.

Issue: May a judge award an additur without the consent of both parties?

Rule: No. A court's request for an additur without the recovering party's consent is a violation of the Seventh Amendment right to the verdict of a jury.

Dissent: (Stone, J.) The Seventh Amendment does not prescribe any particular procedure by which the benefits of a jury trial may be obtained, or forbid any which does not curtail the function of the jury. It does not restrict the court's control of the jury's verdict.

Doutre v. Niec (Mich. Ct. App. 1965)

Facts: Doutre was awarded $10,000 for personal injuries from an improperly applied bleach and color treatment to Doutre's hair by Niec. Niec moved for a new trial limited and the trial judge granted it, but only as to liability.

Issue: Can a new trial be granted only on the issue of liability?

Rule: No. The questions of liability and damages are so closely intertwined that they may not usually be separated. But where liability is clear, a retrial of only the damages issue is proper.

Donovan v. Penn Shipping Co. (S. Ct. 1977)

Facts: In a "slip and fall" case, Donovan obtained a $90,000 verdict. The judge agreed to order a new trial unless Donovan accepted a $25,000 remittitur. Donovan took the $65,000 "under protest" and then sought an appeal of the judge's action.

Issue: May a party appeal from a remittitur that has already been accepted?

Rule: Once a remittitur is accepted, it is binding on the parties.

Hulson v. Atchison, Topeka & Santa Fe Railway (7th Cir. 1961)

Facts: Hulson was granted an extension for filing a motion for a new trial. Both the motions for a new trial and judgment notwithstanding the verdict were subsequently filed three weeks after judgment was entered, even though FRCPs 50, 59, and 60 stipulated that such motions must be filed within ten days of the judgment's entry.

Issue 1: Does ignorance of the FRCP constitute a valid defense to untimely motions?

Rule 1: An untimely motion may be entertained by the court only if its untimeliness was due to "mistake, inadvertence, surprise, or excusable neglect." Consequently, under FRCP 60, ignorance of the Rules does not furnish grounds for relief.

Issue 2: Does the fact that the motion for an extension is agreed to by the opposing party constitute waiver of the timeliness provisions in the FRCP?

Rule 2: Counsel cannot waive the strict requirements of the Federal Rules.

Griggs v. Miller (Mo. Sup. Ct. 1963)

Facts: To satisfy a $2,000 judgment in favor of Griggs, Brookshire's entire farm was sold for $50,000, much less than its market value.

Issue: Is it error to execute a levy upon real property without first attempting to divide the property and sell only that portion necessary to satisfy the judgment?

Rule: Yes. When real property is levied and executed, the property must be divided (if possible) so that only the amount that is necessary to satisfy the judgment is sold.

Reeves v. Crownshield (N.Y. Ct. App. 1937)

Facts: A state statute allowed a court to order a judicial award to be paid in installments. Reeves refused to pay and was held in contempt.

Issue: Is a state statute that allows for imprisonment for failure to obey a court order to pay a debt unconstitutional as violative of due process?

Rule: After evaluating a judgment debtor's family situation, it is not unconstitutional to imprison him for failure to obey a court order to pay a debt out of income. Further, imprisonment results from not obeying a court order, not from nonpayment of a debt.

In re Boston's Children First (1st Cir. 2001)

Facts: The plaintiff group sued in federal court, alleging that Boston's student assignment process was racially discriminatory in violation of state and federal law. The plaintiff's lawyer made public statements disparaging the judge's handling of the case and the judge responded with a newspaper interview indicating that the case was more complex than certain others. The plaintiff moved to have the judge recuse herself on the grounds of lack of appearance of impartiality and the judge denied the application.

Issue: Does the appearance of partiality, without more, constitute sufficient grounds for recusal of the trial judge?

Rule: Yes. Even in the absence of actual partiality, the appearance of partiality is sufficient grounds for recusal under the federal statute requiring federal judges to disqualify themselves in any proceeding in which their impartiality might reasonably be questioned.

CHAPTER 10

Appellate Review

I. FINAL JUDGMENT RULE

A. Generally
1. For the most part, only final judgments are appealable.
2. A final judgment is reached when, on the merits, litigation ends, leaving only the execution of judgment to be completed.
3. Substance, not form, determines if a judgment is final.

B. Interlocutory Appeals Exception
Interlocutory appeals are allowed in cases involving:
1. Collateral Orders
A collateral order is one that:
a. Raises serious legal questions;
b. Involves a danger of irreparable harm; and
c. Deals with an issue unrelated to the basic substantive claims asserted.
2. Multiple Claims or Parties
A final decision as to one or more, but less than all, the claims or parties before the court may be appealed before all claims of all parties have been resolved.
3. Equitable Orders
E.g., grant, denial, or modification of an injunction.
4. Questions of Great Import
If a trial judge certifies, and the appellate court agrees, that the order involves a controlling question of law over which a difference of opinion exists, and that immediate appeal may materially advance termination of the litigation, an interlocutory appeal will be allowed.
5. Possibility of Irreparable Harm
6. Courts admit interlocutory appeals of orders affecting substantial rights that will be lost if not immediately appealed.

7. Writs of Mandamus or Prohibition
   a. When Used
   b. Appellate courts may grant a writ only if the trial court exceeds its jurisdiction or clearly abuses its discretion.
   c. Factors
   d. When deciding a petition for a writ a court will consider:
   e. Mnemonic: **PLACE**
      i. **P**rejudice
         Whether petitioner will be prejudiced in a manner not correctable on appeal;
      ii. **L**aw of First Impression
         Whether the district court's order raises important issues of law of first impression;
      iii. **A**dequate Alternate Relief
         Whether petitioner has other adequate means to obtain relief;
      iv. **C**learly Erroneous Errors
         Whether the district court's order is, as a matter of law, clearly erroneous; or
      v. **E**rror That Is Often Repeated
         Whether the district court's order is an often repeated error or a manifest persistent disregard of the FRCP.

II. PROCEDURES

A. Timeliness
   The time period in which an appeal must be brought begins to run once judgment is entered.
B. Standing to Appeal
   1. Only a party injured (or aggrieved) by the judgment of the lower court has standing to appeal.
   2. It is possible for both parties to be injured by a single judgment. Simply because one party is injured less does not mean it cannot appeal.
   3. Nonparties may not appeal.
C. Notice of Appeal
   1. Notice of appeal must be filed within 30 days (60 days if the United States is a party) of the judgment's entry.
   2. If a court finds excusable neglect or good cause, a 30-day extension to file a notice of appeal will be granted.
   3. Parties to a suit cannot stipulate to alter the time within which to make an appeal.

D. Waiver

A party may expressly or impliedly waive any right to appeal.

E. Rehearing

A court (the Supreme Court, or circuit courts en banc), at its discretion, may order a rehearing of a case if:

1. The petition is timely filed; or
2. The strict application of the rules favoring finality of judgments would unfairly impinge on the interests of justice.

III. SCOPE OF REVIEW

A. Reviewable Issues

Generally, appellate courts only review issues of law, not factual findings.

B. Jury Trials

1. An appellate court must uphold a verdict supported by substantial evidence.
2. An appellate court cannot weigh evidence or pass on witness credibility.
3. An appellate court cannot disturb factual findings.

C. Nonjury Trials

1. If clearly erroneous, a judge's factual findings may be set aside.
2. Questions of witness credibility are solely in the trial court's province.

D. Errors

Appellate courts have jurisdiction only if an error:

1. Involves a legal issue;
2. Appears in the trial record;
3. Affects a substantial right of the aggrieved party; and
4. Is preserved by prompt objection to a court's ruling.

E. Harmless Error

When an error neither prejudices a substantial right of the aggrieved party nor has a significant effect on a case's outcome, courts will not reverse a judgment.

IV. HIGH COURTS

A. Generally

Every state has its high court, generally known as the State Supreme Court, although each state will have its own title. The federal courts are of course led by the United States Supreme Court. Intermediate appellate courts generally exist to relieve the burdens of the high courts, but there are exceptions to every rule.

B. Original Jurisdiction

Every jurisdiction delineates certain areas of the law where the high court has original jurisdiction. In other words, an appeal under original jurisdiction must, as of right, go straight to the top.

C. Discretionary Review

1. Generally

According to Chief Justice Taft, there is no right to appeal all the way to the top. The Supreme Court's function is not primarily to preserve the rights of the litigants. It is to expound and stabilize principles of law. Most state systems express the same view.

2. Certiorari

The Supreme Court exercises its discretionary power by granting writs of certiorari. By requiring certification of a case before hearing it, the Court can select those cases it feels most compelled to decide.

a. Rule of Four

It takes a vote of only four of the nine justices to grant writ. In contrast, it normally requires five justices to decide a case.

b. Factors

In determining whether to grant a petition for certiorari, the justices will consider:

i. State Court Deciding Federal Law

Where a state court is the first to interpret a federal law, or misinterprets it.

ii. Conflict in Court of Appeals

The circuits are in conflict with each other or with the decisions of state courts.

CASE CLIPS

Liberty Mutual Insurance Co. v. Wetzel (S. Ct. 1976)

Facts: Wetzel and others alleged that Liberty Mutual's employee insurance benefits and maternity leave regulations discriminated against women in violation of Title VII of the Civil Rights Act of 1964. The federal district court granted partial summary judgment for Wetzel solely on the issue of liability, without considering the issue of relief. Liberty Mutual appealed under 28 U.S.C. §1291.

Issue 1: Can an order for partial summary judgment limited to the issue of liability alone be appealed under 28 U.S.C. §1291?

Rule 1: No. A partial summary judgment order solely on the issue of liability is not a "final decision" as required by 28 U.S.C. §1291.

Issue 2: May an order for partial summary judgment limited to the issue of liability be deemed an interlocutory order appealable under 28 U.S.C. §1292(a)(1)?

Rule 2: Although this was an interlocutory order, it was appealable under §1292 but only if certain procedural requisites were met, which were not met in the instant case. So the appeal was dismissed.

Sears, Roebuck & Co. v. Mackey (S. Ct. 1956)

Facts: Mackey sued Sears, Roebuck & Company for damages under the Sherman Antitrust Act. Mackey's complaint contained multiple claims. Some of the claims were dismissed and Mackey appealed the dismissals.

Issue: Can a district court in a multiple claim action permit an appeal on less than all claims before final judgment is entered on every claim asserted?

Rule: Yes. Per FRCP 54(b), a district court, in a multiple claim action, may permit an appeal on less than all the claims before final judgment on every claim asserted is entered. It can permit appeal from a final decision on that claim for relief.

Cohen v. Beneficial Industrial Loan Corp. (S. Ct. 1949)

Facts: Cohen brought a shareholder's derivative suit against the Beneficial Industrial Loan Corporation for mismanagement and fraud. Beneficial moved, under state law, for Cohen to post a bond. The district court ruled that the state statute did not apply to an action in federal court. Prior to the case's disposition on the merits, Beneficial appealed the ruling, which was reversed.

Issue: When is a trial court's ruling on law appealable prior to the case's disposition?

Rule: Under the "collateral order" doctrine, an order is appealable when it is a final disposition of a claimed right that is not an ingredient of the cause of action and does not require consideration with the cause of action.

Curtiss-Wright Corp. v. General Electric Co. (S. Ct. 1980)

Facts: Curtiss brought a breach of contract claim against General Electric in federal court on diversity grounds and General Electric filed a counterclaim. The trial court granted summary judgment to Curtiss as to its claim and ruled that this judgment was final. The appellate court reversed, holding that the presence of a counterclaim prevented judgment on the plaintiff's complaint from becoming final.

Issue: Is a trial court's finding that adjudication of one claim in a multi-claim case constitutes a final order reversible?

Rule: Yes, but only under a clearly erroneous standard. FRCP 54(b) allows a court in a multi-issue case to direct the entry of final judgment as to less than all issues in its discretion. The exercise of such discretion is reviewable only under a clearly erroneous standard. Here, the appellate court ruled that the presence of a counterclaim always will defeat the finality of judgment on the main claim and that unduly interfered with the trial court's discretion under FRCP 54(b).

Will v. Hallock (S. Ct. 2006)

Facts: The plaintiffs sued the government under the Federal Tort Claims Act (FTCA) in federal court after their residence was raided and computers were seized and after the plaintiffs were cleared of wrongdoing. While that action was pending, the plaintiffs brought a separate negligence action against the individual agents. The trial judge dismissed the first case and then the agents moved to dismiss the negligence claims brought against them pursuant to a provision of the FTCA that bars suit where a judgment on the claim already had been entered. The trial court denied this motion and the appellate court upheld that ruling on the ground that since the plaintiffs had not properly brought a claim in the suit against the government, no judgment had been entered.

Issue: Where an FTCA claim is dismissed on sovereign immunity grounds and a district court denies a motion of the individual federal agents to dismiss a subsequently filed action against them, does the federal appellate court have jurisdiction under the collateral order doctrine to hear an appeal of the trial court's order denying the agents' motion?

Rule: No. There is no appellate jurisdiction in such an instance under the collateral order doctrine. Only orders that can't effectively be reviewed after a final judgment can be appealed before the trial has been completed.

Lauro Lines s.r.l. v. Chasser (S. Ct. 1989)

Facts: The plaintiffs brought suit in federal court to recover damages they sustained while passengers aboard the Achille Lauro, which was hijacked by terrorists. Lauro Lines moved to dismiss, citing a forum selection clause printed on each passenger ticket that required all suits to be brought in Italy. The district court declined to enforce the clause. The court of appeals would not hear Lauro Lines' appeal on the grounds that the district court's order denying the motion was interlocutory (not a final judgment that ends the litigation on the merits). There is a narrow exception to the final judgment rule, the collateral order doctrine, which allows a party to appeal an interlocutory order if the asserted right would be destroyed if not vindicated before trial.

Issue: Does an order denying a motion to dismiss for improper forum fall under the collateral order exception to the final judgment rule?

Rule: No. An order denying a motion to dismiss on the basis of a forum selection clause does not fall under the collateral order exception to the final judgment rule. The potential costs associated with failure to enforce a forum selection clause (e.g., the expense of relitigating the matter in the proper forum) are not sufficient to warrant immediate appeal.

Concurrence: (Scalia, J.) The result in this case is correct because contractual forum selection is not a sufficiently important right to warrant immediate review.

Digital Equipment Corp. v. Desktop Direct, Inc. (S. Ct. 1994)

Facts: Desktop brought a trademark infringement action against Digital in federal court. The case was dismissed after settlement. Desktop subsequently moved to vacate the dismissal and rescind the settlement agreement based on alleged misrepresentations made by Digital during settlement negotiations. The trial court granted the motion. The circuit court found the order was not appealable.

Issue: Is a trial court's decision to refuse to enforce the dismissal of a settled case subject to immediate appeal under §1291?

Rule: No. This does not end the litigation on the merits and so is not a final order within §1291. And the collateral order doctrine only applies to decisions that resolve important legal questions unrelated to the merits. Here, the right to immunity from litigation provided by private agreement (settlement) is not more important than the interests advanced by the application of the usual final order limitation on the right to appeal.

Gillespie v. United States Steel Corp. (S. Ct. 1964)

Facts: Gillespie sued the United States Steel Corporation to recover damages for the death of her son, basing her causes of action on both the Jones Act and the Ohio wrongful death statute. Holding that the Jones Act provided the exclusive remedy, the district judge struck all references to the Ohio statutes from the complaint. Gillespie immediately appealed.
Issue: May an interlocutory order be appealed as a final decision under 28 U.S.C. §1292(b)?
Rule: Yes. Since a "final" decision does not necessarily mean the last order possible to be made in a case, interlocutory orders dealing with questions fundamental to the further conduct of a case are appealable under 28 U.S.C. §1292(b).
Dissent: The requirements of 28 U.S.C. §1292 are intended to prevent piecemeal litigation of the issues in a lawsuit. If the trial court does not certify issues for appeal, the appellate court has no jurisdiction under §1292(b).

Cardwell v. Chesapeake & Ohio Railway Co. (6th Cir. 1974)

Facts: Cardwell brought an action against the railroad in federal court for her injuries and for the death of her husband. The jury awarded damages to the plaintiff for her injuries but could not agree on the cause of death. Chesapeake moved for judgment notwithstanding the verdict based on insufficiency of evidence on the cause of death. The motion was denied but the trial judge certified that issue for interlocutory appeal.
Issue: Is an interlocutory appeal under 28 U.S.C. §1292(b) available where the regular appellate process would be equally expeditious?
Rule: No. A district court can certify a matter for interlocutory appeal under §1292(b) only when that issue is controlling and an appellate ruling on it would materially advance the ultimate resolution of the case. When issues can be decided as easily on direct appeal as by interlocutory appeal, the courts should rely on the regular appellate process. Here, the trial was over and a regular appeal was nearly available. So interlocutory appeal was inappropriate.

Coopers & Lybrand v. Livesay (S. Ct. 1978)

Facts: Livesay and others alleged that Coopers & Lybrand underreported the net income figures of the Punta Gorda Isles, in violation of the Securities Act of 1933 and the Securities Exchange Act of 1934. After initially certifying the plaintiffs as a class, the district court decertified the class following additional proceedings. The plaintiffs appealed the decertification order.

Issue: Is a district court's determination that an action may not be maintained as a class action a "final decision" within the meaning of 28 U.S.C. §1291, appealable as a matter of right?

Rule: No. An order decertifying a class does not terminate the entire litigation, and thus is not a "final decision" that may be appealed under 28 U.S.C. §1291.

Quackenbush v. Allstate Insurance Co. (S. Ct. 1996)

Facts: Quackenbush, the trustee of a liquidated company, sued Allstate for breach of its insurance agreement with the liquidated company. Allstate removed the case based on diversity and then moved to compel arbitration. Quackenbush moved to remand on the grounds that the federal court should abstain from exercising jurisdiction because its resolution of the dispute might interfere with ongoing state regulation of the liquidated company's insolvency. The trial court agreed that it should abstain but remanded the case rather than issuing a stay. The appellate court vacated that order.

Issue: Is a district court's remand order based on abstention appealable as a final order under 28 U.S.C. §1291?

Rule: Yes. A remand order on abstention grounds is a final order providing immediate appellate jurisdiction. And despite the language in 28 U.S.C. §1447(d) that remand orders are not reviewable on appeal, that provision only applies to remands based on jurisdictional grounds and abstention implies the presence of jurisdiction but the discretionary decision not to exercise that jurisdiction. This remand order ended the matter in federal court and so it is a final order.

La Buy v. Howes Leather Co. (S. Ct. 1957)

Facts: U.S. District Judge La Buy referred a number of antitrust cases to a master for final determination because of his crowded calendar. Howes Leather Company and other parties sought a writ of mandamus from the court of appeals to compel La Buy to hear the cases.

Issue: Does a federal court of appeals, through the issuance of writs of mandamus, have the power to review interlocutory orders of a district court?

Rule: Yes. A court of appeals has discretionary power to issue writs of mandamus to review interlocutory orders in proper circumstances.

Dissent: (Brennan, J.) Writs of mandamus may only be used to review interlocutory orders when the action of a district court frustrates the ultimate exercise of appellate jurisdiction by a court of appeals. The All Writs Act does not confer independent appellate power to review interlocutory orders of a lower court.

Schlagenhauf v. Holder (S. Ct. 1964)

Facts: Holder and other bus passengers involved in a collision between a Greyhound bus and a tractor trailer sued Schlagenhauf (the bus driver), Greyhound (the bus line), Contract Carriers (the tractor owner), McCorkhill (the truck driver), and National Lead (the trailer owner). Contract Carriers and National Lead claimed the accident was due to Schlagenhauf's negligence, and requested, pursuant to FRCP 35(a), that Schlagenhauf submit to four physical and mental examinations. Schlagenhauf then went to the court of appeals and sought a writ of mandamus preventing any examinations.
Issue: When may a writ of mandamus, instead of an appeal, be used by a party seeking remedial action?
Rule: A writ of mandamus may only be used in a remedial fashion when there is a usurpation of judicial power or a clear abuse of discretion. Writs of mandamus should not be used as a substitute for appeals.
Dissent: (Harlan, J.) Once it is determined that the district court acted within its power, the writ of mandamus should have been denied. No other issues but the court's ability to act the way it did should be considered by the appellate court.

Will v. United States (S. Ct. 1967)

Facts: Judge Will ordered the government to provide information to a defendant in a tax-evasion case. The government refused to comply and sought mandamus to vacate Judge Will's order.
Issue: When may an appellate court grant review by means of mandamus?
Rule: A federal appellate court may review a lower court's order through a writ of mandamus only when the record demonstrates that the court usurped power or clearly abused its discretion.

Kerr v. United States District Court (S. Ct. 1976)

Facts: Several California inmates brought a class action against several state agencies. The agencies sought an issuance of writs of mandamus to compel the district court to vacate two discovery orders. The court of appeals refused to issue the writs of mandamus.
Issue: When should a court issue a writ of mandamus?
Rule: To avoid piecemeal appeals, writs of mandamus should be granted only where no other adequate remedies are available.

Atlantic City Elec. Co. v. General Elec. Co. (2d Cir. 1964)

Facts: During pretrial discovery, General Electric submitted interrogatories to discover whether Atlantic City had passed along its alleged damages to its customers. Atlantic City successfully objected to the interrogatories. General Electric appealed the sustained objection under 28 U.S.C. §1292(b).

Issue: Must an appellate court grant a pretrial appeal on issues the party will have full opportunity to appeal at the end of the trial?

Rule: No. An interlocutory appeal should only be granted if the defendant's right to an ultimate appeal would otherwise be prejudiced.

Gulfstream Aerospace Corp. v. Mayacamas Corp. (S. Ct. 1988)

Facts: Gulfstream sued Mayacamas in state court for breach of contract. Soon after, Mayacamas filed a diversity action against Gulfstream in federal court, claiming breach of the same contract. Gulfstream moved to dismiss or stay the federal action pending resolution of the state court litigation. The district court denied the motion and Gulfstream appealed, citing 28 U.S.C. §§1291 and 1292(a)(1).

Issue 1: Is a district court order denying a motion to stay or dismiss an action when a similar suit is pending in state court immediately appealable under 28 U.S.C. §1291?

Rule 1: Since the denial of a motion to dismiss or stay is "inherently tentative" and does not terminate the litigation, it is not immediately appealable as a "final" decision under 28 U.S.C. §1291.

Issue 2: Is a district court order denying a motion to stay or dismiss an action when a similar suit is pending in state court immediately appealable under 28 U.S.C. §1292(a)(1)?

Rule 2: Orders granting or denying stays are not injunctions, and thus are not appealable under 28 U.S.C. §1292(a)(1).

Carson v. American Brands, Inc. (S. Ct. 1981)

Facts: Carson and American Brands negotiated a settlement and consent decree containing injunctive relief. The federal district court refused to enter the decree. The circuit court dismissed the appeal for lack of jurisdiction, holding that the order was not appealable under §1292(a)(1).

Issue: When is an interlocutory order of a district court denying a joint motion of the parties to enter a consent decree an appealable order under §1292(a)(1)?

Rule: An interlocutory order of a district court denying a joint motion of the parties to enter a consent decree is appealable if it contains injunctive relief.

An order refusing an injunction is appealable under 28 U.S.C. §1292(a)(1). This order, though not explicitly refusing an injunction, had the practical effect of doing so.

Firestone Tire & Rubber Co. v. Risjord (S. Ct. 1981)

Facts: Risjord, an attorney, defended the Firestone Tire & Rubber Company in several liability suits. Firestone was insured by Home Insurance, also a client of Risjord. Firestone moved to remove Risjord as counsel in liability actions where the plaintiff was insured by Home Insurance, on the grounds of conflict of interest. The court denied Firestone's motion.

Issue: Can a party, pursuant to 28 U.S.C. §1291, appeal a district court order denying a motion to disqualify counsel?

Rule: No. Orders denying motions to disqualify counsel are not appealable as final collateral decisions under §1291.

J.F. White Contracting Co. v. New England Tank Industries of New Hampshire, Inc. (1st Cir. 1968)

Facts: New England Tank Industries of New Hampshire sued J.F. White Contracting for damages suffered as a result of White's alleged defective construction of oil tanker dock facilities. On appeal, White raised an issue not raised in either the pleadings or at trial.

Issue 1: May an appellate court consider an issue not raised in the pleadings or at trial?

Rule 1: No. An appellate court cannot consider an issue that was neither pleaded as an affirmative defense nor raised at trial. The jury verdict for New England is affirmed.

Issue 2: When may an appellate court reverse the decision of a trial court?

Rule 2: An appellate court may only reverse a trial court's decision if it finds an error that affected the verdict or "the substantial rights of the parties."

Electrical Fittings Corp. v. Thomas & Betts Co. (S. Ct. 1939)

Facts: Thomas & Betts Company sued Electrical Fittings Corp. in federal court for patent infringement. The district court found Thomas & Betts's patent valid, but not infringed. Fearing that the judgment of the patent's validity would bind it in subsequent suits, Electrical Fittings appealed this part of the decision. The circuit court dismissed the appeal on the grounds that Electrical Fittings had been awarded all the relief to which it was entitled and that the trial court decree would not bind it in subsequent litigation.

Issue: Can a party appeal from a judgment or decree in his favor for the purpose of obtaining a review of findings he deems erroneous that were unnecessary to that judgment?
Rule: Yes. A party may appeal an issue actually adjudicated and specifically mentioned in a decree, even though the adjudication was immaterial to the disposition of the case. The order dismissing the appeal is reversed.

International Ore & Fertilizer Corp. v. SGS Control Services, Inc. (2d Cir. 1994)

Facts: International Ore sued SGS in federal court for breach of contract when its fertilizer that SGS contracted to transport was contaminated and the intended buyer refused it. At trial, International Ore lost on the valuable breach of contract claim but won a lesser award of damages on its claim that SGS had negligently misrepresented the condition of its ship. SGS appealed but International Ore did not file a cross-appeal on the contract claim. The appellate court reversed the trial court's judgment on the negligent misrepresentation claim. The remaining question was whether to review the trial court's order on the contract claim.
Issue: Can a federal appellate court decide an issue that the appellee fails to raise via a cross-appeal?
Rule: Yes. Although International Ore could have preserved the issue for appeal by filing a cross-appeal, it was sufficient to raise the question at oral argument in response to questions generated by the opponent's appeal.

Corcoran v. City of Chicago (Ill. Sup. Ct. 1940)

Facts: Corcoran sued the City of Chicago for negligent street maintenance and was awarded a judgment for $5,000. The City of Chicago's motion for a new trial was denied by the trial court, but granted on appeal on the ground that the verdict was against the manifest weight of the evidence. Corcoran claimed that the appellate court's finding that the verdict was against the weight of the evidence denied him his right to a jury trial.
Issue: Can an appellate court set aside a verdict because the findings of fact were not supported by the evidence if a statute permits such review?
Rule: Yes. Both statutory and common law authorize appellate courts to set aside verdicts if the findings of fact are not supported by the evidence.

Pullman-Standard v. Swint (S. Ct. 1982)

Facts: African-American employees brought suit against their employer, Pullman-Standard, alleging violations of Title VII of the Civil Rights Act of 1964. Finding no discriminatory purpose, the trial court ruled in

Pullman-Standard's favor. Making its own factual finding (i.e., determining the ultimate fact, discriminatory purpose), the appellate court reversed.

Issue: Under FRCP 52, can a federal appellate court disturb a district court's factual determination?

Rule: (White, J.) Under FRCP 52, a federal appellate court cannot set aside a district court's findings of fact unless such findings are clearly erroneous.

Dissent: (Marshall, J.) The district court's findings were clearly erroneous and should be reversed.

Bose Corp. v. Consumers Union of U.S., Inc. (S. Ct. 1984)

Facts: Bose sued Consumers Union for defamation in federal court. The trial court found Bose was a public figure and that Consumers Union published with reckless disregard of the truth. The court of appeals undertook a de novo review of the reckless disregard finding and reversed the trial court's judgment for the plaintiff.

Issue: What is the standard of review on appeal from a district court's finding of reckless disregard of the truth in a defamation action?

Rule: The appellate court is to apply de novo review to a finding of reckless disregard in a defamation action. FRCP 52(a) requires special deference to factual findings that can only be reversed under a clearly erroneous standard. But in actions implicating the First Amendment, as here, appellate courts must exercise de novo review of the entire record including factual determinations relative to issue when constitutional issues are involved. So the appellate court acted properly here.

Orvis v. Higgins (2d Cir. 1950)

Facts: In an action for a refund of federal estate taxes, the decision turned on whether two trusts were set up independently or by mutual agreement. Sitting as the factfinder, the trial judge heard both written and oral testimony. The government appealed a ruling that Mrs. Orvis and her deceased husband had set up their trusts independently.

Issue: May an appellate court rule that a trial judge's factual finding was "clearly erroneous" if it was based in part upon the credibility and demeanor of witnesses?

Rule: No. Although an appellate court may review the factual findings of a trial judge if they rest exclusively upon the written evidence, the evaluation of credibility must not contribute to the findings.

Cox Broadcasting Corp. v. Cohn (S. Ct. 1975)

Facts: The Cox Broadcasting Corporation (Cox) reported that Cohn's daughter was a murder victim. Cox argued that the state law permitting

Cohn to sue for damages was unconstitutional. Remanding, the state's highest court held the state law to be constitutional. Without waiting for the case's resolution in lower state courts, Cox appealed to the U.S. Supreme Court.

Issue: Can the Supreme Court regard the decision of a highest state court on a federal issue as final judgment even though other issues in the same case may be pending in lower state courts?

Rule: Yes. When judgment is rendered on a federal issue, the Supreme Court may regard the decision of the highest court of a state as final even though there may be pending proceedings in lower state courts in the same case.

Bankers Life & Casualty Co. v. Crenshaw (S. Ct. 1988)

Facts: At trial, Bankers Life neglected to raise certain constitutional issues in its defense. Bankers Life only vaguely mentioned "constitutional principles" in its brief to the Mississippi Supreme Court, but did finally raise them in a petition for certiorari to the U.S. Supreme Court.

Issue: May the Supreme Court exercise certiorari jurisdiction over an issue not raised below?

Rule: Because of comity and the need for a properly developed record for appeal, the Supreme Court will not exercise certiorari jurisdiction over an issue not pressed or passed upon below. A party may not preserve a constitutional challenge by generally invoking the Constitution and awaiting review to specify the constitutional provision it is relying upon. It is up to the prudence of the court to allow such a claim.

Anderson v. Bessemer City (S. Ct. 1985)

Facts: The federal court found that Bessemer City had denied Ms. Anderson employment in favor of Mr. Kincaid because of her sex. The court's decision was based on the following subsidiary findings: Anderson was better qualified than Kincaid; male hiring committee members were biased against Anderson because she was a woman; only Anderson was asked if her spouse would object to her taking the job; and the reasons offered by the committee for choosing Kincaid were pretextual. The appellate court determined that the trial court's findings were clearly erroneous and reversed its judgment.

Issue: Under FRCP 52(a), when may an appellate court reverse a trial court's findings of fact?

Rule: An appellate court may only reverse a trial court's findings of fact when they are clearly erroneous. A finding is clearly erroneous within the meaning of FRCP 52(a) when, although there is evidence to support it, the appellate court, on the entire evidence, is left with the definite and firm conviction that a mistake has been made. Where the trial court and the appellate court reach different, but equally logical, conclusions from the evidence, the interpretation of the trial court controls. Because the findings of the trial court in this case were based on reasonable inferences from the record, its findings must stand.

FirsTier Mortgage Co. v. Investors Mortgage Insurance Co. (S. Ct. 1991)

Facts: A judge announced that he intended to grant summary judgment, but he had yet to receive proposed findings of fact and conclusions of law, and he did not explicitly exclude the possibility that he would not change his mind before entering a final judgment. Following this announcement, but before judgment was entered, FirsTier filed a notice of appeal. FRAP 4(a)(2) permits notice of appeal to be filed "after the announcement of a decision or order."

Issue: Is notice of appeal premature where a court has announced that it intends to grant a final judgment, but has not yet terminated the litigation?

Rule: FRAP 4(a)(2) permits notice of appeal following a nonfinal decision if the decision is of the type that would be appealable if immediately followed by the entry of judgment.

Harnden v. Jayco, Inc. (6th Cir. 2007)

Facts: Harden filed a products liability action asserting a variety of claims against Jayco, the manufacturer of a recreational vehicle, in federal court. An expert report prepared by a Jayco employee established that the problems were minor and did not stem from the manufacturer. Harnden did not contravene these conclusions. The trial court granted summary judgment to Jayco. On appeal, Harnden objected to the admission of the expert report because it was not in the proper affidavit form as required by FRCP 56(e) and, therefore, was inadmissible hearsay.

Issue: Is the admission of an expert report harmless error where the opponent knew the contents of the report and remanding the case would only result in a change in the report's format and not its content?

Rule: Yes. Admission under these circumstances is harmless error because it did not affect the opponent Harnden's substantial rights since he always knew the contents of the report and could have rebutted it, but had failed to do so.

Bowles v. Russell (S. Ct. 2007)

Facts: Bowles was convicted of murder. The conviction was upheld through all direct appeals. He subsequently filed a habeas corpus petition in federal court, which was denied. Under FRAP 4(a)(1)(A), Bowles then had 30 days to file a notice of appeal. He failed to do so. After the expiration of that period, he moved the federal district court to reopen the period for filing a notice of appeal under FRAP 4(a)(6) and the trial court granted the motion. But while FRAP 4(a)(6) allows for a 14-day extension, the court granted Bowles a 17-day extension. Bowles filed his notice of appeal within the 17 days but after 14 days. The court of appeals dismissed the appeal on the ground that the notice was untimely and, therefore, that it lacked jurisdiction.

Issue: Where a federal district court extends a party's time to file an appeal beyond the time permitted by statute, does the fact that the appeal was outside the statutorily mandated time but within the additional time allowed by the trial deprive the appellate court of jurisdiction?

Rule: Yes. The statutory rules limiting the time for filing appeals is a jurisdictional requirement and the court has no authority to create equitable exceptions such as a claim of "unique circumstances." Thus, failure to file a timely notice of appeal defeats the jurisdiction of the appellate court.

CHAPTER 11

Preclusion

I. INTRODUCTION

Preclusion of both claims and issues is a longstanding tradition of Anglo-American jurisprudence. Litigants get one opportunity to litigate their case, and if they are unsuccessful, preclusion prevents relitigation even if the first trial did not achieve the optimally just result.

A. Policies

The idea that a judgment once made is binding on all future adjudications is rooted in several policies, including:

1. Avoiding multiple suits on identical issues.
2. Compelling single litigation of all factually and legally related matters.
3. Achieving repose for the litigants.
4. Conservation of judicial resources.
5. Conservation of the litigants' resources.
6. Ensuring uniform application of the law.

B. Stare Decisis

This doctrine is not technically one of preclusion, since neither the same claims nor litigants are involved, generally, but many of the same policy considerations hold true. Under stare decisis, courts are bound by prior decisions of law made by superior courts, and will only overturn those decisions in cases of extreme prejudice or injustice.

II. CLAIM PRECLUSION (RES JUDICATA)

After a valid and final judgment, a transactionally related claim may not be relitigated between the parties of the original suit.

A. Same Claim

1. Transactional Test

The claim to be litigated may not involve the same transaction or occurrence, or series of transactions or occurrences, as a claim litigated in a prior suit.

2. One may not "sue hand by hand or finger by finger." For instance, a driver damaged in a car accident could not bring separate suits for damage to the driver's legs, the driver's back, the neck, etc. These are clearly transactionally related. However, damage to an auto and to the driver in one accident would not be transactionally related. Similarly, if the other driver slandered the plaintiff several days later by referring to the plaintiff's poor driving abilities, that would not be transactionally related to the claims of physical injury.

B. Same Parties

1. Generally

Parties are bound by a prior decision only when those present in the second suit, or those in privity with the parties, were present in the first suit.

2. Privity

Parties who represent others or are contractually bound to accept liabilities at issue on the case are considered to have been present at the original suit for purposes of claim preclusion. Typical examples of privity include:

a. Representatives

Trustees, guardians, executors, agents, etc.

b. Class Action Representatives

One of the benefits of a class action is that the claims of many plaintiffs are resolved in one action. To allow class members to relitigate their claims would disembowel the efficacy of the class action.

c. Co-parties Adjudicating a Finite Resource

For claim preclusion to apply, the parties must generally have been adverse to each other in the original suit. The exception to this rule occurs with adjudications of finite resources (water rights, in rem action, etc.). There, although the parties may nominally be on the same side of the litigation, since everybody's share depends on the legal rights of the others, everybody is essentially adverse to each other.

d. Nonparties

In *Nevada v. United States*, parties not present in the original suit were bound under claim preclusion. However, that case was special in that it involved water rights upon which many people had relied to their detriment.

e. Laboring Oar

A party not technically present in the original suit may be bound by claim preclusion if it had been so involved in directing the first suit that it could be said to have had a "laboring oar" in the conduct of the litigation. *Montana v. United States*.

      3. Parties have no duty to join a lawsuit, and if not joined, they will generally not be bound by claim preclusion.

C. Valid and Final Judgment

  1. Validity

  A judgment is valid unless procured through fraud or corruption, or where there existed a lack of personal or subject matter jurisdiction, or there had been no opportunity to be heard.

  2. Finality

    a. Decision on the Merits

    Defining a final judgment is no easy task. Generally, any decision on the merits of the case is final.

    b. FRCP 12(b)(1)-(5), (7)

    Dismissals due to lack of subject matter jurisdiction, lack of personal jurisdiction, improper venue, or insufficient process or service of process, or failure to join an indispensable party (FRCP 12(b)) are not final judgments.

    c. FRCP 12(b)(6)

    Dismissal for failure to state a claim upon which relief may be granted is a final judgment unless expressly dismissed without prejudice.

    d. Unappealed Judgments

    Decisions that could have been appealed, but were not, are final judgments.

    e. Ripeness

    Dismissal because a claim is not sufficiently ripe (see Justiciability) is not a final judgment.

D. Counterclaims

  1. Permissive Counterclaims

  Permissive counterclaims are generally not precluded from future litigation, because they are generally not transactionally related to the case at hand.

  2. Compulsory Counterclaims

  By definition, compulsory counterclaims must be brought in the original suit or be barred from future litigation. They are, by definition, transactionally related to the case at hand, although an exception exists where the court deciding the first suit decided in favor of the defendant but cannot afford that party full relief on the counterclaim.

III. ISSUE PRECLUSION (COLLATERAL ESTOPPEL)

When an issue of fact or law is *actually litigated* and determined by a *valid and final judgment,* and the determination is *essential to the judgment,* the determination is conclusive in a subsequent action between the *parties*, whether on the same or a different claim. *Restatement, Second, Judgments* §27.

A. Actually Litigated
   1. Similar Facts
      Similar facts do not mean that the issue was actually litigated. In *Cromwell v. County of Sac*, the court held that a finding of fraud in the conveyance of one coupon of interest was not preclusive for other coupons of interest, even though the coupons all came from the same municipal bond.
   2. Burdens of Proof
      An issue may not have been actually litigated if the first issue had a lower burden of proof. For instance, just because a defendant was held to have committed assault in a civil case (preponderance of the evidence), does not mandate a finding of assault in a criminal case (beyond a reasonable doubt).
      Likewise, a verdict of not guilty on a criminal assault charge does not preclude a finding of assault in a civil tort case, where the plaintiff's burden is much lower.
B. Essential to the Judgment
   It must be shown that the issue alleged to have preclusive effect had to be decided by the decision maker at the first trial.
   1. Multiple Theories
      Where a decision could have been rendered on any of several theories, without a special verdict no facts may turn out to have subsequent preclusive effect.
   2. Proximate vs. Ultimate Facts
      In *The Evergreens v. Nunan*, Judge Hand noted that not all trivial facts should be given preclusive effect, even if they did turn out to be essential to the judgment. Although he tried to distinguish between proximate facts (no preclusion) that were mere intermediary steps and ultimate facts (preclusion), the distinction remains hazy. Some factors that could be helpful in such an analysis are whether the parties actively litigated the issue, whether the issue is "trivial," or whether the importance of the fact could have been foreseen.
C. Same Parties
   1. Traditional Rule — Mutuality
      As in claim preclusion, the traditional rule had been that in order to assert issue preclusion the same parties or their privies had to have been present at the original case. The general rule was that if you couldn't estop your adversary, they couldn't estop you.
   2. Due Process Requirement
      No party can be precluded from litigating an issue that was resolved in a prior case to which that entity was not a party

or in privity with a party to the first suit. To do otherwise would violate the constitutional right to due process.

3. Modern Rule — Nonmutuality

The doctrine of mutuality has given way to a more flexible standard of nonmutual collateral estoppel. Not all jurisdictions recognize nonmutual collateral estoppel, and some only recognize defensive nonmutual collateral estoppel.

a. Defensive Nonmutual Collateral Estoppel

Where a plaintiff had already received an adverse judgment on an issue, a defendant not party or privy to that first suit could use that judgment to estop the plaintiff from subsequently relitigating that claim.

b. Offensive Nonmutual Collateral Estoppel

Where a defendant has already litigated an issue and lost, a plaintiff not party to the first suit may use that judgment to estop the defendant from asserting the same defense.

c. Mutuality and the United States as a Party

Because there is only one government, requiring the United States to be bound by the first decision on an issue could result in severe public costs. Further, given the limited resources of the government, the Supreme Court has been reluctant to extend the principles of nonmutual collateral estoppel against the government.

i. Defensive Collateral Estoppel

The government may assert defensive nonmutual collateral estoppel when sued, as any private litigant.

ii. Offensive Collateral Estoppel

In *United States v. Mendoza*, the Court refused to allow a private party to assert offensive nonmutual collateral estoppel against the government. However, mutual collateral estoppel is still available. *United States v. Stauffer Chemical Company*. It would be unfair to let the United States use its resources to get favorable legal rulings by bankrupting a single defendant through legal fees.

D. Valid and Final Judgment

The standard here is generally identical as that for claim preclusion, above.

E. Exceptions (*Restatement, Second, Judgments* §28)

1. Party to be precluded could not by law have obtained review of the judgment in the first action.

2. There has been an intervening change in the applicable law.

3. To enforce the collateral estoppel would result in an inequitable administration of law.

4. The second court has very different procedures or rules, war-
ranting relitigation.
5. The party to be precluded had to meet a heavier burden of
persuasion in the first suit, the burden is on another party, or
the party requesting preclusion has a heavier burden in the
second suit.
6. The public interest warrants relitigation.
7. The effects of the preclusion were not foreseeable at the time the
first action was litigated.
8. The party to be precluded did not have a full and fair opportunity to litigate the issues.

IV. INTERSYSTEM PRECLUSION

A. Interstate Preclusion
1. The Full Faith and Credit Clause
The Constitution, Art. IV, §1, stipulates that every court in the
nation must accord "full faith and credit" to the prior decisions
of other courts in the country.
2. Full Faith and Credit Act (28 U.S.C. §1738)
Enacted pursuant to the Full Faith and Credit Clause, this statute clarifies what constitutes a valid decision, and to what deference it is entitled in the courts.
3. Effect
A decision of a sister state is given as much deference as it would
receive in the state issued, even if not enforceable in the forum
state.
4. Child Custody (28 U.S.C. §1738A)
Even though child custody orders are not technically "final"
because the issuing court generally reserves the right to modify
the order to protect the needs of the child, this act prevents
other courts from modifying such orders unless:
a. The state is the home state of the child;
b. No other state would have jurisdiction;
c. The child was abandoned in the state, or some other emer-
gency exists; or
d. The state that originally issued the order has declined
jurisdiction.
B. Preclusive Effect of State Judgments in Federal Courts
Although the Full Faith and Credit Clause only applies to the
states, the Full Faith and Credit Act (28 U.S.C. §1738) extends
the same requirements to the federal courts as well.
C. Preclusive Effect of Federal Judgments in State Courts
Although statutory and constitutional authority is murky, most
observers agree that states must afford federal judgments the same

full faith and credit as afforded to decisions of sister states. This rule has never been seriously challenged.

D. Preclusive Effect of Foreign Judgments

Absent a treaty, judgments of foreign nations are not given full faith and credit. However, the United States has such treaties with most countries.

CASE CLIPS

Rush v. City of Maple Heights (Ohio Sup. Ct. 1958)

Facts: Rush was injured when she fell in an accident. She successfully sued for damages to personal property. Then she commenced a new action against the same defendant to recover for her personal injuries occasioned by that same accident.

Issue: Does claim preclusion apply when the plaintiff brings separate actions seeking different forms of damages arising from a common event?

Rule: Yes. A plaintiff may maintain only one action arising from a single transaction or occurrence. Suing for separate types of injury (personal versus property) does not transform the claims into separate causes of action. This is an attempt to split a single cause of action, which is prohibited by claim preclusion when the claim is against the same defendant.

Frier v. City of Vandalia (7th Cir. 1985)

Facts: Vandalia towed four of Frier's cars because they were blocking traffic. He brought an action for replevin in Illinois state court and lost, the court having determined that the City had the right to tow the cars. Frier then brought a §1983 action for damages in federal court alleging that the towing of his car deprived him of his property without due process in violation of the Fourteenth Amendment.

Issue: Does claim preclusion bar a suit that is based on the same facts as a prior suit, but which propounds a different legal theory?

Rule: Yes. A suit is barred by claim preclusion if it arises out of the same core of operative facts or the same transaction that gave rise to the original suit, even if the first suit was decided on different legal grounds than those advanced in the second suit.

Manego v. Orleans Board of Trade (1st Cir. 1985)

Facts: Manego was denied permission to open a disco in Orleans because of its impact on a nearby skating rink used by children, so he sued individuals and entities involved in the denial in state court. The court dismissed that case. Subsequently, Manego filed an action in federal court under federal antitrust laws, alleging a conspiracy to prevent him from competing with the skating rink. The trial court dismissed the case on claim preclusion grounds.

Issue: Has the plaintiff filed a different cause of action, and thereby avoided claim preclusion, by changing the legal theory of his claim that is based on the same facts that gave rise to the first lawsuit?

Rule: No. Whether or not it is the same case is transactionally based and does not depend upon the legal theory asserted for relief. Thus, he attempted to split a single cause of action and that is precluded by claim preclusion. The trial court's ruling is affirmed.

Mathews v. New York Racing Association, Inc. (S.D.N.Y. 1961)

Facts: Matthews sued two employees of the New York Racing Association alleging assault and libel. After the conclusion of that suit, Matthews sued the Racing Association itself alleging assault, kidnapping, false arrest, and false imprisonment. The first suit dealt with actions occurring on April 4 and 10. The second action only related to actions of April 4. The Racing Association moved to dismiss the action against it on claim preclusion grounds.

Issue: When are parties viewed as "in privity" so as to invoke the doctrine of claim preclusion?

Rule: Res judicata bars subsequent suits involving the same parties, or those in privity with them, based on a claim that once reached a judgment on the merits. The first claim was against the employees; the second suit was against their employer. Both claims arose out of the same event so the claim was the same. The parties are deemed to be in privity for preclusion purposes because the employees were the agents of the company and the company's liability was based on the employees' negligence, i.e., vicarious liability. Thus, privity exists and the defendant's motion to dismiss is granted.

Federated Department Stores v. Moitie (S. Ct. 1981)

Facts: Moitie and others all lost in separate suits against the Federated Department Stores. The other independent plaintiffs gained reversal on appeal. Without appealing, Moitie brought the present action, alleging the same injury and facts. The Federated Department Stores asserted claim preclusion.

Issue: Does res judicata bar relitigation of an unappealed adverse judgment when other plaintiffs in similar suits against the same defendants successfully appealed the judgments?

Rule: Res judicata bars the relitigation of an unappealed adverse judgment, even though other plaintiffs in similar suits against common defendants successfully appealed the judgments against them.

Concurrence: (Blackmun, J.) Sometimes, but not here, the doctrine of res judicata must give way to "overriding concerns of public policy and simple justice." Second, res judicata applies not only to those claims that were actually litigated, but to all claims that could have been litigated.

Jones v. Morris Plan Bank of Portsmouth
(Va. Sup. Ct. 1937)

Facts: In a prior suit, Morris Plan Bank had obtained a judgment against Jones regarding two unpaid installments on a note secured by a conditional sales contract containing an acceleration clause that made the whole amount of the note immediately due upon a default on a single installment). After obtaining judgment, Morris Plan brought, and won, a second action for a subsequent unpaid installment. When Morris Plan took and sold Jones's auto, Jones brought the present action for conversion in state court alleging that in bringing the first action to recover the first two defaults, Morris Plan had waived its right under the acceleration clause to bring further suits for the balance.

Issue: Where an installment contract containing an acceleration clause is breached, does the doctrine of claim preclusion require that the party sue for all installments in a single action and not sue for past due installments in one case and separately sue for subsequently defaulted installment payments in another?

Rule: Yes. Claim preclusion applies when the cause of action in the two suits is the same, i.e., a plaintiff cannot split a single cause of action. The sales agreement constituted a single contract. Since, under the acceleration clause, the entire note became due upon a single default, all attempts to recover payment under the contract form part of a single indivisible cause of action. So Morris Plan lost its right to bring subsequent actions for remaining installments after its first suit.

Mitchell v. Federal Intermediate Credit Bank
(S.C. Sup. Ct. 1932)

Facts: In a previous suit between Mitchell and Federal Intermediate Credit Bank, Mitchell's answer contained no counterclaim. After winning that suit, Mitchell brought an action against Federal Intermediate Credit Bank, asserting a counterclaim based on the subject matter of the original suit.

Issue: Is a party barred from litigating a claim that could have been asserted as a counterclaim in a previous action between the same parties when the counterclaim is based on an allegation that was asserted as a defense to the plaintiff's claim?

Rule: Yes. A party may not split a cause of action by using one portion in defense of a complaint while reserving the remainder for offense in a subsequent suit against the same party. A party cannot use an issue as a defensive "shield" in the first suit and then as an offensive "sword" in a subsequent suit against that same party.

Martino v. McDonald's System, Inc. (7th Cir. 1979)

Facts: McDonald's sued Martino because Martino breached a provision in their franchise agreement that provided he would not acquire a financial interest in a competing self-service food business. The suit was terminated in favor of McDonald's by a consent judgment (on the merits) before an answer was filed. Martino brought the present action, alleging that enforcement of the franchise restriction violated the Sherman Act. The trial court agreed with McDonald's that the new action was barred by claim preclusion and the compulsory counterclaim rule of FRCP 13(a).

Issue 1: When does FRCP 13(a) bar a claim arising out of a transaction that was the subject of a prior suit?

Rule 1: FRCP 13(a)'s rule about compulsory counterclaims does not apply when the action was terminated by a consent judgment before an answer was filed. Thus, it is not a basis for precluding the assertion of the counterclaim in a separate action.

Issue 2: Does claim preclusion bar a counterclaim claim that arose out of a transaction that was the subject of the complaint in prior suit, but that was not asserted in that prior suit?

Rule 2: A consent judgment is a judgment on the merits that is subject to claim preclusion. Res judicata treats a judgment on the merits as an absolute bar to relitigation between the parties of every matter that was offered or could have been offered to sustain or defeat a prior claim. Similarly, precedent and policy require that res judicata bars a counterclaim when its prosecution would nullify rights established by a prior action. Martino's antitrust claim would have been an appropriate defense in his first suit, and its successful prosecution might have nullified rights established in the prior action. Thus, Martino was not permitted to bring the antitrust claim in a second action.

Searle Bros. v. Searle (Utah Sup. Ct. 1978)

Facts: In a divorce suit, a court determined that the Slaugh House property was part of the marital property and awarded it all to Mrs. Searle. Searle Brothers, a partnership comprised of Searle's sons, brought this action against her in state court to claim that they had a one-half interest in the property, having purchased it with partnership funds. The trial court ruled that their claim was precluded, even though they were not parties to the divorce action.

Issue: May collateral estoppel be applied against a party who was not a party to the original action?

Rule: No. Because a party is only subject to judgments or decrees of courts if its interests were legally represented, collateral estoppel can only be asserted against a party in a subsequent suit who was a party or in privity with a party in the prior suit. A person is in privity with another if its interests are so closely identified that they represent the same legal right. Collateral estoppel was not properly applied to Searle Brothers because it was not a party to the first suit and there was not sufficient evidence to show that its interest in the property was ever litigated.

Cromwell v. County of Sac (S. Ct. 1896)

Facts: Cromwell brought an action to cash in four bonds and four coupons for interest on those bonds. The bonds had been issued by the County of Sac. In a previous action brought by Smith, the original bondholder, other interest coupons from the same bonds had been held to be fraudulently issued, and thus null and void. Cromwell was estopped in his case from establishing that he had given value to obtain the bonds.

Issue: When does the doctrine of collateral estoppel preclude litigating that issue in a subsequent suit?

Rule: Where the second suit involves a different cause of action, the only relevant doctrine of preclusion is issue preclusion. Issue preclusion can only be invoked if the same issue was actually decided in the first case and its resolution was necessary to the result in that case. Here, in the case against Smith, the issue that was decided was whether Smith had given value for the bonds. The issue in the second case was whether Cromwell had given value for the bonds. Thus, the issue is not the same and so issue preclusion cannot apply.

Russell v. Place (S. Ct. 1876)

Facts: Russell had a patent covering two types of processes. He sued Place for patent infringement and obtained a general verdict for damages that did not indicate which of the two patented processes had been infringed. Place continued to produce the product. Russell sued again and tried to estop Place from denying infringement.

Issue: When does a prior judgment effect an estoppel in a subsequent suit between the parties?

Rule: In order to invoke issue preclusion, one must know with certainty how the issue was resolved in the first adjudicated case. Where, as here, the first case results in a general verdict that does not explain which of two alternative theories (infringement of which patented process) formed the basis of the judgment, one cannot invoke issue preclusion. The issue must have been unambiguously decided and it was not in this case. So there can be no estoppel from asserting defenses.

Hardy v. Johns-Manville Sales Corp. (5th Cir. 1982)

Facts: Plaintiffs sued several defendants for injuries resulting from asbestos exposure. They alleged, inter alia, failure to warn. In a prior case against the same defendants, the jury had found a failure to warn of the danger of asbestos, although it was unclear as to when the jury believed that the duty to warn arose. The plaintiffs moved to estop Johns-Manville from relitigating the issue of its failure to warn.

Issue: Is a prior adjudication of an issue entitled to issue preclusive effect when that issue could have been resolved on alternative bases?

Rule: No. If the factfinder based its decision on one of several possible bases, there can be no issue preclusion because the finding on that issue must be unambiguous.

Illinois Central Gulf R.R. v. Parks (Ind. Ct. App. 1979)

Facts: Mr. and Mrs. Parks brought a suit against Illinois Central following a collision between their car and a train. Mrs. Parks successfully sought damages for personal injuries. Mr. Parks unsuccessfully sought damages for loss of Mrs. Parks' services, consortium, etc. Thereafter, he brought a second suit against Illinois Central seeking damages for his own personal injuries. The trial court ruled that Parks was not estopped by issue preclusion from litigating the issue of his non-negligence.

Issue: When does issue preclusion apply?

Rule: When there is an unambiguous adjudication of the issue common to both suits. Here the judgment against Parks in his suit against Illinois could have been decided on alternative grounds, i.e., no damages or plaintiff negligence. Where, as here, a judgment could have been based on alternative grounds, there can be no issue preclusion a party needs to have an unambiguous decision on the same issue in the initial litigation.

Rios v. Davis (Tex. Ct. App. 1963)

Facts: A car accident involved Rios, Davis, and the Popular Dry Goods Company. In the first suit, Popular sued Davis for negligence for damage to its truck. Davis responded with a defense of contributory negligence by Popular and Rios, as well as a third-party claim against Rios for negligence. The jury found negligence on the part of all three litigants, thus denying recovery both to Popular Dry Goods (on its complaint) and to Davis (on his third-party claim). In the second suit, Rios sued Davis for negligence arising out of the same accident that was the source of the first lawsuit. Davis's defense included an assertion that the first jury's determination of

Rios's negligence precluded Rios from reasserting his non-negligence and, therefore, because of the applicability of the doctrine of contributory negligence, mandated dismissal of Rios's claim.

Issue: When does a finding on an issue in a previous trial have collateral estoppel effect in a second suit involving that same issue between the same parties?

Rule: To be entitled to collateral estoppel effect, a finding must be essential to the judgment in the first adjudicated case. Here, the issue of Rios's negligence in the suit filed by Popular was not essential to that judgment since Davis lost on his third-party claim against Rios (because of his own negligence) even though the jury found Rios negligent. Thus, Rios's negligence was irrelevant to the result in the first suit, and cannot therefore be subject to estoppel.

Halpern v. Schwartz (2d Cir. 1970)

Facts: A court found that Halpern committed "an act of bankruptcy" after a creditor alleged that she had committed three such acts, one of which was transferring property with the intent to hinder, delay or defraud. Any or all of them would have been grounds for the court's finding. A creditor brought a second action to prevent Halpern from receiving a bankruptcy discharge, also on the grounds that she transferred property with the intent to hinder, defraud or delay.

Issue: When a prior judgment is based on more than one independent, alternative ground, is a party precluded by collateral estoppel from relitigating any of those grounds?

Rule: No. Although an issue may have been fully litigated in a prior action, the prior judgment will not preclude reconsideration of the same issue if that issue did not necessarily determine the prior judgment. This is because an issue that was not essential to the prior judgment may not have been subject to the careful deliberation and analysis normally applied to essential issues, since a different disposition would not have affected the judgment. Also, a decision on an inessential issue is not subject to the safeguard of appellate review.

United States v. Moser (S. Ct. 1924)

Facts: A Civil War statute granted retired Civil War veterans three-quarters the salary of the rank above theirs. In the first suit, Moser, a graduate of the U.S. Naval Academy, sued the United States and received his back pay. In another suit, Jasper, also a U.S. Naval Academy cadet during the Civil War, lost because the government discovered another retirement statute that precluded recovery. The United States stopped payments to Moser, and Moser brought yet another suit to reinstate the payments.

Issue: Is a party barred from relitigating an issue where, in the prior judgment, the law had been wrongly determined?

Rule: Yes. Res judicata bars a party from relitigating an issue, even though the decision was based on an erroneous application of the law.

Commissioner of Internal Revenue v. Sunnen (S. Ct. 1948)

Facts: The IRS unsuccessfully sued Sunnen for failure to report royalty income that he had assigned to his wife who did report the income on her tax return. In that case, the Tax Court upheld the assignment and found the income was attributable to the wife. Two years later, after a change in the governing tax law, the IRS brought another action against Sunnen for subsequently received royalty payments.

Issue: Where the facts, issues, and parties are identical but applicable law changes in the time between two suits, does collateral estoppel apply?

Rule: Collateral estoppel only applies where the matter raised in the second suit is identical in all respects with that decided in the first suit and where the controlling facts and applicable legal rules remain unchanged. Since the law changed between the time of the two lawsuits, there can be no preclusion on the issue of whether the assignment was valid or not. There is no claim preclusion because the two suits were brought concerning nonpayment in different years, which constitute separate causes of action.

Hanover Logansport, Inc. v. Robert C. Anderson, Inc. (Ind. Ct. App. 1987)

Facts: Hanover agreed to lease certain property to Anderson, but Hanover failed to deliver the premises on the contract date. Anderson filed suit for breach, seeking "specific performance or in the alternative money damages." Before trial, Hanover offered to convey the property to Anderson. Anderson accepted with a reservation retaining his right to recover damages from the breach. The parties consented to have their settlement entered as a judgment on the record. Subsequently, Hanover attempted to have the remaining breach action dismissed, arguing that the prior settlement constituted a judgment that prevented any further litigation.

Issue: May a plaintiff who accepts an offer of judgment that awards one type of alternative relief contained in his complaint reserve the right to additional damages from the same cause of action?

Rule: In order for a plaintiff to successfully reserve a claim, the reservation must be incorporated into the offer of judgment and must be an inherent part of the original complaint. This rule avoids protracted litigation by allowing reserved claims only after insuring that it is both parties' intention to continue litigation after a consent judgment is entered. Here, Hanover did not agree to the attempt by Anderson to reserve the right to bring a claim for damages. Thus, having not been expressly codified, the reservation is unassertable.

Holmberg v. State, Division of Risk Management (Alaska Sup. Ct. 1990)

Facts: Holmberg filed an administrative appeal from a state agency's denial of his disability application. Pending this appeal, another state agency awarded Holmes total disability. Holmberg then maintained that the second agency's finding of disability precluded denial of that issue by the first agency.

Issue: Is a decision by one state agency binding on another agency of the same sovereign on the grounds that these agencies of the same state government are in privity?

Rule: Yes. Litigation before one state agency is generally binding on another agency of the same state on the grounds of privity. But in this case there can be no issue preclusion because these two agencies perform different functions and thus they are not in privity. The second agency had jurisdiction over a private funding source whereas the first agency's decisions controlled the dispersal of public funds. Thus, these two agencies are not in privity and there can be no issue preclusion.

Bernhard v. Bank of America National Trust & Saving Association (Cal. Sup. Ct. 1942)

Facts: Before her death, Sather transferred money from her bank account to her executor, Cook. Bernhard, representing the beneficiaries of Sather's estate, sued Cook for the money alleging that Cook did not have Sather's permission, and lost. Bernhard, administrator of Sather's estate, then sued the bank for wrongfully transferring the money.

Issue: Must a party invoking issue preclusion have been a party, or in privity with a party, to the first suit in which that issue was adjudicated?

Rule: No. A party asserting res judicata need not have been a party, or in privity with a party, to the earlier action (i.e., mutuality is not always required). But due process requires that the party sought to be estopped from relitigating an issue did have to be a party, or in privity with a party, to that initial suit.

Blonder-Tongue Laboratories v. University of Illinois Foundation (S. Ct. 1971)

Facts: Blonder-Tongue Labs sued a third party for patent infringement. The court declared Blonder-Tongue's patent invalid. Subsequently, Blonder-Tongue sued the University of Illinois for patent infringement.

Issue: Can a defendant assert nonmutual issue preclusion?
Rule: Yes. There is no mandate of mutuality of estoppel. If a plaintiff has, after fairly and fully litigating his claim, received an adverse judgment, he may not relitigate the issue against a different defendant in a subsequent suit.

Parklane Hosiery Co. v. Shore (S. Ct. 1979)

Facts: Shore brought a stockholder's class action against Parklane Hosiery for damages caused by a materially false and misleading proxy statement. Before this action came to trial in state court, the SEC filed suit against Parklane Hosiery in federal district court alleging the same violations, and won. Under the governing law, trial by jury is not available in actions brought by the SEC. Shore moved for partial summary judgment on the issues that had been resolved in the SEC action against Parklane.
Issue: Can one who was not a party to the first suit offensively assert nonmutual collateral estoppel to prevent a party from relitigating issues resolved against it in the first suit?
Rule: Yes. A litigant who was not a party to a prior judgment may use that judgment offensively to prevent a party from relitigating issues resolved against it in an earlier suit. The trial court has discretion over whether to invoke offensive nonmutual collateral estoppel (issue preclusion). To avoid "wait and see" plaintiffs, such preclusion should not be allowed where the plaintiff in the second suit could have joined the first action, where application of estoppel would be unfair to the defendant because it had no incentive to fully litigate the issue in the first suit (because it could not have foreseen the subsequent case), or where the procedures available in the subsequent suit were not available in the originally adjudicated action.
Dissent: (Rehnquist, J.) The Seventh Amendment requires that in order to estop a claim, it must first have been litigated before a forum where a jury trial is available and Parklane did not have a right to jury trial in the action brought against it by the SEC.

Martin v. Wilks (S. Ct. 1989)

Facts: A job discrimination suit brought by the National Association for the Advancement of Colored People (NAACP) and seven African-American firefighters against Birmingham was settled by way of a consent decree that contained race-based affirmative action programs including the hiring of African-American firefighters. Seven white firefighters sought an injunction to intervene, but were denied relief due to the late filing of their petition to intervene. Another group of white firefighters brought suit alleging that the affirmative action programs constituted unlawful racial discrimination under federal antidiscrimination statutes. The trial court dismissed this action on preclusion grounds, but the appellate court reversed.

Issue: Is a consent decree entitled to preclusive effect barring a suit challenging some of its terms that is brought by individuals who were not parties (nor in privity with parties) to the suit that produced that decree?

Rule: Parties are not bound by previous litigation unless they are joined. FRCP 24 does not make intervention mandatory. There is no duty to intervene in the lawsuit, even if parties know their rights may be affected. And Rule 19 was not invoked in the first suit to compel the joinder of the white firefighters. So the white firefighters who were not party to the suit that generated the consent decree are not precluded from bringing an action to challenge its application to them.

Benson and Ford, Inc. v. Wanda Petroleum Co. (5th Cir. 1987)

Facts: Wanda prevailed in an antitrust action brought against it. Thereafter, Benson and Ford filed a similar action against Wanda and they were represented by the same attorney that had unsuccessfully filed the first suit against Wanda. The trial court dismissed the action on the ground that issue preclusion barred relitigation of the issue of Wanda's liability.

Issue: Can issue preclusion be invoked against a nonparty to the first proceeding simply because that party is represented by the same attorney that represented the losing party in the first suit?

Rule: No. Identity of legal representation is not enough to permit issue preclusion against someone who was not a party to the first proceeding and who, therefore, never had a chance to litigate that issue. To do otherwise would violate the Due Process Clause.

Stephenson v. Dow Chemical Co. (2d Cir. 2001)

Facts: A class of all U.S. military personnel exposed to Agent Orange during the Vietnam War, including those who had not yet manifested injuries, was certified to sue the manufacturer of Agent Orange and others. A settlement was reached providing veterans or their families with ten years of payments. After the fund was depleted, Stephenson discovered that he was injured. The trial court dismissed his claim as barred by the settlement agreement.

Issue: Is a collateral attack on a class action judgment not precluded by claim preclusion if the class did not adequately represent the plaintiff?

Rule: Yes. If the class did not adequately represent the plaintiff in the subsequent action, then that plaintiff is not deemed to have been a party to the class action suit and therefore claim preclusion is inapplicable.

Hart v. American Airlines, Inc. (N.Y. Super. Ct. 1969)

Facts: A number of wrongful death actions were brought in various courts against American as a result of an airplane crash in Kentucky. The first case to be tried resulted in a judgment of liability against American that was affirmed on appeal. Subsequently, in the present action brought by other survivors, the plaintiffs sought to estop American from relitigating the issue of its liability based on the judgment returned against it on that issue in the first case.

Issue: Is offensive nonmutual issue preclusion (collateral estoppel) applicable to this case?

Rule: Yes. American had a full and fair opportunity to litigate the issue in the first case. A party is estopped from relitigating issues decided in a prior suit in another state, if he had a full and fair opportunity to defend and the issue in the previous suit is decisive of the issue in the present suit. American is estopped from relitigating the issue of its liability.

Thompson v. Thompson (S. Ct. 1988)

Facts: Susan Clay (formerly Susan Thompson) and David Thompson had joint custody of their son, Matthew, but the California court gave Susan temporary custody until the case could be reviewed. Susan took Matthew to Louisiana, where a state court awarded her sole custody. Two months later, the California court modified its order and gave custody of Matthew to David. David filed suit in federal court under the federal Parental Kidnapping Prevention Act (PKPA), seeking a declaratory judgment that the California order awarding him sole custody trumped the Louisiana court order. The trial court dismissed his case on the grounds that the PKPA did not create a private federal right of action and this ruling was upheld by the appellate court.

Issue: Does the PKPA provide a private federal right of action?

Rule: No. It was enacted to establish a rule of decision for courts in adjudicating custody disputes but not to create a new cause of action.

Allen v. McCurry (S. Ct. 1980)

Facts: McCurry had been charged with illegal drug possession and unsuccessfully challenged the admission of evidence in that state court prosecution on the grounds that the police search was unconstitutional Subsequently, he brought suit for damages under 42 U.S.C. §1983 against the police officers, claiming that the same search was unconstitutional. The trial judge granted summary judgment of dismissal on the grounds that the constitutionality of the search already had been litigated in the criminal case and was therefore subject to issue preclusion.

Issue: Is a party precluded (i.e., collaterally estopped) from litigating an issue in a §1983 claim in federal court if he previously and unsuccessfully litigated that issue in a state criminal case?

Rule: Yes. The normal principles of issue preclusion apply when the issue was initially adjudicated in a state court proceeding and is sought to be reasserted in a federal court action. All such requirements are met here. The only constitutional issue is whether the party sought to be estopped was a party to or in privity with a party to the first action and McCurry was a party to both proceedings.

Dissent: (Blackmun, J.) Section 1983 had been passed before nonmutual collateral estoppel had been established, so nonmutual estoppel should not apply.

United States v. Mendoza (S. Ct. 1984)

Facts: The Nationality Act provided that noncitizens who served honorably with the United States during World War II were exempt from some nationality requirements. Due to political pressure, however, the Attorney General revoked the authority of the Immigration and Naturalization Service to grant these exemptions. In the first suit, 68 Filipino war veterans challenged the Attorney General's action and prevailed. In the second suit, Mendoza, a Filipino war veteran not included in the first claim, asserted the same claim as the previous 68 veterans.

Issue: May a plaintiff invoke nonmutual issue preclusion against the federal government?

Rule: No. A private party may not assert offensive nonmutual collateral estoppel against the United States Government.

United States v. Stauffer Chemical Co. (S. Ct. 1984)

Facts: In the first suit, the Environmental Protection Agency (EPA) tried to inspect a chemical plant owned by Stauffer in Wyoming (Ninth Circuit). Stauffer challenged the EPA action and won. In the second suit, Stauffer challenged an attempt by the EPA to inspect Stauffer's plant in Tennessee (Sixth Circuit).

Issue: When may a party assert collateral estoppel against the federal government?

Rule: Although nonmutual estoppel may not be asserted against the government (see *United States v. Mendoza*, above), mutual collateral estoppel may still be asserted, to prevent the government from using its massive resources to bankrupt a single defendant, and thus win its action.

Marrese v. American Academy of Orthopaedic Surgeons (S. Ct. 1985)

Facts: In state court, Marrese alleged that the American Academy of Orthopaedic Surgeons violated his common law associational rights. The court dismissed the suit for failure to state a cause of action. Subsequently, in federal court, Marrese alleged that the academy had violated the Antitrust Act, an allegation not raised in state court.

Issue: Does a state court judgment have preclusive effect on a federal claim that could not have been raised in the state suit because it falls within the federal court's exclusive subject matter jurisdiction?

Rule: No. A state court decision will not have preclusive effect on a cause of action that could only have been brought in federal court because of exclusive subject matter jurisdiction.

Rinehart v. Locke (7th Cir. 1971)

Facts: Rinehart sued various private detectives and police officers in federal court alleging false arrest. The court dismissed the claim for failure to allege lack of probable cause. Rinehart subsequently brought a second action in federal court against the detectives and officers for false arrest but this time he alleged lack of probable cause.

Issue: When does the dismissal of a complaint for failure to state a claim preclude bringing a second suit on the same facts even though the complaint has been modified?

Rule: Per FRCP 41(b), an order dismissing a complaint for failure to state a claim that does not specify that the dismissal is without prejudice, is presumed to be with prejudice, i.e., is deemed an adjudication on the merits and is thus entitled to preclusive effect.

Little v. Blue Goose Motor Coach Co. (Ill. Sup. Ct. 1931)

Facts: Blue Goose successfully sued Little for property damage to Blue Goose's bus that occurred when Little drove his car into the bus. Little's appeal was dismissed for lack of prosecution. But before it had been dismissed, Little commenced an action against Blue Goose for personal injuries arising out of that accident. Little died before trial and his executrix then commenced a successful wrongful death action against Blue Goose alleging both negligence and willful and wanton negligence. The judgment in favor of the executrix was reversed on appeal.

Issue: When does a judgment preclude a subsequent suit that involved the same parties and issues?

Rule: Though based on a different legal theory, preclusion arises when material issues in a subsequent lawsuit have been determined in a prior suit between the same parties or their privies.

Hilton v. Guyot (S. Ct. 1895)

Facts: Guyot, a Frenchman, sued Hilton, an American, in a United States circuit court to recover judgment rendered by a French court. Hilton unsuccessfully contended that the merits of the case should be re-examined.

Issue: Is a judgment of a foreign nation's court entitled to full credit and conclusive effect when sued upon in the United States?

Rule: A foreign judgment that was the product of proceedings that comport with broad notions of due process will be enforced in the United States if that foreign country recognizes American judgments.

Gargallo v. Merrill Lynch, Pierce, Fenner & Smith (6th Cir. 1990)

Facts: Merrill Lynch sued its investor Gargallo in state court for debt collection. Gargallo filed a counterclaim alleging violation of federal securities laws. The state court dismissed the counterclaim with prejudice for failure to comply with discovery requests and orders. So Gargallo filed the securities claim in federal court, and the court dismissed it on claim preclusion grounds based on the state court judgment.

Issue: Is a state court judgment issued by a court lacking subject matter jurisdiction entitled to claim preclusive effect in a subsequently filed action?

Rule: No. A judgment rendered by a court without subject matter jurisdiction is not entitled to claim preclusive effect because it is not a valid adjudication on the merits. The state court did not have subject matter jurisdiction over Gargallo's securities act counterclaim because such claims are subject to exclusive federal court subject matter jurisdiction. So the trial court decision dismissing the claims on preclusion grounds is reversed.

State Farm Fire & Casualty Co. v. Century Home Components (Or. Sup. Ct. 1976)

Facts: A fire that started in Century Home Components' shed damaged many nearby properties. Century won the first two actions that reached judgment, but it was found negligent in the third. State Farm, which was not a party to the two prior actions, sought to use the third judgment to collaterally estop Century Home from denying liability in the instant action.

Issue: Can issue preclusion apply if prior suits have reached inconsistent verdicts regarding the issue in question?

Rule: No. Where there have been several lawsuits with varying verdicts, issue preclusion will not apply, even if the identical-issue and fully-and-fairly-litigated requirements are satisfied.

Kovach v. District of Columbia (D.C. Ct. App. 2002)

Facts: After thousands of motorists had been issued citations for running red lights, the District of Columbia decided to dismiss outstanding fines where infractions had been recorded by camera. But it did not reimburse those individuals who had paid the fine. Kovach, who had paid his fine, sued the District arguing that the decision to forgive unpaid fines but to not reimburse paid fines violated his constitutional rights to equal protection. The trial court ruled that his payment of the fine precluded him from contesting the decision.

Issue: Does admission of a violation in an administrative proceeding preclude relitigation of issues that were and could have been litigated in that proceeding?

Rule: Yes. Admission constitutes a valid adjudication on the merits and is entitled to claim preclusive effect, which applies to issues that were or could have been adjudicated as part of that claim. But the issues raised in Kovach's suit could not have been presented in the administrative proceeding regarding the ticket and so claim preclusion does not apply.

Durfee v. Duke (S. Ct. 1963)

Facts: Durfee brought a suit in Nebraska state court against Duke to quiet title to land beneath the Missouri River. There was a question of fact as to whether the land was in Nebraska or Missouri. If the land was in Missouri, Nebraska would not have subject matter jurisdiction. The Nebraska court determined that the land was in Nebraska and ruled in favor of Durfee. Two months later, Duke filed a suit to quiet title to the same land in Missouri state court, which was subsequently removed to federal court on the basis of diversity. The federal court held that although the land was in Missouri, since the Nebraska case had adjudicated all issues, it was entitled to claim preclusive effect and dismissed the case. The appellate court reversed, ruling that the district court did not need to give full faith and credit to the Nebraska judgment and that claim preclusion was inapplicable because the Missouri court was free to reassess the issue of the Nebraska court's subject matter jurisdiction, i.e., the location of the land.

Issue: Must courts give full faith and credit to decisions rendered in other jurisdictions?

Rule: Yes. The Constitution requires every state to give a judgment at least the res judicata effect that the judgment would be accorded in the state that rendered it. This even applies to challenges to the other court's jurisdiction, so long as the question was fully and fairly litigated and finally decided in the court that rendered the original judgment. Thus, the district court must enforce the Nebraska judgment because Nebraska would enforce the Nebraska judgment.

United States v. Beggerly (S. Ct. 1998)

Facts: The United States brought quiet title action against Beggerly in federal court and the case turned on whether the land had been deeded prior to the date of the Louisiana Purchase. If not, the United States would own it. The case was settled before trial with judgment entered based on the agreement. Beggerly subsequently sued to set aside the settlement on the ground that the government had not made a sufficient effort to respond to his discovery request for proof of title before the case was settled.

Issue: Under FRCP 60(b), can a judgment be reopened when doing so would conflict with claim preclusion principles?

Rule: Yes. The opportunities for reopening judgments under FRCP 60(b) involve situations that demand departure from adherence to claim preclusion doctrine in order to avoid a miscarriage of justice. Here, Beggerly's allegations do not meet this standard. He only alleged that the government failed to thoroughly search for the document he requested. That is not enough to reopen the judgment.

Semtek International Inc. v. Lockheed Martin Corp. (S. Ct. 2001)

Facts: Semtek sued Lockheed in state court for breach of contract and tort and the case was removed on diversity grounds. It was then dismissed as barred by the California statute of limitations. Semtek then refiled the suit in Maryland, which had a longer limitations period. The Maryland state court dismissed on claim preclusion grounds. Its decision was upheld by the state court of appeals.

Issue: Does federal common law govern the claim preclusive effect of a dismissal by a federal court sitting in diversity?

Rule: Yes. Federal common law governs the claim preclusive effect of a dismissal by a federal diversity court and that federal common law rule should be that a state rule of claim preclusion applies to dismissals by state or federal courts unless state law is incompatible with federal interests. No such conflict with federal interests exists here and so state preclusion doctrine should apply.

CHAPTER 12

Alternative Systems

I. ANALYSIS

A. Characteristics of the Traditional System

  1. Adversarial Method

    The traditional civil proceeding involves a plaintiff and defendant whose interests are adverse. The proceedings are thus designed to use that natural animosity to encourage each side to get at the truth. However, sometimes parties do not want the truth, but a fair resolution of their dispute. Further, an adversarial tack can be very damaging to a longstanding relationship that the parties may want to preserve beyond the resolution of the one dispute.

  2. Advocacy

    Professional advocates (attorneys) represent the parties in court to help them get through the often complicated legal maze. As a result, however, a client's concerns may become subordinated to the legal issues relevant to the case.

  3. Adjudication

    Although a judge-mandated resolution of disputes may be useful for adverse parties, in some instances it might be better to encourage parties to resolve their differences voluntarily to both parties' satisfaction. In adjudication, more often than not, one party leaves satisfied, while the other does not. In close relationships (neighbors, family, etc.) this may not be a desired result.

B. Need for Alternative System

  1. Delay

    With the massive increase in litigation in recent years, courts have been overwhelmingly backed up. Given their time constraints, many courts focus on triage-type scheduling. Criminal cases are prioritized, then cases involving the court's power of injunctive relief. As a result, many civil suits involving traditional damages may not be resolved for months, or even years.

2. Economics
Litigation gets more and more expensive every year. Although delay is responsible for much of the cost, many would-be litigants simply cannot afford the attorneys' fees.

3. Complex Litigation
Multiplicity of parties, issues, jurisdictions, and laws all present unique situations that are not readily translatable into the adversarial relationship. As such, several alternative dispute resolution methods have been developed to deal with these issues.

II. ALTERNATIVES

A. Arbitration

1. Court-Ordered Arbitration
Although most arbitration is voluntary, some states have experimented with mandated arbitration as a means of freeing much of the court docket. However, since arbitration does not grant many of the procedural protections of litigation (especially the right to a jury), it is not a widespread or favored practice of states.

2. Arbitrability

a. By Agreement
When looking at whether a given contractual dispute is arbitrable, courts will look first at the arbitration agreement in the contract, and construe it as broadly as possible. Almost everything relating to the contract is arbitrable, including the validity of the arbitration clause itself.

b. Subject Matter
Some specific matters are not generally arbitrable. These include:

i. Family Matters
Including child custody, alimony, guardianship, etc.

ii. Punitive Damages
Some, but not all, courts have decided that punitive damages are not arbitrable on policy grounds.

iii. Antitrust Claims
The Supreme Court reasoned that private antitrust suits are an important part of the enforcement of antitrust policy that would be hindered through allowing arbitration of the claim. Interestingly, the Court did not extend this reasoning to RICO claims or Securities Exchange Act violations.

iv. Fraud in the Arbitration Agreement
Although a claim of fraud in the contract itself is arbitrable, courts will hear claims that the arbitration clause itself was fraudulently entered.

3. Procedure

Although specific arbitration associations supply their own arbitration procedure, state and federal law does not require any specific procedure.

a. Evidence

Arbitrators are free to hear or exclude any evidence they like.

b. Witnesses

They may hear from witnesses orally, in writing only, or not at all.

c. Examination

They may allow attorneys to perform all questioning, or they may participate. Cross-examinations are discretionary.

d. Opinions

They need not even write an opinion explaining their decision (and some associations discourage such opinions to prevent a court from overturning).

e. Arbitrator

One arbitrator may decide, or a panel. Dissenting and concurring opinions are neither promoted nor discouraged by law.

4. Judicial Review

Judicial review of awards is very limited, and occurs only after the rendering of an arbitral award. A court will only overturn a decision where enforcement would violate basic notions of morality and justice. However, very few situations survive this standard.

5. Enforcement

Courts will enforce the award as long as there was some possible basis for an arbitrator to have reached that decision. There need not be an arbitral opinion.

B. Family Courts

These courts attempt to bring about a mutually acceptable resolution of family issues, so as to lessen the adverse affects of divorce and separation on children. If mediation fails, the case may be adjudicated.

C. Small Claims

To lessen costs to litigants, these informal courts serve to resolve disputes of less than a statutorily specified amount. The amount varies from jurisdiction to jurisdiction, depending on the state's acceptance of this form of dispute resolution (which often varies proportionally to the backlog in civil courts).

D. Negotiations

Many courts have rules designed to encourage settlement of disputes before trial. However, a judge must be careful not to favor one side too heavily, thus impinging on rules regarding impartiality.

E. Local Resolution

Some jurisdictions have set up neighborhood courts that informally mediate disputes between neighbors, spouses, and local merchants in close neighborhoods. This serves to maintain a sense of community and stability, as well as offer individualized remedies. Mediators are given wide discretion in arriving at a mutually acceptable solution. If a solution cannot be found, the dispute may then be litigated in court.

F. Rent-A-Judge

A favorite of complex litigation, all parties split the cost of hiring a retired judge to act as a more formal arbitrator of their dispute. Often, but not always, the proceedings are held with many of the rules of civil procedure and evidence, hybridized from the various jurisdictions.

G. Other Countries

Foreign nations have different philosophies of jurisprudence. Civil law countries, for instance, are governed almost entirely by statute, with little or no common law. Many countries do not have trials, judges take an active role in questioning parties, and witnesses may appear seldom or only in writing. Some commentators have advocated that certain of these rules or approaches be transplanted into the American system.

CASE CLIPS

Gilmer v. Interstate/Johnson Lane Corp. (S. Ct. 1991)

Facts: As a prerequisite to employment with Interstate, Gilmer registered as a securities representative with the New York Stock Exchange. The NYSE registration application required Gilmer to arbitrate any dispute arising from his employment with or termination by Interstate. At age 62, Gilmer was fired by Interstate, and Gilmer sued under the Age Discrimination in Employment Act (ADEA). Interstate moved to have the matter arbitrated, based on Gilmer's NYSE registration application and the Federal Arbitration Act, which required courts to enforce arbitration agreements.

Issue: Are non-collectively bargained agreements to arbitrate statutory claims enforceable under the FAA?

Rule: Non-collectively bargained agreements to arbitrate statutory claims are presumptively enforceable under the FAA. However, the agreement may not be enforceable if a party can show that Congress intended to preclude a waiver of a judicial forum for the statutory claim at issue. In this case, the Court found no such waiver in the ADEA and held the arbitration agreement to be enforceable.

Ferguson v. Writers Guild of America, West (Cal. Sup. Ct. 1991)

Facts: Ferguson was hired to write the screenplay for *Beverly Hills Cop II*. Members of the Writers Guild agreed that the task of determining the relative contributions of the various writers would be handled by Writers Guild committees. When the picture was completed, the Writers Guild determined that Ferguson should share credit for the screenplay; credit for the story was given to two others. The Writers Guild had elaborate rules for making such determinations and arbitrating subsequent disputes. After Ferguson was unsuccessful in the arbitration proceedings, he brought suit in state court.

Issue: What is the scope of judicial review of arbitration proceedings?

Rule: Where parties have agreed among themselves to bring a matter before a specially skilled arbitration committee and not to litigate the matter, judicial review is limited to whether the arbitrators exceeded their powers and whether the procedures employed deprived the objecting party of a fair opportunity to be heard.

In re African-American Slave Descendants' Litigation (N.D. Ill. 2003)

Facts: Plaintiffs alleging that they were descendants of formerly enslaved African Americans sued several corporations alleged to have profited from slave trade or slave labor in federal court. They sought restitution for profits the defendants gained through participating in the institution of slavery. While the defendants' motion to dismiss was pending, the plaintiffs moved to have the court appoint a mediator to try to settle the case. The defendants opposed the motion.

Issue: Should a federal court order mediation over the objection of a party in the absence of any statutory authorization?

Rule: No. A federal court should only exercise its inherent authority to order mediation over a party's objection, in the absence of statutory authorization, under very limited circumstances and this is not one. Ordering mediation is not likely to help end this case in light of the pending motion to dismiss. Perhaps the motion would be more timely later in the suit.

Lockhart v. Patel (E.D. Ky. 1987)

Facts: A teenager who lost an eye brought a medical malpractice action. After several formal and informal pretrial conferences, the judge ordered the defense counsel to bring a representative, "not some flunky" from the insurance company, who was authorized to enter into a settlement. They sent a flunky. Consequently, the court struck the defendant's pleadings and declared it in default.

Issue: May a court order parties and their insurers to attend settlement conferences?

Rule: FRCP 16 authorizes courts to order parties and their liability insurers to attend settlement conferences, and to impose sanctions for disregarding such orders.

TABLE OF AUTHORITIES